Avoiding Responsibility

Avoiding Responsibility

The Politics and Discourse of
European Development Policy

Nathalie Karagiannis

Pluto Press

LONDON • ANN ARBOR, MI

HD
75
.K366
2004

First published 2004 by Pluto Press
345 Archway Road, London N6 5AA
and 839 Greene Street, Ann Arbor, MI 48106, USA

www.plutobooks.com

British Library Cataloguing in Publication Data
A catalogue record for this book is available from the British Library

ISBN   0 7453 2190 9 hardback
ISBN   0 7453 2189 5 paperback

Library of Congress Cataloging in Publication Data
Karagiannis, Nathalie.
   Avoiding responsibility : the politics and discourse of European
development policy / Nathalie Karagiannis.
      p. cm.
   ISBN 0–7453–2190–9 (cloth) — ISBN 0–7453–2189–5 (pbk.)
   1. Economic development. 2. Developing countries—Economic
conditions. 3. Developing countries—Social conditions. 4. European
Union countries—Foreign economic relations—Developing countries.
5. Developing countries—Foreign economic relations—European Union
countries. 6. Economic assistance, European—Developing countries. 7.
Postcolonialism. I. Title.

   HD75.K366 2004
   338.91'401724—dc22
                                                        2004001405

10   9   8   7   6   5   4   3   2   1

Designed and produced for Pluto Press by
Chase Publishing Services, Fortescue, Sidmouth, EX10 9QG, England
Typeset from disk by Stanford DTP Services, Northampton, England
Printed and bound in the European Union by
Antony Rowe Ltd, Chippenham and Eastbourne, England

5411467

For Armin

Contents

Acknowledgements

I am very grateful to Shereen Essof, Armin Rabitsch, Eugenia Siapera and Peter Wagner who read, and always fruitfully commented upon, the various versions of the manuscript. In doing so, they taught me ever richer understandings of responsibility, solidarity and giving.

Raj Patel, Jean-Antoine Karagiannis, William Outhwaite, Philip McMichael and Julie Stoll offered very valuable comments and friendly support across chapters and continents.

1
Europe and Development Revisited

> Madam Zachanassian: you forget, this is Europe.
> You forget, we are not savages. In the name of all citizens
> of Guellen, I reject your offer; and I reject it in the name
> of humanity. We would rather have poverty than blood
> on our hands.[1]
>
> Friedrich Dürrenmatt, *The Visit*

The above extract comes from the beginning of a play that concludes with 'the offer' being tragically accepted. The offer is made by Claire Zachanassian, a rich old lady who returns to her natal village to ask for justice. In her youth, she was wronged by a man whose murder will, she thinks, compensate for the damage done to her. To this end, she offers a great amount of money to the village of Guellen. Despite the initial resistance of the community, epitomised by this extract, the murder is committed and the community is paid, all in the name of humanity, whose location is Europe.

As an introduction to the following discussion of the ties woven between Europe and less economically developed countries, the above extract reminds us not only of the image that Europe may have of itself ('in the name of all citizens of Guellen' is the same as 'in the name of humanity') and how tragically erroneous this has been and can be, but also how Europe can relate itself to the caricature of the bloody and greedy savages, its purportedly absolute 'other'. The reference to a community (that of Guellen, Europe) and to the 'external' offer (but with ineffaceable origins within it) made to this community also neatly fits the European discourse towards the African Carribean and Pacific (ACP) countries, a discourse that has oscillated between a picture of development as a domestic matter and a depiction of development relations as ruled by unavoidable and irreversible external forces. Registering the full meaning of this oscillation is the task of what follows.

POLITICAL AND SOCIAL THEORY IN DEVELOPMENT

This book argues for introducing social and political theorising into studies of development, as well as for introducing development into an area of theorising where it has been neglected until now. Thus, avoiding both a strictly normative interrogation on development ethics and a political-scientific version of development studies, it attempts to imaginatively look at the question of development. This opens up the space for political discussion on these issues, issues that, to paraphrase Arendt, are too important to be exclusively left to development scientists and professional politicians. What *we, we Europeans*,[2] do with giving, responsibility, efficiency – among the most important issues in development – is largely a question of grasping other possibilities than the ones we thought were imposed on us; it is largely a question of choice.

A look at the writings in social and political theory that have included development (discourse) in their reflection reveals a capacity to challenge developmentalist clichés. Social and political theory alone have managed to contextualise ethical questions around development by inserting them into a broader interrogation on capitalism and modernity. Thinkers like Touraine, Castoriadis or Bauman have looked at two persistent questions in development, namely its 'rationality' and 'the reason for helping/giving', that is, the question of community.[3]

Concerning rationality, Castoriadis effectively challenges the premises of a rational path to economic growth and of the idea of unlimited progress, on which the idea of development is based.[4] Development is defined by him as the achievement or actualisation of a virtual state, a process also implying the definition of a 'maturity', i.e. of a determined state that exists. Castoriadis shows that, by contrast, the present understanding of development is devoid of any definition of a 'maturity'. Present-day 'development' expresses the injection of infinity into the social-historical world, and seeks exit from finite states in order to attain ever renewable states. Additionally, he denounces the idea of mastery over things as leading to absurd results when it purports to be total: thus, development is based on the fallacy that a constant acquisition of more is not subject to any limits. But as Castoriadis underlines, no technical improvement can avoid the risk of being used in a direction opposite to that originally planned. Consequently, not only is development less rational than is usually thought because it strives for control that can annihilate it, but it is also absurd in the never-ending process that it creates.

Intellectually similar to the spirit of the Castoriadian critique, an impressive array of literature emerged in the mid-1990s which strongly insisted on looking at how development discourse works.[5] The observation that, now, this literature has created its own *topoi* (or common places) of *anti*-development discourse, and thus that those that criticise a discourse produce a discourse in its own right does not seem to strike a lethal blow to this 'anti-development discourse'.[6] Ultimately, in the realm of development studies, this literature attempts to ally empirical observation with socio- and politico-theoretical insights as well as explicit ethical questioning. These authors have uncovered that the social sciences are political philosophy applied,[7] and they have attempted to both hang on to the possibilities proper to the social sciences and simultaneously re-discover political philosophy. It is the persistence and importance of this work, over a period of 30 years, that reveals how similar interrogations around development, modernity and capitalism remain: in this sense, there is a 'third spirit of capitalism' underlying the three decades that are considered separately in the following chapters.[8]

The second question that is posed through social and political theorising is that of *community*. We may indeed envisage development (discourse) as creating a community seeking to answer the profoundest uncertainty of a future world lived in unequal conditions, alarming for security reasons for some, intolerable because of poverty, oppression, sickness for others. This view does not presuppose a pre-existing closed 'space' but rather one that is self-instituted, also in the present. This means that what happens to this community is by no means predetermined; that its space is malleable and its inequality avoidable. Indeed, development cannot achieve some of the basic requirements of a common world, and this, while there already is one. The paradoxical situation of development discourse is that as long as it condones itself, in the view of achieving equality of conditions in this unequal community (in the form of interminable stages to be reached), it condemns the members of that community to perpetual inequality. The very words that we use to characterise members of this community are witnesses to this.[9] This paradox is more than a mere witticism; it contains the seeds of tragedy. What are we[10] to do with the less economically developed countries? Once their relation to the more economically developed countries is revealed to be bogus, should we send them home, so to speak? What would that home be, in a world fashioned to a great extent by what we used to call 'the West'?

For the moment, we must place this question in brackets, not because it is unanswerable (it should be the central question because it is the only question that *must*, in the end, be answered) but because we should examine this community before looking at its dissolution. The Walzerian view of community, as a good to be distributed, provides us with two crucial insights in terms of the development community. The first concerns the element of mutual aid that Walzer identifies as constitutive of the community. Indeed, if we look at the development discourse of the European Union (EU) towards the ACP countries, mutuality of 'giving' (help, aid, debt, exchange) is present as a crucial justification of the very existence of the community. The second insight is that the distribution of community is decided from its inside, from within it.

> The community is itself a good – conceivably the most important good – that gets distributed. But it is a good that can be distributed only by taking people in, where all the senses of that latter phrase are relevant: they must be physically admitted and politically received. Hence, membership cannot be handed out by some external agency; its *value depends upon an internal decision*.[11]

This is crucial to an understanding of what is considered 'domestic' in this relation and what 'external';[12] to a critique of who decides who can enter the community;[13] and to an interrogation of the imaginary sources of the duty to give in the community (vocations).[14]

Another way of looking at community is of Hegelian inspiration: the community of development discourse becomes one of 'interdependence'. Although the word is currently used in a distinct effort to depict equality in the relations between the more economically developed and less economically developed countries, it has roots in a conceptualisation of master–slave relationships. According to the Hegelian vision, the master is at least as dependent on the slave as the slave on the master. In fact, the master is deprived of the slave's satisfaction of being able to change reality through work.[15] Thus, there is an interdependency between the powerful and the powerless. It is in Marx that we must locate the first use of this idea with regard to the relationship between colonisers and colonised.[16] Later, the intellectual development movement that was most explicitly inspired by the idea of interdependence was the Latin American 'dependencia'. But in a twist, the 'dependentistas' insisted on Latin America's dependency situation *vis-à-vis* the capitalistic centre. Inheriting this understanding, the current development discourse emanating from the EU hastily adds 'inter' to 'dependency' without realising that it comes back to a formulation that was originally set up to denounce inequalities.

 · In the end, these are all questions that point an accusing finger to the vast majority of development relations. For indeed, who else than those who are 'developed' instigates, creates and chooses to continue or discontinue relationships of aid? And if this question is only rhetorical, then we must proceed to accomplish a 'double movement' – one towards the explicit acknowledgment of responsibility by the 'developed', a responsibility painted in the colours of solidarity – and one, seemingly opposite, that attempts to found this solidarity in the others of the 'developed'. The political aim of the first part of the movement is to insist anew on the necessity for the more economically developed countries to accept the responsibilities that are their own, both on historical grounds and because of the power they hold. The political aim of the second part of the movement is to acknowledge and strengthen the extraordinary potential that less economically developed countries present in the shaping of the world that unites them with, and separates them from, the more economically developed countries. One cannot go without the other.

DEVELOPMENT AS DISCOURSE

The origins of this book reside in various texts of European development policy; development is viewed as discourse.[17] Most authors who included themselves, or were included, in the 'argumentative turn' of political science or in the 'discursive turn' in other social sciences shared an interest in going back to texts and in looking at what there was instead of what there wasn't. This did not mean relinquishing critical concern with possibilities that were not fully actualised, 'changing the world' or *changer la vie* as a poetically attuned '1968' had put it. Quite to the contrary, it very often meant uncovering openings that could lead to such change.

The variety of philosophical approaches informing these social-scientific 'turns' is great; we must clearly distinguish between Jürgen Habermas' and Karl-Otto Apel's discourse ethics, on the one hand, and the critical and post-structuralist current most stringently expressed by people like Jacques Derrida, Ernesto Laclau and Chantal

Mouffe, Judith Butler or Slavoj Žižek, on the other. The main point of contention concerns the common good. The first current is indeed devoted to an understanding of discourse as a medium for attaining a political consensus, the common good. The second current would, on the contrary, advocate a somewhat less instrumental place for discourse, and one that insists on the incessant play of difference that it produces; the 'common good' is better expressed in the plural, goods that are placed in different situations and are never quite as fixed as we think they are (nor should they, for that matter, be). If the second 'discursive' current is often too formalistic, its insistence on difference and non-fixity is theoretically valuable.[18]

This book is based on an understanding of discourse informed by the second current: development discourse is conceived as a whole whose ambiguities, richness and the critique it receives change it through time. Such change comes about through the changes in the relationships between the components of the discourse. Inspired by Laclau and Mouffe, the components of discourse that are stopped, as it were, in their movement, are called 'moments' and the relationship between them 'articulation'. Two such moments or instances of justification are responsibility and efficiency. The two concepts were chosen to be submitted to more detailed study because of their utmost significance and their frequency in the discourse, and their belonging to entirely different strands of justification. Indeed, responsibility pertains to the moral, political, reasonable fields, whereas efficiency is an amoral, economic, cognitive concept. Although this book departs from formalism, it is led by the ideas that talking generally about 'discourse' is self-defeating since this takes for granted a static bloc of 'discourse' without disentangling its changes through time, across actors and between ideas or concepts; that there is thus a need to locate precise discursive components; and that this must be done in a way that takes time into account. Such an approach clearly shows that, although it is these attempts at fixity that render a discourse recognisable as such, these attempts are always undermined.[19]

However, it must be noted that most authors who have used or studied 'development discourse' refer to a Foucaultian understanding: very often, it is rather a Foucaultian inspiration, because Foucault's own writings on discourse are varying and are seldom referred to. In many ways, the use of discourse here is also influenced by Foucault's work, particularly insofar as it interrogates the forms of moral and scientific knowledge that are used by the development institutions.[20]

To identify the 'European development discourse' this book relies on three sorts of texts, the first two large, programmatic policy papers and articles of the *ACP-EU Courier* emanating from the European institutions; the third coming from think-tanks and publications that are close to the European Commission.[21]

A SHORT HISTORY OF EUROPEAN DEVELOPMENT POLICY

Even though this book investigates 'European development discourse', it is one of its contentions that the dialogue between the ACP and the EU emerges implicitly and constantly through this discourse. Indeed, one of the main properties of discourse is justification; and this justification, the European justification, always addresses someone else: the designed 'partners'. Additionally, living in one of the ACP countries, Zimbabwe, during the writing of this text has necessarily influenced my view of the European discourse, and information on the 'ACP side' is inserted in endnotes to make clear the book's focus as well as the need to separate two (albeit hybrid) 'voices' in this dialogue. The term 'European' must thus evidently be problematised: reading through the text, one must always keep in mind that notwithstanding a wide political and literary thinking on 'Europe', such thoughtfulness is not often present in European development discourse, and this, despite a constant play with ambiguity which crucially demarcates it from American development discourse.

In the precise case of the EU-ACP relations, 'Europe' is more united, more 'one' than the ACP states; hence, more 'one' than a philosophical tradition that insists on its diversity would have it. It is represented, besides the member states of the EU, by the European Council and the European Commission; by contrast, the ACP countries are not legally represented by their Secretariat or any other institution that could somehow 'unite' them: this difference plays a significant role in the unitary perception that the ACP countries have of Europe. This is another instance, one may argue, of the distinction between European and non-European that has characterised nineteenth-century colonial culture and is still very present in countries like Zimbabwe. The concluding remarks return to this question; for now, the particularity of this 'European' development discourse must be stressed, if we deny it and equate this discourse to the other international discourses, we erase a (post-)colonial past that weighs heavily on both sides, a past that is, in a distinct way, European and neither American nor international.

Related to the brief historical overview that follows, we must briefly raise the issue of time, an issue that haunts development, starting from its very name that speaks of stages in time. A detailed critique of this name is out of place here, but we may cursorily point to the element of promise within it; the promise to develop. Hannah Arendt has seen promise as the invention that counters human action's unpredictability in the future, an island of stability in the ocean of uncertainty that the future is, as she says.[22] It gives continuity and durability to people's relationships as it binds the one who makes a promise to the one to whom it is addressed. The relationship between the EU and the ACP countries can be seen as a constantly renewed promise of development, in fact, a constantly renewed promise to give. The multilateral contractual form that this promise takes is emblematic of a will to bind all parties. By contrast, the tendencies towards disengagement are a breach of a promise, very generally understood, and hence they provoke a mounting feeling of uncertainty; and of disaffection.

Forgiveness is the second crucial feature of development that relates to time and irreversibility (of action in time). It is a distinctly Christian remedy, another island of security situated this time in the midst of a sinful past. With regard to development discourse, forgiveness is first of all a crucial reminder of the religious roots of the duty to help; without this in mind we would be at pains to explain our current concept of responsibility, for instance. But the instrumentalisation of the power to forgive has also been very significant in terms of how relevant the colonial past of development has been understood to be. Finally, the currently 'mediatised' demands of less economically developed countries to more economically developed ones to erase the former's debts are as intimately linked with forgiveness as the very worldly community of development is linked to religion.

To revert to a more straightforward understanding of time for readers who are not familiar with the EU development policy: the chronological frame of the book starts a little earlier than 1975, the year of the signing of the first Lomé Convention between the EU (then European Economic Community, EEC) and the ACP countries. The end of the Lomé system is marked by the Cotonou 'Agreement' of the year 2000, and the change of the treaty's name is of symbolic importance rather than of legal significance, as it announces the gradual European disengagement and the liberalisation of the trade relations between the partners (or, in other words, the increasing openness of the ACP markets to European products). The Lomé

Conventions, that cover the 1970s, 1980s and 1990s, arise out of various aspects of dissatisfaction with the previous systems of 'association' and of changes in the relative negotiating power between European, 'developed' countries and mainly African 'developing' ones. Briefly: the 1970s were characterised by the strongest position the ACP ever had in the past, which is related to the two oil crises and the OPEC position. Their demands and doubts are taken seriously: the colonial past is discussed, (Afro)Marxist influences are perceptible and there is a strong belief in the novelty of the Lomé formula. The 1980s saw hopes for the African continent decline. It was the decade of the emergence of the Structural Adjustment Programmes (SAPs), and the Europeans searched for 'social' palliatives to the constraints imposed by the SAPs on the one hand; on the other, they praised the systematic search for efficiency. In the 1990s, the Europeans displayed ambiguity again: whilst they claimed an inability to resist 'globalisation' and thus started dismantling the Lomé system (to the great dismay of the ACP); whilst the (post-)colonial ties were deemed irrelevant; and whilst the ties between the EU and the ACP leaned towards the market exchange, the Europeans increasingly asserted their autonomy on the international scene, particularly *vis-à-vis* the US that lagged behind in terms of regional market arrangements.[23] However, throughout the years, the primary objective of the Convention on the European side remained to ensure the continuation of the economic patterns established under colonisation and the solution to the lack of primary resources and control over the region. And on the ACP side, the same objective also prevailed: exports and preferential market access. In this regard, it is interesting to note that the bigger former British colonies like South Africa and India (since the geographical scope of the ACP was understood ever more loosely) always posed a particular problem. Thus, India never became part of the Convention and South Africa still does not have preferential market access and is not part of the important protocols that accompany the current Agreement.

The decades examined in this book can be inserted in a broader chronological framework in which three main periods in the European development policy *vis-à-vis* the ACP states stand out: the period from 1957 (Treaty of Rome) to 1973 when Denmark, Ireland and the UK joined the Community, the period from 1973 to the Treaty of Maastricht (1992), and the period from 1992 to the year 2000. Part 4 of the Treaty of Rome established an Association between the EEC countries and non-European territories that maintained 'special relationships' with Belgium, France, Italy and the Netherlands[24] that are marked by the successive African independences. Two types of divergences between EEC member states can be noted at this stage; a first divergence between, on the one hand, France and Belgium that insisted on the creation of a development policy concentrated on Africa, and, on the other hand, Germany and the Netherlands that promoted a worldwide policy; the second divergence concerned the already existing 'aid or trade' question, the first option being supported by France, Belgium and Italy and the other by Germany and the Netherlands.[25]

Thus, the consensus needed to create this association launched by France was reached with difficulty, a situation that was to be repeated in every future negotiation involving the member states' different interests *vis-à-vis* their former European colonies. It must be noted that the Treaty of Rome stipulating the Association did not mention 'a development policy' because it was aimed at a very specific number of countries, which were naturally following their metropoles into the European Community. By contrast, the Treaty of Maastricht defines a European development policy which is, in principle, open to any country that wishes it.

Decolonisation and economic growth led to the first Yaoundé Convention being signed between the EEC and 18 independent states in 1963, the year of the failure of the first attempt of the UK to join the EEC. In 1973, four years after the signature of the second Yaoundé Convention, the UK (and Ireland and Denmark) eventually joined the Community, which produced a massive extension of the geographical scope of EEC development cooperation. After this enlargement, the Germans strengthened their positions on trade and 'globalisation' of policy whilst the Danish (along with the Italian) influence urged for increased generosity of aid.[26] The first Lomé Convention was signed in 1975 between the EEC and 46 ACP states. Its Preamble announced the establishment of 'a new model for relations between developed and developing states, compatible with the aspirations of the international community towards a more just and more balanced economic order (…)'.[27]

EEC Commissioner Cheysson characterised the Convention as 'unique in the world and history'. Thus, although the Convention had strong similarities to its Yaoundé predecessors, it was presented as establishing a particular relationship between the North and South. Its major innovations were the introduction of a method to stabilise the export earnings of the ACP for selected products and the world market price for primary agricultural commodities (better known as

STABEX), and the provision for guaranteed access to the Community market of certain quantities of sugar from certain ACP countries. The big scale of the Convention was another reason why particularity was claimed to exist. As Lister shows, the borrowing of the terminology of the discourse on the New International Economic Order (NIEO) enhanced this impression of the Convention as being revolutionary: the term 'partnership' which was used from then on to describe the contract was chosen with difficulty after the terms 'Association' and 'Cooperation' were rejected because they explicitly referred to the previous contracts under the strong French influence.[28]

Here, some brief remarks on the actors of the EU-ACP relationship are necessary. Although the expression EU is used more or less invariably throughout the book, it should be mentioned that it is the EEC that signed the first and second Conventions, the EC that signed the third and the fourth, and the EU that very recently signed the Cotonou Agreement. The Conventions were signed by the heads of the member states, the Council and the Commission, all of which play an important role in the formulation of the policy.

Within the European institutions, the division of labour in the institutional triangle (the Council, the Commission and the Parliament) is of interest. The formulation of the development policy can be traced along the line linking the Council to the Commission: as in almost all the other European policies, the Council mandates the Commission, which, in turn, proposes texts (including those authorising it to negotiate with the ACP countries) that are then amended by the Council.

More precisely, the Council reflects the inter-state *problématique*, namely the necessary considerations of who pays what and how. For instance, only three member states fulfil the UN objective, giving more than 0.7 per cent of their GNP to less economically developed countries: Denmark, Sweden and the Netherlands. On the other hand, while Ireland makes 34 per cent of its aid transit through the EU, only 6.6 per cent of the Danish aid is likewise distributed. This consideration also involves the division between the 'trade-not-aid' group (Germany, UK, Netherlands and the Scandinavian countries) and the others (France, Belgium, Spain).

In the era of the Lomé Conventions, there were different dynamics within the European Commission that went from the opposition between DG (Directorate General) VIII (now DG Development) and the other DGs responsible for external affairs (DG I, DG IA, DG IB – now DG REL.EX.) to DG VIII's internal ideological/national divisions.[29] It must also be noted that the European Community Humanitarian Office (ECHO) is responsible for the EU's humanitarian aid and a strong competitor as far as public image and media are concerned. The fact that the European Development Fund (EDF) is outside the EU budget, and hence outside effective control of the European Parliament, considerably reduces the role of the latter.[30]

On the other hand, the ACP group as such was created shortly after the signature of the first Convention; the primary aim of the group's constitution was to give its members bargaining power *vis-à-vis* the EU. In the long run, a more unitary interlocutor would also have facilitated the EU. But this group is not an example of regional integration: in no way should it be assumed that these countries correspond to a unity, be it cultural, economic, ethnic or political. On the contrary, their internal divisions are numerous, ranging from their relations with their previous colonial authorities to their political regimes. In such a context, the correspondence between an 'adequate' response to the EU policy and the effectiveness of the ACP institutions can be questioned, not least because of the acknowledged malfunctioning of the latter; but also because in the expression of the ACP demands, their peoples' needs are not necessarily accurately reflected.

Although the Lomé Convention was not the sole instrument of Community cooperation during the second half of the 1970s, the criticisms to European development aid that emerged then were focused on it. The major part of these criticisms concentrated on the 'neo-colonial' nature of the Convention. Neo-colonialism was detected because the parameters of the relationship between the ACP states and the Community were set by the latter; because the Convention fostered ties between the former metropoles and their former colonies instead of weakening them; because Lomé's provisions did little to change the economic weakness and dependency of the ACP; because the relationship did not involve the EEC and ACP populations but was only established on an elite to elite basis; and because by creating divisions between the ACP and other less economically developed countries, it regionalised selected countries.[31] However, 'development policy continued to be supported in Europe at political and diplomatic levels'.[32] This support was one of the elements guaranteeing the stability of the relation; the other was that of 'political neutrality'.

The second Lomé Convention was signed in 1980 and it did not make any important modifications to the previous one. The major innovation was the institution of a system of project and programme aid in the ACP mining sector (SYSMIN). Apart from some improvements in the area of trade, the general impression was one of disappointment, especially on the side of the ACP as they were denied free and unhindered access to the Community market for all their agricultural products during the negotiations.[33] According to Lister,

> [m]uch of the disappointment occasioned by Lomé II was the result of misunderstanding the nature of Lomé I. Lomé II was regarded as a disappointment because it did not radically differ from Lomé I and did not seem to promise any fundamental re-structuring of relations between developed and developing countries. However, Lomé I itself had not actually been the radical reform which some of its enthusiasts had claimed.[34]

More significant changes occurred in 1985 when the third Lomé Convention was signed. First of all, the *acquis* Lomé appeared: this was constituted by a series of objectives and principles that characterised the relationship. Thus, equality of partners, respect for their sovereignty and the right of each state to determine its own policy options were part of this *acquis* which, in turn, guaranteed the security of the parties' relations. A second important innovation was the Joint Declaration of the parties on Article 4, which expressed the parties' 'deep attachment' to the protection of human rights. Thus, Lomé III initiated a tendency to insert political elements into the relationship, which was against the previous principle of neutrality.

At the European level, the period 1981–86 is characterised by southern enlargements of the Community (Greece 1981, Spain and Portugal 1986). From the viewpoint of trade, protectionism and agricultural exports, these new EC member states were rightly considered as competitors of the ACP.[35]

The end of the 1980s was punctuated by events that influenced the negotiations of the fourth Lomé Convention. The end of the cold war, the generalisation of the use of the concept of globalisation, the explosion of the ACPs' long-term debt due to the energy crises, the growing gap between import expenses and export revenues and the demographic growth in the ACP countries certainly shaped the next Convention. In terms of development doctrine, modernisation theories equating economic growth with poverty alleviation were severely challenged.

The particularities of the 1989 Convention included an increased emphasis on the human rights issues and support for structural adjustment. The Declaration annexed to Lomé III was transformed into an insertion in Article 5 of the Convention, and the parties reaffirmed their existing obligations and commitment to international law. Article 5 has been used by the Community to suspend its cooperation with some countries (Liberia, Sudan, Nigeria and Zaire) accused of non-respect of human rights or democratic rule. 'Of course, [the understanding of the Article] cannot be too broad (...) because the number of countries that would suffer from the restrictions would be too many.'[36] The new support for Structural Adjustment Programmes was presented as a pragmatic choice; instead of fighting the Bretton Woods institutions, of which the European states are a part, the Community would try to correct them. Let it be noted that, formally, the members of the EU and the ACP together could form the majority at the World Bank: however, 'in the mid-1990s, the ten richest industrial states controlled 52 per cent of the votes, and 45 African countries controlled just 4 per cent of the votes'.[37] Both of these steps – insistence on human rights issues and support for the SAPs – radically altered the previous conception of Lomé; the first meant definitely breaking with the tradition of neutrality whilst the second departed from the discourse of 'exceptionality' of the Convention, until then understood as the difference between EEC cooperation and that of the other international donors.

The scheduled revision of the fourth Lomé Convention took place in 1994, two years after the signature of the Treaty of Maastricht establishing the European Union. The basic principles of the European development policy such as sustainable development, poverty alleviation, consolidation of democracy and respect of human rights, good governance and rule of law, and the development of commerce instead of the system of preferences were for the first time laid down in this Treaty.

These changes that aimed at ending the EU's political neutrality led Commissioner Pinheiro to proclaim that 'this is the last of the Conventions as we have come to know them'. At the same time, the new northern enlargement of the EU accentuated the interest in eastern Europe; significantly too, it brought in countries (Finland and Sweden) that were critical of the colonial basis for development aid and favoured a policy based on poverty alleviation.[38]

The announcement of the termination of Lomé was the starting point of a debate on the future relationships between the EU and the ACP countries launched by the Commission through the issuing of the Green Paper. This debate officially lasted a year, after which the Commission withdrew to begin the negotiations for the next Agreement. In this debate two main positions were clearly perceptible: one contended that the Lomé partnership had become an anachronism. The second one advocated for some transformation but supported the preservation of the Lomé Convention in the form it had had for the last 20 years. In both the first and the second argument, the general principle of change was admitted; what differed was judgement over the necessary degree of change.

The increased attention of the EU to the countries of central and eastern Europe as well as the renaissance characterising the EU's relations with the Mediterranean, Latin America and Asia constituted the change in the focus of the development policy. At that turning point, there were several interpretations of the way in which this change could take place. Some claimed that there would be a further 'Europeanisation' of the development policy towards the ACP states.[39] Others predicted that the development policy would shift from the first pillar of the Treaty of the European Union (TEU) towards its second pillar.[40] Yet another interpretation suggested that the major change for Europe would be the emergence of a coherent external policy made up of the Common Commercial Policy, cooperation in the area of foreign policy and development cooperation policy.[41] Finally, a different possibility was advanced, which considered that coherence between the various external policies or within the development policy could be achieved through a dichotomy between their components.

A distinction between the economic and political aspects of European development policy was indeed operated, on the occasion of the restructuring of the European Commission. The Lomé Convention had for a long time been presented as a predominantly legal and economic instrument, its political aspects allegedly non-existent. The EU's attachment to neutrality, stipulated for a long time in the Convention's text, had been the major justification of this approach. This position reveals one of the more ambiguous points of the European discourse during the Lomé era. On the one hand, the EU continuously stressed the historical ties linking it to the ACP countries and, on the other, it denied the political nature of the agreement. Interestingly, when the last Convention included political conditionality, the historical ties that were referred to were those of the last 20 years and not those of the colonial past. Today, a political impact of the Agreement (ex-Convention) is admitted and, thus, a future clearer division between the components of the EU development policy is rendered possible. Some of them would become part of the European foreign policy decided by the governments while others, less politically controversial, would remain under the Commission's responsibility. The artificiality of such a distinction is clearly perceptible in former Director General Frisch's examination of the political dimension of the Convention. To the questions of whether the Lomé Convention has been an instrument of the European foreign policy, whether it has a political dimension which is 'more closely related to development', and whether there is a political dimension in the operationalisation of the policy, Frisch answers 'yes'. If then, at all these levels, the Lomé Convention is political as a whole, this distinction between more or less political aspects of the policy can be reasonably criticised.[42]

Nevertheless, it is this change that took place institutionally after the 2000 reshuffle of the Commission: DG Development (formerly VIII) has been reduced to 'contributing to the formulation' of development policy, while the coordination of all development policy was transferred to DG REL.EX. under foreign policy, and all trade aspects of trade in development were put under the responsibility of DG Trade. There is thus a true division of development matters by subject, and the fear that development policy will increasingly tend to lose its specificity as opposed to foreign and trade policy. Apart from the difficulties that this reorganisation represents for the ACP, this also creates an institutional tension between the first pillar, under which development and trade fall, and the second pillar, that of foreign policy.[43]

This overall change in the European development discourse is the first step towards a new era of the European development policy, one of increased coordination between the EU and its international partners, one where the EU aspires to become a strong political actor on the international scene. This involves a price: giving up the particularity of the EU approach to development (e.g. partnership and contractual relations, non-reciprocal preferential agreements); a particularity, however that was not strong enough to produce attempts at imitation. It must be underlined, for instance, that the current international economic regime (towards which the EU leans) undermines – with few exceptions – preferential market access for the least developed countries. Similarly, since Lomé has become 'a donor-driven mechanism of development assistance, based on a growing number of political and economic conditionalities',[44] the principle of equal 'partnership' seems to pertain to the realm of rhetoric.

It can be argued that this approach has not always been as particular as it has been presented to be. Indeed, Gabas observes that despite differences in the approaches of the EU and the Bretton Woods institutions and despite the fact that EU aid is superior to the latter's aid, the EU like all the other aid donors had to adapt to the leader's objectives.[45] Given that the competition between aid donors is strong and there exists an 'oligopoly of aid',[46] by not proposing a strategic alternative to the adjustment logic the EU has distanced itself from its own objectives. Torn between its own development policy, the development policy of its member states and the strategic choices of the multilateral financial institutions, the EU has blurred its own objectives and rendered them more vulnerable to the other institutions' goals. But here again, the simultaneous belonging of the European states to the EU and to the other institutions partly explains this lack of coherence.

Nevertheless, the EU has always insisted on the uniqueness of its policy-making. The Lomé Convention was presented as the proof *par excellence* of the specific European approach of the North-South relationship. Its termination could mean the end of this particularity or the beginning of a normalisation of the North-South relationship *à l'européenne*. Therein lies the European development discourse in all its ambiguity, between European specificity and normalisation on the international scene, between domesticity in relations with the ACP and a purportedly wild globalisation that Europe cannot resist, between promise and forgiveness, unpredictability and irreversibility, between ultimate irrationality and the necessity to always re-create community. These poles express the tensions in which the European development discourse is caught but far from regretting them or simply denouncing them, one can work with them and unfold the richness that they contain; and then resist some and build a different understanding of European solidarity on the basis of others.

ARCHITECTURE OF THE BOOK

As a background to the analysis of European development discourse, Chapter 2 offers a historical-conceptual overview of the development discourse of the US, one of the most salient development discourses both in its influence and in the critiques it has raised. The chapter focuses on three fundamental features of American philosophy: pragmatism, the social question and the idea of community, and shows how the specific ways in which they have unfolded in the development discourse since the Second World War have been detrimental to a rich understanding of America's role in development. This is what can be termed the 'American suppression of ambiguity'. By contrast, European development discourse, which is widely and erroneously considered as a mere imitation of its US equivalent, displays doubts and a distinct self-reflexivity that leave space for resistance to it and for the elaboration of a more solidaristic approach of the relations between 'developed' and 'developing'.

Chapter 3 examines, first of all, the untenable double characteristic of development disciplines, namely their occluding of their ethical or political components. In other words, strictly splitting development from its ethics fails to grasp the profoundly ethical – and often moralising – roots of development discourse, visible in this discourse's modernisation, in (neo-)Marxist or in most current versions. In turn, the recent re-emergence of an ethical questioning in development studies also both necessarily pulls us towards the search for an edifying and universal happy ending and fails to see that ethics and politics can artificially be separated only at the expense of a political reflection. A conceptualisation of development discourse as a regime of justification is proposed, where responsibility and efficiency play central roles. The notion of 'regime of justification' serves both to escape pitfalls of conceptualisations associated with underlying structures, real interests and power and to effectively denounce the tyranny of development discourse.

The fourth chapter focuses on the concept of responsibility as a vocation. Responsibility is a concept that has a very practical resonance for whomever has as much as visited a less economically developed country: it is a concept that relates to our immediate experience as witnesses of the past and ongoing practice of development (and behind it always hangs the question of colonialism). Responsibility is the most insistent conceptual question that is and will constantly be posed for the future of the more economically developed and less economically developed countries: this question haunts a wide array of burning political issues from the demand for 'reparations' of ex-colonies and current less economically developed countries to the impossibility of circumscribing a limited (geographically, at least, if not culturally, economically and politically) responsibility for global terrorism (the supposed apanage of the 'underdeveloped'). Bringing together experience and intellect, the issue of the decision in responsibility is a third layer of significance: responsibility is not only something that we can feel and not only something that we must think about, but also something that we are required to act through. The moment of decision, one of the most fascinating moments of action, is at the same time profoundly moral and amoral, grounded in knowledge and out of its reach, reasonable and 'mad': responsibility is what permits the decision and it is also its outcome. Theoretically, at least two strands of thought[47] have investigated responsibility: the most explicit is political theory. In political theory, responsibility, in the guise of justice, is a time-honoured theme relating to the fate of the community, and it has a distinctively deontological flavour: it is a principle, a should-be. Implicitly, most often under the form of 'autonomy' or 'freedom', a key characteristic of modernity, responsibility has also concerned social theory: the issue, here, is rather how possible such 'autonomy' actually is and how people achieve it, under conditions of modernity and capitalism. Bringing these two theoretical trains of thought together and applying them to the European development discourse reveals that responsibility has been increasingly used in a vague manner, has been gradually understood as less collective, and has not often been looked at pragmatically, that is, with an insistence on the precise occasions on which it is retrieved as an issue, as well as, more generally, on the dialogue from which it always arises.

The idea of a call preceding responsibility is obscured in the modern understanding of the concept, whereas it was quite present in classical or Christian understandings. In Chapter 4, after investigating the broader meaning of this idea of the call (or the vocation), the European uses of responsibility are interrogated: we observe a movement from a hierarchical to an egalitarian responsibility, accompanying the autonomisation of the EU. Finally, the political implications of global responsibility are looked at: first, how democratic is global responsibility if the idea of representativity is upheld but without mandates on the one hand, and if no direct participation in decision-making is possible on the other hand? And second, what does global responsibility mean if it always addresses a future (and therefore indeterminate) state of affairs but never the (precise) past?

Chapter 5 inquires into how efficiency has become a passion. Efficiency has hardly ever been investigated by political and social theory, in contrast to economic theory, and, at first sight, it seems a considerably less interesting concept than responsibility. This lack of thought on efficiency is surprising: efficiency haunts development discourse, at least as much as responsibility. The omnipresence of this concept and its oppressiveness (or its disciplinary aspect) is puzzling: most visitors in a less economically developed country wonder, in the best case benevolently, at the inefficiencies surrounding them. From a *conceptual* point of view, efficiency is just not challenged: activists, development bureaucrats and social scientists alike may fight over principles or, most often, their precise application in development but nobody ever claims the irrelevance of efficiency. In terms of action, efficiency is also situated before and after the decision: but contrary to responsibility, it does not create the decision, nor is it created by it. It merely serves to calculate the means necessary to an end, so as to make (not to ontologically enable) a certain (rational) decision smoother. After the decision, it is again present as exactly the same modality of calculation, but for the past.

Whereas efficiency was originally a means of calculation, it is increasingly presented as an issue that will determine the viability of the relationship between the EU and its 'developing' counterparts, in the future. How to make theoretical sense of this change? Weberian social theory offers one tool that we can use to look at efficiency: instrumental rationality. By the same token, and looking at more recent social theoretical efforts, we may paste onto efficiency modernity's second characteristic (next to autonomy), mastery. From the viewpoint of political theory, efficiency is the epitome of consequentialism, that is a vision that stipulates that action should be taken on the basis of the consequences that it will (may) bring about. Looking at efficiency through these lenses shows how irrational the concept's use has become, as it has been transformed from an instrument to an objective.

In Chapter 5, efficiency is first defined as that which relates the means to the ends (the objectives) of an action. This perspective gives us a grip on the relation between efficiency and capitalism's morality: efficiency is 'doing better what we do now'. Then, looking at what 'European efficiency' has meant, we notice the double movement from a consequentialist to a deontological understanding of efficiency and the spreading of the concept from the economic to the political field. This empirical observation is then reformulated in political terms and efficiency is conceived as having evolved from an interest to a passion. This is not only absurd but also dangerous. The consequences of this conclusion are considered: first, the threat that efficiency and the technification of development discourse has posed and poses to democracy; second, and perhaps more important than all the above, the picture of 'the barbarian' that efficiency depicts. The novelty of such an investigation resides in three aspects: it shows the damages that a single, supposedly innocuous development concept like efficiency can provoke; it shows that this sort of knowledge is, in principle, accessible to everybody; and insists on grounding resistance to development by uncovering ambiguities that are often reinforced by critical discourse.

The sixth chapter formulates the articulation of responsibility and efficiency as commitment to 'giving'. The articulation of these completely different concepts, practices and principles of action is puzzling. To think that one shelters an overwhelming significance in things political, social or developmental, and that the other does not, is not only misguided but also the central problem of many efforts that look at important themes of development discourse: efficiency is as significant as responsibility, and they are also significant together. This should not be misunderstood as claiming their equal normative or even conceptual role: evidently, in both these regards, responsibility is infinitely more challenging and ultimately always open to new questionings. To the contrary, efficiency's question can be ultimately answered. But if by saying that efficiency is 'politically significant', we mean that it matters to how the community envisages itself, then the fact that efficiency closes *a priori* any discussion on itself as determining this vision along with the fact that it does actually determine this vision, and increasingly so, confirm that we can unambiguously say that it is.

However divergent, and in some regards antithetical, the two concepts may be, they are also closely related, and in a manner that covers a wide surface of what development discourse is. As this book's interest lies also in the possibility of ultimately making sense of the vastness that 'development' is, the articulation of responsibility and efficiency, expressed by the ambiguous, multiform and omnipresent idea of 'giving', is extremely significant. The different forms of giving, borrowed from Pierre Bourdieu,[48] bring responsibility and efficiency together in different ways, in more detailed articulations. Luc Boltanski and Laurent Thévenot's conceptualisation of 'worlds' and 'compromises'[49] is then brought close to the Bourdieusian forms of giving. The formal movement of the research is one that goes from a decomposition of various elements to their recomposition into the development discourse. Once again, this opening up and ensuing reconstruction serves to show that however tyrannical (overwhelming) European development discourse may be, it is grounded in a plethora of different understandings of what development is.

In the concluding remarks (Chapter 7), it is suggested that having hindsight into where the European development discourse comes from and how it takes shape, enables one to point in a more decisive and accurate way to the shortcomings of the discourse's or development policy's usual analyses. More significantly, it offers the opportunity of considering certain components of the discourse in ways that permit us to imagine political debates, procedures and outcomes that give the everyday possibility of questioning which development, if any, is wished for. As a consequence, understanding responsibility in a solidaristic manner, for instance, as opposed to a liberal-individualistic or a paternalistic (interventionist) one, yields radically different results both in terms of the theoretical understanding of this discourse and with regard to very concrete practices. The same applies to the choice of restricting the use of efficiency to economic reasoning that, in turn, could be subjected to more debate, and therefore to more political consideration. 'Giving' in development can eventually be conceived in an equal way. Using such tools can ultimately benefit both political theorists who can mould their reflection in a pragmatic way that seriously matters and development practitioners who can find new argumentation against ongoing development practices.

2
Out of America

I recently heard the story of a small town of 7000 people, in which there are 44 churches. The 44 churches represent different dogmas, and propose different understandings and explanations of earthly matters to their believers. But they all agree on one point: that the recent war in Iraq was a good thing. For next to the 44 churches, there is another building: a bomb manufacturing plant. This is the factory where the largest number of conventional bombs in the US are manufactured. Most of the active population in this town works in, or relies, in one way or the other, on the factory. When there is war, there are jobs. When there is no war, there is unemployment. But the town's population is not that cynical: their interest in the factory is not only a matter of rational choice. They believe in war in the same way they believe in the religion that their church represents. When several of them, including a priest and a Vietnam veteran, were asked whether they see any contradiction or ambiguity in such beliefs, they reacted almost as if they did not grasp the sense of the question. What becomes clear to a non-American listener, viewer or reader in this and other stories is the suppression of ambiguity: in the US, ambiguity (its admission and, worse, its richness) is a forbidden area.[1]

Why does this chapter look at the US, placed as it is at the beginning of a book that talks about the relationship between Europe and the less economically developed world? There is a widespread belief in development studies and broader international relations disciplines, that development discourse not only originates in, but also can be equated with, American development discourse. This book argues that this is not so today, first of all, because of the distinctiveness of the European development discourse, which is substantiated in all the following chapters. However, does development discourse really originate in the US? Assuming for a moment that a quest for origins is not a futile endeavour, we may point to President Truman's famous address of 1949, for instance, and declare that his Point Four is at the root of American, international, and thus European, development discourse.[2] But one may prefer digging in the nineteenth century for the beginnings of developmentalist thought and uncover European texts by European authors, such as Marx, Comte or Saint Simon, at the origins of European, international and thus American, development discourse.[3] This chapter assumes that the peculiarities of American self-understanding – and in particular, their translation through American foreign assistance and development discourse (intimately tied as those two are in the US, by contrast to the European situation) – can be understood through America's constant interaction with Europe, an interaction that, in recent times, has taken place in the context of the American confrontation with the former Soviet Union and with the most neglected 'Other' of America: the less economically developed countries.

Concerning earlier periods, talking about the precedence of America's 'invention' over its existence[4] – the vagaries that surrounded its 'discovery', the tales and myths to which the quests gave rise before actual settlement: a purely European invention – becomes significant when one listens to the echoes of this 'invention' in development discourse of the last decades. Similarly, the enthusiasm with which the American revolution was received in Europe may seem a well-trodden theme, but it becomes less obvious at a second look, when following the ups and downs of European opinion about America, and when trying to make sense of the rupture within the 'West' over the last Anglo-American war in Iraq. Examples can be multiplied, ranging from the peculiar dialogue of European intellectuals with America, a dialogue wrought in fascination, admiration and rejection, to the complicated relations between the US and Europe during the cold war, and to the anti-colonialism of the US that ended up taking the place of Europe in the colonies. It is in the history of the relations between the two that one can draw some lessons for understanding current differences and commonalities. But for the reader of the two development discourses one thing stands immediately out: that if Europe understands and even feels comfortable with ambiguity, America does not.

Establishing this as the main distinctive criterion between Europe and the US does not in any way amount to overlooking the plethora of American paradoxes. To the contrary, it means looking with fascination both at the co-existence of churches and bomb manufacturing plants and at the suppression of any feeling of discrepancy related to this state of affairs.

In this chapter, three exemplary themes will be discussed to uncover the American suppression of ambiguity: they are all peculiar to

American self-understanding, they all clearly speak of a difference with Europe and all have very significant consequences for foreign aid and the development discourse. The first such theme is the relation between principles and their application, in the guise of pragmatism and the principle of freedom. The second is the, broadly understood, social question. And the third is the idea of community in America.

In the following attempt to disentangle the political-philosophical, the social and the cultural in the American discourse, two things must be borne in mind: that this is an attempt to shed light on elements that are historically bound to one another; and that the strongest factual difference between American and European development policies is that, in the former case, military assistance and development aid are tied together.

PRAGMATISM

The peculiarity of American pragmatism

One of the things that shocked some Americans and the majority of Europeans in George W. Bush's discourse on the war in Iraq was the frequency and intensity of his religious language blended with the famous vow to 'liberate' the Iraqi people. The reason why this was shocking was that it represented an apparently radical departure from the stance with which Americans are familiar: pragmatism, whilst retaining both the reasonableness of its tone and a repeated reference to a principle that is self-evident to Americans: freedom.

Pragmatism was described by Louis Hartz as 'America's great contribution to philosophic tradition'[5] and this description has many followers, whether they are concerned with the cultural history of America or with American philosophy.[6] But pragmatism did not spring out of nowhere: its direct ancestors are eighteenth-century British utilitarianism and empiricism, which were directly opposed to continental humanism. Utilitarianism's fundamental principle was that, in order for the greater good to be satisfied, sacrifices of the lesser goods were permissible. Significant as its theoretical objective may have been, utilitarianism left unanswered what the 'greater' good meant, who defined it, how such a criterion was practically to be applied, and last but not least, what exactly were those goods or interests that society could afford to sacrifice. Pragmatism inherited a concern with given situations rather than situations that could be wished for, as well as a focus on the materiality of social life rather than on humanity.[7] However, this is only the first of three phases in the relation between American pragmatism and Europe.

The second phase, in early to mid-twentieth-century Europe, is one of the rejection of pragmatism, in the name of Marxism or Hegelianism and, more rarely, of liberal humanism, too. During this second phase, the effects of which can still be felt today, pragmatism is not only criticised on philosophical grounds; its critique turns pragmatism into the most telling example of the aversion of the American mind towards concepts, and of its obsession with material aspects of a capitalistic reality. This is a phase that, in some of its versions, denounces the slide in the interest of American pragmatism from action to practice, and from practice to usefulness, a slide that unambiguously points back to early and contemporary utilitarianism.[8]

For more recent European thought, and for a prominent current of American thought, pragmatism becomes attractive again because it coincides with the aporias of the time. It marks a fundamental break with more conventional philosophical endeavours, placing a strong emphasis on context and on situations. Herein lie the origins of the third phase. Instead of beginning with predetermimed principles before application, pragmatism argues that one should start with what is objectively given to us, the 'pragmata', and attempt to deploy a reasoning on that basis. The commonalities with post-structuralism may have been overstretched, but one can easily see how post-modernism's rejection of 'grand narratives' may be made to correspond to pragmatism's uneasiness with pre-established principles. But if one drifts away from political and cultural theory towards the discipline of international relations (IR), another originally American contribution to academia, it is striking to observe that it is not constructivism (the rough equivalent of the post-modernist stance) that is closer to pragmatism but its opponent, realism. Indeed, realism means exactly the same as pragmatism from an etymological point of view. IR realism is thus a cousin of consequentialism, and takes into account the consequences of action rather than their guiding norms. As such, IR realism is opposed to Kantianism, and more generally to deontology, which privileges principles.

What does this tell us? First of all, that American pragmatism, broadly understood, is a big bag into which a lot of different things are thrown, depending on the 'disciplines' which reappropriate it. Thus, Dewey's pragmatism has indeed little in common with Rorty's[9] or with Keohane's. If then pragmatism is the only truly American contribution to philosophy, it speaks of a multifaceted US.

Secondly, pragmatism stands in an ultimately uneasy relation to its own most basic stance. Another way of putting this is to say that although pragmatism is not concerned with principles, it nevertheless functions on their basis, primarily on the basis of the understanding that principles can only always be derived from situations. And this is not only a problem of logic.

Myrdal has said that 'America is … conservative … But the principles conserved are liberal.'[10] Far from being an easy condemnation of American politics or, worse, the American mind, this reveals something extremely important to our discussion: that American pragmatism, in fact, allows (liberal) principles to remain unquestioned. By attempting to supersede principles, pragmatism ends up neglecting their presence, but it cannot eradicate them. That is how pragmatism, perhaps even more than utilitarianism, even more than consequentialism, closes a trap on itself; and that is how it eventually suppresses the fundamentally ambiguous relationship between principles and their application. It is to this performance of pragmatism that we must turn in order to understand why American development discourse has construed development as a problem to which a solution must be found, while never raising the question of development's creation, its founding principle. It must be clear that, far from being a merely theoretical device, pragmatism has fed, in the guise of political theory, development theory or international relations, the cautious anti-colonialism of the US after the First World War[11] or during the cold war and the relations of the US with Europe during that period. It is not by chance that, seeking to convince the Americans of the potential of a united Europe, Jean Monnet's first point was that the future belonged to a pragmatic venture.[12] Predating European theory, European bureaucracy had started entering a third phase in the relation between the US and Europe. But as will later become evident, this third phase, a third step, remained suspended.

Efficiency

The predominant place of the concept of efficiency in American development discourse is a good case in point. A fundamentally consequentialist principle, efficiency may also be seen as an offspring of pragmatism. Indeed, by definition, efficiency gives precedence to the relationship between means and ends over the question of the validity of ends. Translating this in pragmatic terms amounts to not problematising guiding norms. Efficiency is an eminently problem-solving device. It is not preoccupied with the correct formulation of the problem, it only seeks the best solution.

In 1970, the US Task Force on International Development wrote: 'If the goal is economic development, the issue is one of efficiency, not ideology.'[13] No statement of American development discourse could be clearer than this one, as far as the relationship between efficiency and principles are concerned. Efficiency is not only considered to be non-ideological, but the exact opposite of ideology. It should already be evident from the previous discussion on pragmatism that efficiency is as much a part of an ideological (here, economic liberalism) apparatus as any other principle. What is more striking is the context in which the above statement is written. The preceding phrase reads: 'Each nation must fashion its own policies and institutions to meet its own needs'.[14] Under Nixon's presidency, the delayed ending of the Vietnam war is not a felicitous background: development aid is all about economics, is the message the Task Force wants to convey, not about imposing US politics. Thus, this report seeks to keep development aid separate from military assistance, which, nevertheless, 'should be determined on a cost-benefit analysis'.[15] To the reaction of the American left (no war) is answering the reaction of the American right (no waste).[16]

But left and right are not so easily distinguished in the American foreign aid discourse.[17] Some years earlier, in 1963, the Clay Report, addressed to President Kennedy, was rightly accused of the opposite bias. Significantly, it is also a document that speaks very bluntly in favour of cutting down aid. The justification of this position is efficiency:

> If our assistance strengthens the will and capacity of a country to remain independent and helps it move towards political and economic stability, our money will have been wisely spent. If our aid simply postpones the inevitable day of financial reckoning then we have wasted our resources.[18]

This seems like a straightforward, politically 'liberal', reliance on efficiency. But here is the next paragraph:

> We believe the United States should not aid a foreign government in projects establishing government-owned industrial and commercial enterprises which compete with existing private endeavours ... The observation of countless instances of politically operated, heavily

subsidised and carefully protected inefficient state enterprises in less developed countries make us gravely doubt the value of such undertakings in the economic lives of these nations.[19]

Comments as to the ideological nature of efficiency seem superfluous.

Two decades later, under Reagan's presidency, the close integration of economic and military assistance was advocated.[20] The Commission writing this new report 'believes that foreign cooperation programs must not only be effective and efficient, but must also make Americans proud of their role in the International Community'.[21] Under the Reaganite mix of social conservatism and economic neo-liberalism, efficiency of aid is so self-evident that it does not take precedence anymore. It has become an almost undiscussed (and undiscussable) goal. To this extent, and in a context of fervent militarisation of the American development discourse, the concern with it may actually decline.[22] In that sense, Irene Gendzier may be right when she observes that, along with psychology, this discourse's preoccupation with efficiency was only a tool of romanticisation of the Third World by US development theorists.[23] In this way, American pragmatism in development matters may well have become romanticist: it has been turned on its head, having refused the principle of its own position, and having turned efficiency into another conserved principle. If, according to Hartz's aphorism on American pragmatism, 'it is only when you take your ethics for granted that all problems emerge as problems of technique', could it not also be that problems of technique become your taken-for-granted ethics?

AMERICAN FREEDOM AND RESPONSIBILITY

Freedom

After the Second World War, the US agreed to back European states in their efforts to retain their influence in their colonies where liberation movements were becoming increasingly vocal. But 'over the years, Washington's support for the European colonial states gradually resulted in America assuming imperial responsibilities for a large number of Third World client states'.[24] Although nobody would object to such a description of the West's dealing with colonies, it is striking to see that traditional American distaste for colonialism and imperialism is always waved away in the face of realpolitik and

America's 'real' interests (in this case, securing border zones against the perceived Soviet threat). However, despite the explanatory potential that realism may have, insofar as Reaganite hawks believed in it and used it, and notwithstanding the virtues of an approach that would favour a sharp divide between rhetoric and reality, the constant, unfailing proclamation of America's attachment to its own freedom and the freedom of others is mind-boggling.

For freedom is the ultimate value of American development discourse. The references to 'freedom-loving nations', 'free countries' and 'free peoples of the world' in Truman's 1949 speech are well known. But it is Dean Acheson's discourse, in 1950, that marked an unavowed ambiguity between the principle of freedom and the context in which the US pursued it through the cold war: 'The free way of life is under attack in every part of the world, including those areas of the world which we call underdeveloped.'[25] Later, in the 1960s, when the Kennedy administration initiated the blurring of the distinction between development aid and military aid,[26] the rhetoric of freedom became less prominent. It became a conserved principle, to use Myrdal's expression, and although it resurfaced in the 1970s, it was under the guise of a moderate understanding, closer to everything that is supposed to be traditional in the American taste for freedom: so,

> participation in international development can promote progress toward the kind of world in which each country can enjoy the rewards of its own culture and the fruits of its own production in its own way, without impinging on the right of any other country to the same freedom for national fulfillment.[27]

But it is interesting to note how the second escalation of the cold war caught up with this, and under Reagan, development discourse's freedom became threatening once more:

> [T]his country has an ethical interest in the long-term economic and social development of these countries that springs from our basic national values. The United States – founded on principles of freedom, democracy and humanitarianism – cannot be indifferent to the international neglect of these same principles without imperiling its own future.[28]

This last phrase reveals something which is doubly problematic in America's relation to freedom, within development discourse and in its self-understanding at large: that it cannot but see itself as founded on the principle of freedom and thus functioning on the secure basis of this *acquis* (to borrow a European development discourse term), whilst at the same time having to fight for it and this in a way that takes freedom away from others. In other words, imperial expansion becomes necessary for freedom at home.[29] The long history of American support for, or even instigation of, Latin American *coups d'état*, like in Chile or Nicaragua, witnesses this.

The small town with 44 churches and a bomb factory lives on the echoes of what Nathan Glazer has called the 'first American epic'. This epic

> emphasizes the newness, the vastness, the openness of America – the freedom thereby granted Americans. It is the old, or at least the older story about America. Connected with it are such terms as the American idea, or the American creed, or the American dream or Manifest Destiny [...] an ever available frontier denoting free land, free institutions, free men.[30]

These 'free men', however, are colonisers and settlers who only need to downplay the existence or virtues of those who are brutally colonised, when later writing the epic. This epic plays the tune of the conquest of freedom achieved without prejudice, and thus of a perfectly legitimate and unquestionable freedom. Unquestionable, indeed, since it is precisely the ambivalence between a freedom achieved (over others) and a freedom granted (by whom?) that must be suppressed, lest the question of the alien, unintelligible and tortured other is raised. This is one of the best examples of the conservatism in American pragmatism, and it is not different from the issue of America's foundation.[31] Ultimately, America will always have to perform that which it presents as given: its own Americanness, or, its American freedom, but it will always have to pretend that what matters is not what it is but what it does.[32]

The observation of such suppression of ambiguity helps make more sense of what is expressed in the American vow to 'liberate' oppressed people all over the world, as was the case in the 2003 war in Iraq. America's 'liberal dogmatism', to use Hartz's words, accommodates the simultaneous championing of freedom at home, which must be protected from infection from the outside, and the championing of freedom abroad. Dogmatic as it is, it erases the ambiguity that an operation like 'Shock and Awe' is inherently made of, namely the ambiguity between the liberation of people that must be then considered the same as Americans since they deserve freedom as much as anybody else, i.e. Americans, and the preservation of America's exceptional freedom, a freedom that is not only unequalled by anybody else but also radically different from any other people's freedom.

Responsibility

The theme of responsibility for the less economically developed countries and more generally, of geopolitical responsibility, is directly relevant to the issue of freedom, as one cannot be responsible without being free, according to the classic philosophical position. But responsibility is inscribed in a wholly different fashion in the American and the European discourses. It changes from a paternalistic to an egalitarian stance in the European case over time, whereas the American philosophy remains stable. The difference between the two points to different self-understandings in terms of autonomy, another version of 'freedom'. Europe's understanding of the acuteness of its responsibilities *vis-à-vis* less economically developed countries fades away as Europe itself gradually becomes more autonomous and constitutes itself as a political body. The US, in contrast, rising unambiguously as a superpower after the Second World War, fully accepts global responsibility as the price to pay for its undisputed autonomy. Thus, in 1949, after having declared that the US will 'keep [its] full weight behind the European recovery program', President Truman stated: 'The United States is pre-eminent among nations in the development of industrial and scientific techniques', and that is what endows it with responsibility for helping other people.[33] Again in the 1970s, one reads: 'the size and power of the United States gives us a special responsibility'.[34]

Having said this, we must trace the two directions in which the theme of American responsibility is forged. The first concerns the responsibility of the less economically developed countries: it is to them that responsibility for their own development is attributed. Thus, the 1967 Foreign Assistance Act reads: 'Development is primarily the responsibility of the people of the less developed countries'.[35] In the important 'New Directions' Act of 1973 (which represents a break with past policy due to its emphasis on poverty and needs), we find again the same assertion: 'Development planning must be the responsibility of each sovereign nation.'[36] The slide from this rather egalitarian understanding of responsibility to its precise application – ever closer monitoring of aid, political and military conditionalities, and, dating back further than anything else, the idea of 'Food for Peace' – is noteworthy; however, in no instance does the discourse ever vacillate from the principled position.

At the same time, however, the theme of American responsibility is firmly entrenched in the context of the cold war. During that period – the post-cold war period bears this legacy – there were innumerable frictions between Europe and America. The US seemed to be torn between its self-affirmation as a global power bearing global responsibilities and constant calls on Europe for burden-sharing. Thus, in 1973, the year of the adoption of the 'New Directions' in US policy, Kissinger also launched 'The Year of Europe'. On this occasion, he suggested that 'the United States has global interests and responsibilities. Our European allies have regional interests'.[37] Ten years later, this seems confirmed under Reagan's presidency: 'While our mutual assistance programs reflect our global responsibilities, those of other Western countries tend to reflect former colonial relationships and regional interests', although on an earlier page of this report, other countries are presented as increasingly sharing this global responsibility.[38]

Indeed, during the cold war, the trade-off is clear for both Europeans and Americans. After European recovery, Europeans must accept to extend responsibilities beyond their continent if they want to keep Americans in Europe.[39] But this is without taking into consideration two important factors which are the source of an important misunderstanding. The first is chronological variation, the different phases of the cold war, and specifically détente. As Palmer says, '[w]hereas for the Americans, [détente] meant legitimising the superpower status quo, for the Europeans, and in particular the West Germans, it involved exploring to what extent a new relationship might be possible across the Iron Curtain'.[40] Indeed, rather than suffocating and feeling 'squeezed' between the two superpowers, Europeans accommodated themselves rather well with the situation. Additionally, and this is the second factor, European radicals increasingly urged a rupture within the West, and a de-linking of Europe from both the US and USSR.[41] The consequences of this misunderstanding were far-reaching, as they announced the strengthening and autonomisation of the EU which was to come, the leaning of European governments to the left which spanned almost two decades, and the reactions that ranged from passive non-compliance to downright rejection of America's occasional military excursions. These consequences were far-reaching as they confirmed the very different stances of America and Europe *vis-à-vis* ambiguity.

But in terms of development discourse, a paradoxical gap was created in this context. While Europeans increasingly refused to take into account their colonial past as a justification for contemporary responsibility, the Americans' stance changed in the opposite direction. Until then, they had constantly deplored colonialism and imperialism. Truman, for instance said: 'the old imperialism – exploitation for foreign profit – has no place in our plans. What we are envisaging is a program of development based on the concepts of democratic fair dealing.' But then they slowly substituted their own influence (be it financial or military) in the ex-colonies for that of the Europeans.

How can this evolution co-exist with America's passion for freedom? American foreign aid and development discourse performs two things simultaneously. First, it sees the less economically developed countries as inexorably alien; and second, it proclaims its own universality by ignoring America's own multitude. There are different ways to attempt to remedy such a conceptual problem and one of them, proposed by Michael Walzer, would see in American freedom an exlusively political freedom.[42] But for reasons that will become clear, this is not satisfactory. For beyond the conservation of the founding political freedom, America must deal with social and cultural freedoms as well.

THE AMERICAN LEAP OVER THE SOCIAL QUESTION

'Born equal'

The refusal to face its domestic social question is a very significant part of America's self-understanding. Americans are 'born equal', wrote a fascinated Tocqueville on his return from the US, and he was talking about a society where the inheritance of a pursuit of liberty had crossed the ocean without being accompanied by a feudal ethos. On these premises, 'social freedom, social equality' in America came to be seen as the 'distinctive element in American civilization', a self-evident characteristic for Americans.[43] And whether Europeans wholeheartedly enthused in the results of the American Revolution, or whether they later sometimes deplored American vulgarity or bourgeois commonness, they always did it from a vantage point that took this freedom to be self-evident.

When Americans had proceeded to a bourgeois revolution, they had not done so against an aristocracy within their society, but against something they considered radically external to that which they were going to found: and how neatly that tied with the first epic of America's creation, of the conquest of a vast, free land! But how blind it was to the aporia that had been previously produced, an aporia that encompassed Europe: 'the very gratification they found in differentiating themselves from the Europeans by opposing innocence and corruption simultaneously jeopardised the identity they claimed as Europeans in opposition to primitive Indians'.[44] As a result, only one revolution was deemed necessary to install the only possible class, the bourgeoisie; one revolution and no other. From the outset, the irreproachability of this revolution was such that the mere idea of internal dissent and opposition was unthinkable.[45] But additionally, no revolution could ever be understood after this, because suddenly America found itself with an 'inherited' freedom.

In later years, the second American epic emerges, which 'emphasises racial and ethnic diversity', an epic that Glazer qualifies as 'somewhat more problematic'. Problematic as it produced an unheard-of tide in the calm sea of American oneness. But it may also be problematic for a reason that Glazer does not see, because it still does not raise the question of the American social fabric in terms of social conflict. That both Glazer and Walzer, as well as other American theorists, see the immigration waves as a phenomenon posing an exclusively cultural question is, I find, significant. To a European eye, the separation of racial, ethnic and 'cultural' issues from social ones is rather dubious. This returns us to what has been considered a fundamental difference between the European and the American experiences. On the one hand, we have the portrait of a culturally homogeneous society with social rifts; and on the other, the image of a socially similar society with cultural ruptures. Both of these paintings are poorly drawn. For if, on the one hand, Europe's nationalisms were successful only against the background of other intra-European identities that were erased (and whose contemporary resistance we see in the Basque or the Corsican movements, for instance) and of sustained colonialism, America's successive waves of immigrants were invariably made of people poorer than those who had preceded them. In America, capitalism was the bourgeoisie's morality but the established bourgeoisie found its working class in every newcomer.

The leap

What then is the significance of this other suppression of ambiguity, in the realm of the American treatment of less economically developed countries? In development discourse and development theory, it is first of all expressed by the long-lasting impression that the US never had to undergo any similar 'development'. Once the revolution had ended, 'America' was seen as free of the Old Continent and its corruption but having kept all its development baggage, as it were. This belief is in turn translated by unwaving trust in social and political stability, as no revolution other than the American one can be good. 'We should seek to use the social and economic tools available to us in ways that will reduce the explosive power of forces pressing for revolutionary change to the point where necessary changes can be accomplished without uncontrollable instability', writes the National Security Council in 1952.[46]

In 1957, Millikan and Rostow, two leading theorists, re-state this in a way that simultaneously higlights the awkardness of Americans *vis-à-vis* European colonialism:

> We should be more vigorously on the side of freedom and independence for subject peoples. But, leaving aside the difficulties of direct political intervention in the affairs of our Eurpopean allies, it is not at all clear that we contribute to the peace and stability of the world by encouraging colonial [sic] peoples to rally their energies around the goal of violent revolution. There is some merit in the argument of the colonial powers that to turn loose their colonies before they have acquired the capacity to deal with their own affairs is to do the colonies as well as the world at large a disservice.[47]

Thirty years later, in 1983, the Commission on Security and Economic Assistance puts it the other way around: 'Threats to stability impede economic development and prosperity', and 'foreign assistance … can temper social and political unrest …'.[48] But in all these texts, as in any other document produced after the Second World War by American development policy, stability is cherished and revolution abhorred. Even at times when it is broadly understood that stability may at the very least not be a fact, which is very far from admitting that the US itself may comprise instability, it is always seen as an undoubtedly valid objective to be fulfilled by other countries.[49]

The second, concomitant idea of a development discourse that does not accept the possiblity of social conflict is an inherent fear of mass participation. Irene Gendzier has shown the stance of American academia on the relationship between participation and development. Starting out with the contrast made by modernisation theory between a purported smooth evolution of western societies and the 'disorderly, revolutionary-prone process of transition in Third World countries', American theorists declared such hints of revolution a grave concern for American policy.[50] While in principle democracy was declared to be a universal aim, worthy of all, strong doubts were expressed as to the possibilities of less economically developed countries to have access to it. And when these countries were portrayed as possible candidates for democracy, they were nevertheless understood to experience 'problems which the US has long since outgrown or which it never faced'; and mass participation remained such a problem.[51] In later years, as premises of modernisation theory were revised or even exposed as erroneous (as by Charles Tilly) and this theory's own revolutionary potential was denounced, concern for mass participation focused mainly on one thing: the dangers it represented, dangers of 'turbulence'.[52]

Beyond the well-documented problem of the definitional gap between development as economic growth and development as democracy, what must retain our attention here is the wider refusal of American discourse to consider social conflict as a source of potential improvement. The 'leap' may be taken in three successive steps: the refusal to acknowledge possible good effects of social conflict anywhere in the world is the first step; the imposition of elimination of social conflict by the US outside home (and any book by Chomsky shows that Huntington's preference of a rapid *coup d'état* over a long revolution was turned into practice in American foreign policy) is the second step; the ultimate negation of the conserved principle of freedom beyond America's territory is the third step. Ultimately, the only type of change that is acceptable to the American developmentalist is the non-revolutionary one: this bridges the gap between an image that America cannot have of itself (bringing about revolution in other countries and thus negating freedom, but also accepting others' social conflict as it should accept its own) and the image it wants to have (promoting its own spotless example).

Thus an author like Nicholas Eberstadt who strongly criticises the anti-liberal leanings of American development aid, can, without seeing any contradiction, quote Eric Hoffer: 'There is an America hidden in the soil of every country and in the soul of every people. It is our task to help common people everywhere to discover their America at home.'[53]

AMERICAN INTERNATIONAL COMMUNITY

American Community

As David Campbell says, America is the imagined community *par excellence*.[54] It is simultaneously a nation, an idea and a power. But how easily can we transpose the expression of 'imagined community' to the US, whose simultaneous oneness and multiplicity are at the core of its identity?

Rather than pointing to a well-trodden path of thought that sees the international community as so irrevocably and deeply influenced by the US that it is equivalent to an 'American Community', the title of this section seeks to convey something different. The idea is, to the contrary, to outline a resistance to such thought by underlining the ultimate impossibility of the US to 're-create the world in its image'.[55] And to return to our initial expression, this impossibility is originally due to the suppression of ambiguity in America's own self-understanding.

The specificity of America's founding position *vis-à-vis* its own newness that did not have to oppose something internal to it also 'inspired [Americans] with a peculiar sense of community that Europe had never known', a 'knowledge that they were similar participants in a uniform way of life'.[56] In this description of the American community, one is immediately arrested by the spectre of unanimity – which had been depicted in milder and slightly different tones by Tocqueville as conformism and the danger of a tyranny of majority – a unanimity that pertains to the way of life. Is this community an 'American' community or is it the community of a plural noun?

America's self-understanding as a community is profoundly divided, but this division is only seldom acknowledged, and never in development discourse. Walzer, whose efforts to understand what it means to be an 'American' are backed by a sustained thinking about pluralist community, proposes as characteristic of the American community, the 'many-in-one'.[57] American oneness is, according to this author, a oneness of citizenship that is strictly political and truly liberal since it allows for 'manyness'. He adds: 'If the manyness of America is cultural, its oneness is political.' When, however, is political oneness really oneness? And is the cultural face of America really so plural?

From the point of view of development discourse, political oneness arises for the outside world only on the occasion of America confronting its others. In other words, America becomes an America characterised by oneness only when it must face that which is outside it. This is due to the discomfort America has when faced with difference, a discomfort first sensed and unavowed with regard to its own domestic situation: not accepting its own heterogeneity, it will always feel threatened by that which may produce such heterogeneity from the outside. America cannot bear doubt. The result is that against the background of their absolute national morality, Americans either do away with alien things or radically transform them, as Hartz suggests.[58] We immediately grasp the close connection between a conceptualisation of America as a community and its conceptualisation as a renegade of social conflict; and we immediately see its relevance, in development discourse and foreign policy more generally. When faced with its others, who are by definition different, there is one thing that American development discourse cannot do, and that is accept to live comfortably by its others' side. It cannot accept the uncertainty that this creates for its supposedly homogeneous interior, and it cannot accept the ambiguity contained in the revelation of America's manyness. As Campbell says:

> For political actors who are most comfortable with a discourse of certitude and who decry the strategic danger of ambiguity, the flux of a political space without a concomitant political order is too much to handle. Indeed, this key condition had become the new domain of danger ... the threat is uncertainty.[59]

That is how, in 1950 for instance, Secretary of State Dean Acheson could not think that it was ambiguous to, on the one hand, see the USSR as directly competing with the US for the hearts and support of less economically developed countries, that is, *competing on the same grounds*, and, on the other hand, promote liberal individualism as the American characteristic that will convince those countries: '[Increasing numbers of people] are interested in practical solutions to their problems in terms of food, shelter and a decent livelihood. When the Communists offer quick and easy remedies for all their ills, they make a strong appeal to these people'; and some paragraphs later: '[T]he peoples of the underdeveloped areas ... associate economic progress with an approach to the problems of daily life that preserves and enlarges the initiative, dignity, and freedom of the individual.'[60] The same deep, unacknowledged ambiguity is present in the Proposal by Millikan and Rostow.[61]

The purely negative expression of this double collapsing of America into the (only possible) good and of the others into America, is the old fear of infection from the outside; or the threat. Such a fear is not particular to America, and Mathy has shown the fright that European intellectuals have occasionally expressed over the possibility that the Old Continent may be invaded by the polluted germs from across the ocean; more significantly, this rhetoric has recently emerged in other parts of the world as well. Nevertheless, the fear, the threat of infection has taken a peculiar twist in the US, not least because of the systematicity in its reccurrence. If the American Revolution has been depicted as the consequence of the only possible escape from the infected Old World, the cold war has been portrayed as the sustained series of efforts not to be contaminated by Communism. The 1963 Clay Report reads: 'We live in a world ... where relentless Communist imperialism manipulates this misery to subvert men and nations from freedom's cause.'[62] Twenty years later, another report denounces 'a changing environment that threatens American security and prosperity in every part of the world'.[63] And if McCarthyism was unique in its ostracism of the infected, one can hear echoes of the past in the recent hesitations of prominent members of the American showbusiness industry to talk against the latest American war. Pearl Harbor, the Twin Towers: that is what holds Americans in terror, the crossing over of the infection to domestic soil.

Thus, if America is bent on recreating the world in its own image, as Diana Schaub puts it, then it is bent on re-creating the world (or the countries with which it is in touch, including the less economically developed countries) in the image of this community. But if America's oneness only arises for America's outside (for external purposes), it seems sensible to expect that it will always immediately be diffused into actual 'manyness' once it has reached the others' domestic situations, simply due to the others' plurality. This is the inescapability of interpretation and the inevitable variation of translation, which American development discourse cannot see since it cannot see the others' difference with itself and among them.

The hated image of America

Simultaneously, America is always received and perceived as one. How can this observation co-exist with the certainty that 'Americanism' is differently perceived in France, say, or in Zimbabwe? In contrast to what Walzer says, it can be advanced that by sheer virtue of crossing the oceans, political oneness also becomes cultural oneness. If disentangling the elements of nation (community, political) and idea (cultural) were indeed possible, we would still always have to bear in mind a third element: power. And on the weaker side, resistance to the diptych will always forcefully emerge. For ultimately, why should any other people want to exchange their oneness for another's oneness? America's intimate and unshakable faith in its own values is as unconvincing, in the realm of reason to which it purports to belong, as any other faith; and it is absolutely inoperative when it addresses other dogmatisms. Thus, unless this 'oneness' is destroyed, unless its co-existence with internal manyness is fully fledged, America will always face a hatred that it does not understand.[64]

It is not the 'paradoxical nature of American civilization' that 'justifies the extreme polarisation of the judgments passed on it', as Mathy says, for if paradoxes never fit with common sense, they are nevertheless communicable. In the 'pragmatism-idealism' couple, only one will be the point of reference, or common sense; only the other will be paradoxical. Instead it is the American refusal to admit ambiguity that is at the root of the hated image of America, since ambiguity is the multiplicity of senses, rather than the discrepancy of one sense relative to that which is 'common'. Such a multiplicity is often uncomfortable for those who hold it; but refusing it is lethal for their interlocutor who cannot make any sense of those who face him or her because s/he is not genuinely invited to.

The conquest of the minds, the concern with America's image in the world has been a particularly fertile terrain for suppression of ambiguity in development discourse. Acheson states: 'And finally, the peoples of the underdeveloped areas will begin to see new opportunities for a better life, and they will associate those opportunities in their minds with the helping hand of the American people.'[65] In the Clay Report, there is a strong acknowledgement of the need to preserve a good American image worldwide, even if inversely, as it were:

The Committee recognises that its recommendations to decrease or to abolish aid in a number of countries and otherwise tighten standards will be difficult to implement and provoke charges that they are 'politically impossible' in terms of good US relations with countries concerned.[66]

Later, and in particular at the height of the Vietnam war, a 'credibility gap' was dug in American foreign aid policy and the image of the US quickly deteriorated around the world, and in the national public opinion too.

In Eberstadt's view, this is one example of the more general situation in which American foreign aid has found itself: one where the American example abroad is not an example to follow. This is also why American development discourse keeps on placing a strong accent on the diffusion of a good image, or visibility, to the extent that, in recent versions, it may occasionally sound like a marketing lesson. Referring to the programme PL 480, also known as 'Food for Peace', the 1983 Commission on Security and Economic Assistance wrote: 'By feeding the needy, the program is a clear demonstration of US compassion and willingness to help. By its sheer volume and persistence over time, it provides highly visible and indisputable evidence of the productivity of a free society.'[67]

And when, abroad, American expatriates faithfully re-create 'home',[68] it is deplorable but no wonder that they become the first targets of anti-Americanism. They bring the US into less economically developed countries, in all its splendid oneness. In his detailed exploration of the functioning of CARE, Eugene Linden is right in saying that the American religion is the American standard of life. And Gendzier says something very similar when she points out that development theory evolved not on the basis of observation of less economically developed countries, but in a strictly domestic fashion. This is, in the end, what drives Hartz to ask: 'Can a people "born equal" ever understand peoples elsewhere that have to become so? Can it ever understand itself?'[69] The answer to the first question will always be no, until the answer to the second question is yes, i.e. America must face its multiplicity and thus, its inequality, before hoping to understand and convincingly address that of others.

Thus, if development discourse is always faced with the need of creating a community, it is a community of inequality between the developed and the developing. In the case of American development discourse, the inequality of the community is inescapable as long as

America's self-understanding remains separate from the understanding of others. Paradoxically, it is because of its colonial origins and the profoundly problematic relations that tie the Europeans to less economically developed countries, that European development discourse may ultimately be able to create solidarity instead.

European solidarity

In European development discourse, 'solidarity' is an often encountered word. In this, we must first see the expression of a discourse that has leaned, generally, much more to the left than its American equivalent. Other influences are also perceptible; in the 1970s for instance, plain Marxist expressions are occasionally found side-by-side with more traditionally paternalistic attitudes towards less economically developed countries. One must return again to geopolitical considerations. For a long time, Europe's position has fallen between the two superpowers and this affects it both materially and intellectually, despite America's constant efforts and military bases. In any case, while the European left is absent from governments, it expresses a dissent that is mirrored by European discourse. This is the big difference to American discourse, European discourse accommodates dissent.

But there is more to it. If the European messianic spirit is anything to go by, if the echoes of European Enlightenment can still be heard in development discourse, then the fact that this spirit arose against a previously oppressive way of life, and that it 'betrayed an inescapable element of doubt'[70] accompany it as well. Doubt is another word for the acceptance of ambiguity, and it is this doubt, or this ambiguity, which is the historical, intellectual baggage of Europe. Looking succinctly at Europe's understanding of the relation between principles and their application, at its view of internal social conflicts and at its understanding of community, fleshes out Europe's contrast to the US. It shows us how the most savagely colonial group of countries could and can construct a different relationship to less economically developed countries.

The relation between principles and their application is, in the European voice, expressed through development discourse, a rather tortuous one. The pot-pourri of ideologies and intellectual traditions that are to be found in this discourse has already been briefly mentioned and it will become apparent in the following chapters. Although the relative weight of economic liberalism, or of social-democratic views, changes in Europe, there is one red thread that clearly demarcates it from American pragmatism: principles are often questioned. This is not only due to the discourse's internal richness but also to another exceptional feature: the voices of the less economically developed countries, which often emerge in the European discourse, whether directly reported or indirectly referred to. Confronting the problem that development is for Europe, too, this discourse multiplies the back-and-forths between established principles and their application or their context. The very rare exceptions of principles becoming unjustifiably rigid, like the notorious *acquis communautaire*, or as the evolution of 'efficiency' betrays, are only there to confirm the rule. The case of freedom is telling, since, in its European version, freedom is somehow always only deposited in the hands of those who have it: and thus, it must always be re-conquered. Such a stance will forever prevent Europeans from talking of liberation of the oppressed people of Iraq; rather they will talk of occupation.

If, in Europe, freedom must always be re-conquered, this is both because it can easily be eroded and because it must be regulated. The European welfare state traditions all denote this belief in the necessary co-existence of freedom and the striving for equality, in a society that admits to having been born unequal. Indeed, social conflict is a theme that is inescapable for Europe. Directly translated into development discourse, this can take, for instance, the guise of protectionism when European farmers and peasants from the poorest European regions (those of the 'structural funds') are subsidised and encircled by barriers against competition from the US and less economically developed countries. More positively for the less economically developed countries, the Lomé Convention represented the largest multilateral treaty through which advantages were granted to recipients. Examples abound, but the best seems to be the northern European support of civil society in less economically developed countries, not only because it speaks of a direct concern for mass participation, but also because it shows the diversity within Europe. Such themes were far less prominent before the intense involvement in development matters of the northern Europeans who denounced former colonialist practices. However, in the end, it is paradoxically to the violent encounters between Europe and its colonies that we must revert, in order to see why social conflict cannot be 'leapt over' or neglected by the Europeans. Their long confrontation with their own 'others' abroad and at home, however violent and exterminating, kept reminding them of the conflictuous structure of their own society and the other societies to which they relate. If solidarity can be seen as the characteristic feature of a society that was held together by organic ties, it can also be seen as the characteristic feature of the relations between this society and its developing counterparts. For, by definition, solidarity admits inequality (and thus, conflict) and tries to overcome it.

It is then impossible for Europeans to see in their own community, political, social or cultural, an image that could be re-created in the rest of the world. This is not to say that the EEC did not propose its example as one to be followed, in the frame of development discourse (and one of the most diligent applications of the lesson can be found in the Southern African Development Community, SADC).[71] But it means that Europe will always tend to admit its weaknesses as the reverse side of its strengths. In development matters, the colonial past cannot but be regretted but will always serve as a point of reference for familiarity of relations (paternalistic earlier, egalitarian now). The absence of any significant military power is, at the same time, a state of affairs that some deplore and the strongest shield against attacks of the kind that the US is bound to continue experiencing. The lukewarm European attitude *vis-à-vis* immigration is neither one that pretends to have a historical claim to be a 'land of immigration' nor one that, in actual fact, leaves no hope for contemporary immigrants; and if, in a war like the 2003 war in Iraq, some European governments back the US, their citizens massively demonstrate without fear of being called non-patriotic. In the end, those citizens know that there are other European governments and other European citizens who are against the war too.

For if Europe is justifiably received by its counterparts as having one voice, it can never erase its internal diversity. It does not seek this. And every time it is confronted with its own invention, 'America', and with its successive actualisations after America's creation, it always looks at and for something that inevitably says something about Europe itself.

3
The Failed Myth
of Development

Ladies and gentlemen, don't feel let down:
We know this ending makes some people frown.
We had in mind a sort of golden myth
Then found the finish had been tampered with.
(...)
Ladies and gentlemen, in you we trust:
There must be happy endings, must, must, must.[1]
Bertolt Brecht, *The Good Person of Szechwan*

The failed, golden myth of Szechwan relies on the ideal of a 'good humanity' ruled by respected deities, where greediness and calculating meanness are absent and where solidarity reigns. In European development discourse, too, there is a community (more economically developed and less economically developed countries) with its regretted sins (colonialism and its corollaries), its absolving gods (the EU) and the final emergence of the good (development). Or so it seems. But hasn't development's 'finish ... been tampered with'? No need, here, for a *deus ex machina*: intervention, of the explicit type, is also within the definition of development. The hiatus between a development that functions predictably and a development that needs constant probing and intervention is at the centre, as it were, of development discourse.

Brecht's epilogue does not leave its audience satisfied because it is not being assured that good will eventually triumph over evil. The distorted image pictures hopelessly unserious gods, split personalities and a fundamental uncertainty over what should be done. Can we escape from this uncertainty? The answer lies in the spectators' decision, says Brecht. The same, fundamental issue of uncertainty has also haunted the social sciences. Development can thus be seen as an ever-renewed attempt to prevent us from taking the position of Brecht's audience; uncertainty can somehow be tackled and the moment of decision postponed.

Denunciations of a 'myth' of development are common in critical development studies, but most such discussions denounce a myth that is never quite successful (or otherwise it could not be denounced); but this, these studies fail to see. Rist, for instance, who sees '"development" as a part of the *modern* myth', adds that 'the myth is shared by all, it is never challenged, and it is a ready-made plan of action which is available in any circumstances'.[2] In this account, the West is self-depicted as 'a society' whose outstanding feature is rationality. The twist is that western modernity – typified by 'development' – is also built on foundations pointing to the obsolescence of myths and seeing success as depending entirely on human (rather than metaphysical) factors.[3] It is argued that discerning how the myth of development attributes meaning to its own existence within a world rendered meaningful by the same token enables resistance to such a myth. The question, however, that must be posed to such an approach is how this 'discerning' comes about. Thus, on the one hand, for the mere possibility of denunciation of a myth to exist, the premise of the perfection (as a closed system) of a myth must be relaxed. On the other hand, it is in the historicity of myths and the passage of time, as well as in the space for criticism that crises open up, that such an approach could gain credibility. For only then would such an approach be able to explain the birth, but also the erosion of myths. Most often, reasoning in terms of myth is done in a quasi-structuralist fashion that hints at 'hidden' layers of truth. Thus, instead of criticising the myth as a meaning that can be challenged by other meanings,[4] this approach often challenges the myth as a falsehood, as a non-truth. Additionally, while referring to it, a denunciation of development in terms of myth misses how exceptional development's justification is by relying on rationality. A look at capitalism makes this clear. As Castoriadis says: 'le capitalisme est le premier régime social qui produit une idéologie d'après laquelle il serait "rationnel". La légitimation d'autres types d'institution de la société était mythique, religieuse ou traditionnelle.' ('Capitalism is the first social regime that produces an ideology according to which capitalism is "rational". The legitimation of other types of institution of society were mythical, religious or traditional.')[5] Thus, like for capitalism, to attack 'development' credibly one must attack its claim to rationality rather than its mythical essence.

By contrast to critiques that insist on the myth's unfelicitous results, the current emphasis of development studies on ethical questions systematically looks for a 'happy ending'. Indeed, having followed the infamous impasse of development studies of the late 1980s and, later, the strong political flavour of the 1990s discourse, ethics of development seems to gain a prominent place in the academic and the institutional worlds. However, talking about development ethics entails splitting (the practice or the politics of) development from its ethics and fails to grasp the profoundly ethical roots of development discourse.

Alternatively, development discourse can be conceptualised as a regime of justification. This formulation aims, first, to resolve both the difficulty of viewing development as a myth and the problematic separation that development ethics operates between itself, development economics and sociology. Second, this formulation seeks to interrogate the capacity of survival of development while denouncing and resisting its tyrannical elements: hence, it insists on the plurality and the diversity of registers of argumentation, it examines how justifications unfold, and it argues that a lucid and fruitful political critique must acknowledge its dialogical position *vis-à-vis* 'standard' development discourse.

THE SOCIAL-SCIENTIFIC ETHICS OF DEVELOPMENT

Ethics, economics and sociology

There are two important reasons why there cannot be a separation between what is and what is not 'ethics' in development. The first pertains to knowledge and the second to responsibility: they are both political. The first reason is contained in Walker's discussion of International Relations as political theory.[6] In 1993, Walker states that although ethics in international relations asks fundamental questions about the link between modernity and community, it is quickly dismissed as trivial, either because the world is how it should be (the 'modernistic' argument) or because 'how it is to be known' and 'how it should be' are seen as separate. Thus, 'questions about ethics are either deferred as mere theory and philosophy or simply subsumed into an account of the way the world is presumed to be'.[7] A decade later, this is no longer true with regard to development discourse and development studies; ethics is gaining an increasingly prominent academic position. Nevertheless, Walker's observation still holds insofar as the separation between ethics and 'non-ethics' is as strict as it had been before and, of course, as unacknowledged. It is vital for political debate to recognise that accounts of how the world is, in fact contain an ethical suggestion about how the world should be. What Walker says about international relations can equally be applied to development theories: they are 'a crucial site in which attempts to think otherwise about political possibilities are constrained by categories and assumptions that contemporary political analysis is encouraged to take for granted'.[8]

In a short text called '*Le cache-misère de l'éthique*' ('that which hides the poverty of ethics'), Castoriadis gives us the second reason, by equating what he sees as a 'return to ethics' with a rise of individualism, the increasing dominance of the private over the public sphere and a rejection of politics.[9] Despite the fact that Castoriadis' dichotomy between all types of ethics and politics is unconvincing (because of the sharp divide between the individual and the collective that respectively correspond to the ethical and the political), the emphasis that he places on two elements must be retained for our purposes. The first is his aversion towards universalistic individualist thought, as human beings are social beings. The second element is his observation that ethics may exonerate from individual and political responsibility.

These strong reasons and warnings are not heard clearly enough by writers preoccupied with development ethics; and neither is it sufficiently underlined, in these writings, that the current emphasis on ethics is only one of a long historical series. For indeed, the current ethical (re)formulation of issues related to development is certainly not the first such questioning that was historically induced by development discourse. However, the current questioning markedly differs from the other three broadly identifiable periods during which 'ethics of development' emerged.

In comparison to the first period – that of colonialisation at the end of the nineteenth century[10] – the current era differs significantly in moral explicitness; it is less explicit in its avowed conformity to standard moral codes. Nevertheless, the justifications used by both 'conservative' and 'progressive' developmentalists still reveal strong religious and other moral beliefs. In the second period – the post-Second World War period up to the 1970s – an advance in capitalistic development meant a retreat in socialist development. By comparison, the current ethical questioning is not situated by opposition to an enemy.[11] Finally, in the late 1970s an anti-development agenda emerged, founded on a radical ethical questioning of development discourse: the view of development as a myth springs from this tradition.[12] By contrast, the current (mainstream) ethical questioning does not reject the idea of development.

Thus, issues of ethics became more salient at political and intellectual times of crises.[13] But this neither meant that such issues were not present when they were less salient nor that they ever existed beyond the context of development practices and knowledge. Thus, it is impossible to talk about ethics of development without talking about development sociology, and it is impossible to talk about development economics without including ethics. The difference, for instance, between neo-classical and Marxist economics is, among others, ethical.[14] Observing this entails uncovering ethical presuppositions where they are concealed (as they are in the concept of efficiency) and 'historicising' and 'socialising' ethical reflections where they are abstracted from their context (an abstraction expressed in the common use of the concept of responsibility).

If ethical issues are involved at every level of development discourse, what has gone wrong with the other development theorising (allegedly non-ethical)? In the search for an answer to this question, one needs to look at the predominance of economics in the field of development as knowledge: development studies started as '*de facto* development economics'.[15] Although Marxism did to some degree challenge mainstream development economics, it was actually neo-classical economics that dominated the discipline. Other contenders, structuralist economics or dependency theory, gained momentum particularly in the 1970s only to lose it later.[16] With few exceptions, the philosophical presuppositions of these economic approaches all shared one fundamental and straightforward ethical stance, that of contempt.[17]

Hirschman narrated 'the rise and decline of development economics'. He claims that development economics as a broad social-theoretical endeavour failed because it did not eliminate the colonisers' contempt towards the colonised:

> with the new doctrine of economic growth, contempt took a more sophisticated form: suddenly it was taken for granted that progress of [the developing] countries would be smoothly linear if only they adopted the right kind of integrated program ... these countries were perceived to have only interests and no passions.[18]

In a similar vein, Gasper, too, adopts this metaphor of interests and passions; he shows how the economistic world-view and its reductionist conception of people downplayed the importance of violence and suffering.[19] The partial discrediting of economics, whose simplifications were only understood after they had done a lot of damage to the less economically developed countries, is an important explanation of the rise of development ethics. But at the same time, we now see how in fact development economics was woven into a particular development ethics, one which spoke contentedly about the superiority of the 'developed'.

The second social-scientific realm that was involved in development theorising, (macro)sociology, was equally reductionist. As in economics, different 'third ways' were attempted between modernisation theory (later transformed into rational choice/ institutional theory) and (neo-)Marxism.[20] Although for a long time dominated by development economics, development sociology adopted the assumptions that still underpin development thinking, namely a strict separation between modernity and tradition and specific, linear directions in change. The ethics of these theories range from the preference for the 'western model' of the later diffusionism to the belief in superior societal forms of evolution, to the idea that structures (and institutions) count more than people's choices in the shaping of social life in structural functionalism.

The different strands of the sociology of development diluted with political economy and political science gave birth to 'development theory'. This took shape with a practical orientation, towards new countries that had to be won over in the cold war context. When the solidity of these elements was shattered, development theory faced a crisis too. Not being exclusive to development theory, this crisis touched most social sciences, including other forms of sociology, under the combined attack of post-modernism and (neo-)Marxism. This crisis brought development theory into an impasse that stirred great controversy in the departments of development studies.[21] But, like other social sciences, 'development studies' ended up producing a wealth of empirical studies – focused on a great variety of subjects and groups – that showed an apparent aversion towards grand theoretical narratives.[22] Again, as with other broad areas of sociology, the mainstream theoretical foundation of these studies was (neo)institutionalism and marked a predilection (at least for a certain time) for rational choice theory.[23] But the crisis did not end.

The 'standard model of development' and critique

The crisis did not end because three circumstances were simultaneously present. The first is the fact that development's ultimate irrationality was not effectively attacked. As we saw in Chapter 1, this ultimate irrationality is an argument which is abstractly strong enough to put an end to the crisis, but it does not offer a constructive reappropriation of the 'problem' of development. The second circumstance is that development discourse proved more resistant to repeated critiques than had been expected, unveiling a certain continuity of development, which in turn, underlines some of its fundamental aspects, as we will see. The third circumstance is that critique did not give up denunciation.

Is there a 'standard model of development'[24] in the Sisyphean resistance of development discourse to strenuous critique? And if there is, how can we account for the historical plurality of developmental paradigms? Such richness belies the 'standard' characteristic of the model. A 'standard' underlying so much change places the 'truth' of development discourse and practice in tension with the meaning bestowed on it by different historical paradigms.

But through the patterns and ruptures in development discourse, one discerns a degree of continuity that underlines some significant features of development. One such feature is the persistent relationship between the more economically developed and the less economically developed. This persistence allows us to conceptualise the relationship as one which creates community (a community containing both more economically developed and less economically developed countries) and thus draws from it an obligation of mutual aid and an interdiction of disengagement. It also poses the fundamental question: once development is successfully criticised, what will happen to the less economically developed countries? Straight 'anti-developmentalism' is a theoretical temptation that has dramatic practical results, if stretched to the limit. Both these issues are relevant to the conceptualisation of development discourse as a regime of justification. As we will see, a 'regime' or 'set of rules' corresponds to a certain continuity, even as this continuity is traversed by incessant movement.

Another feature underlined by this continuity is the long success of development discourse in mobilising enormous amounts of money and a plethora of jobs. In practical terms, development can indeed be called an industry, a machine,[25] something that constantly regenerates itself and has huge consequences for the domains it touches.

These technical metaphors point to yet another fundamental aspect of development: its close relationship to capitalism. Although capitalism has undergone changes in its practices and its 'spirit', its relation to development has not changed.[26] The relationship in the

European development discourse is rather straightforward: it stipulates that the quickest, best and most laudable path to development is the capitalistic way. If development's resistance is problematic (or mysterious), this is largely due to capitalism's own endurance. An analysis of capitalism that highlights the irrationality of capitalism is a first step to theoretically unmaking this resistance.[27] Given the current overarching presence of capitalistic thought in development discourse, such an analysis is enough to show development's own irrationality. Earlier, when strong alternatives to capitalism were still upheld it would have been necessary to show the fallacy on which development as such is founded.

This last feature of development that becomes clear to us through the continuity expressed in development's resistance to critique, which is the second factor of the crisis, is also closely related to the third factor of the crisis: the persistence of critique. Bob Sutcliffe has summarised the attacks on development as polarisation, attainability and desirability critiques.[28] Polarisation critique adopts the centre-periphery model, according to which the periphery is 'exploited' from the centre; it is a critique that focuses on economic imperialism. Attainability critique takes an ecological or environmentalist stance and denounces the non-sustainability of current development practices as well as the future limits of natural resources. Finally, desirability critique fundamentally attacks current versions of development on the grounds that they exclusively originate in the West/North and impose themselves on other cultures. If they involve issues of development ethics, such ethics originate in the capitalistic model denounced by the critiques. Indeed, capitalism contains strong philosophical (and ethical) premises about how the world should work and how this must be achieved, ultimately, the proper human conduct. Examining a concept such as efficiency (Chapter 5) discloses this in an exemplary way.

Sutcliffe suggests that these most recent tendencies of the debate on development result from the increased importance of the attainability and desirability critiques.[29] This gives us a general picture of development critique (and studies) where economics becomes less prominent and where environmental and cultural studies are increasingly important: thus, imperialism in development, when denounced, is ecological or cultural rather than economic. This evolution relative to the development debate, is similar to that noted by Lawrence M. Mead with regard to the welfare state debate: the 'social' is increasingly taking over the 'economic' in the management of the welfare state;

and such change is disturbing because it closes fundamental debates like the debate about capitalism, and because it deeply intervenes in people's lives.[30] Not only can this evolution be found in areas other than development *stricto sensu*, but it is also noted in earlier historical periods. Indeed, another of this tendency's expressions is the crisis of political economy that gave birth to social economy in the nineteenth century.[31] In these past and current moments of crisis, the response is always simultaneously an attempt at control of 'the social' and a renewal of explicit ethical questioning.

But is the 'polarisation critique' (against economic imperialism) increasingly losing momentum with respect to the other critiques? It is not certain that it is: the alternative development type of critique, represented prominently by Asian scholars and by those western scholars who feel inclined to a different 'spirit' of development, argues for development forms not based on western standards of reason, knowledge and progress. In fact, it is built on a denunciation of the imposition of these standards all over the world, and in particular in the ex-colonies. This strand of critique encompasses proposals for different production patterns. In the most recent cultural critique, the centre-periphery scheme is very present too. Thus, the 'myth of development' approach focuses on development as a legitimising device of the West, as we saw. It can be compared to the critique of development being an illusion. Finally, the recent efforts of bringing post-structuralist conclusions into critical insights also contribute to the polarisation critique, through an insistence on the different perceptions of time and space in the 'North' and the 'South'. But none of these critiques accepts 'the standard model' as desirable.

The agreement, throughout the different strands of critique, on the dichotomies that development produces and the consequent need to change this denotes the long-standing influence of socialist thought, a thought often persisting in the 'South' and gaining a new vigour in the 'North'. Writing in 1990, Stauffer predicted this:

> Socialism has lost [the appeal of promised deliverance from capitalism] – at the moment – but with its historical ability to be the most creative source of a coherent critique of the direct human costs of capitalist development, it can be expected to provide a central component of any future pulling together of the currently fragmented voices demanding alternatives to the future that the capitalist road promises to deliver.[32]

It did, in the same year – and the date is significant because of the contemporary changes in the political landscape of Europe and also because of the breath that the social sciences started to recover after the 'post-modernist' attack. Hettne expressed a similar view: 'As long as the system of production and distribution seems irrational from the point of view of human needs and ecological sustainability, the socialist tradition will constitute a source of criticism and utopia.'[33] Here too, an ethical background is discernible, and it does not only clash with the 'standard model of development'; both the 'standard' capitalistic model and the socialist tradition embrace a belief in progress and in human improvement and share epistemological similarities (which are not unrelated to ethical questioning or the silencing thereof). We thus unavoidably encounter the drawbacks of the 'standard model' perspective on development.

In this context of a crisis that has continued for a long time, development studies are at stake. The relation between academia and development agencies returns to the shape it had at the beginnings of US development theory when the latter was designed to closely monitor government policies. The demise of development economics – other than the mechanistic version of efficiency-seeking – and that of development sociology has brought development studies to a narrower, problem-solving and eclectic position. This is the result of 'development [having] been consigned to the realm of low politics'; unless 'the international order, as it has been constructed, is threatened'.[34]

Precisely because the international order seems threatened, development ethics gains academic importance, and development as a set of globalised conceptual issues seems to outgrow the university departments that are supposed to study it. This is an encouraging tendency, because it indicates an increased awareness of how issues of the 'South' relate to the 'North', not to mention the very presence of the 'South' in the 'North'.[35] As Hettne emphasised more than a decade ago, '[t]he "development problem" comes closer and closer as world space and national space interweave. Development will therefore be a concern for all the social sciences, drawing them together, if not merging them into one unified social science.'[36]

DEVELOPMENT DISCOURSE AS A REGIME OF JUSTIFICATION

If conceptualising development as a myth is too holistic an approach; and if looking at development's ethics never dares to ask the bolder questions that must be asked, then looking at development discourse as a regime of justification enables us to do several things at the same time: identify its different justifications; expose the non-fixity of its moments and thus open up spaces for political discussion; but also take it in as a whole by stepping out of it and seeing what is thought to be 'standard' about it. We can thus begin to formulate an idea on why it is that attacks of development discourse on one specific account of injustice, rather than several, have left it wounded but intact.

Justification

It is the political-scientific history of ideas that provides us with the expression 'regime of justification'. In his study of the ideas of post-colonialism, Jackson observes that '[n]ineteenth century colonialism was not only a system of power for the pursuit of western national or commercial interests; it was also a *regime of justification* expressed by domestic and international law'.[37] The expression 'regime of justification' seems very useful because it underlines that this justification is constitutive of a set of rules. In other words, a regime of justification must be understood as an arrangement of *a priori* understandings of what is just and what is unjust in development discourse. *A priori* does not mean that these understandings are forever fixed in a normative framework of development discourse; to the contrary, justifications change over time. *A priori* means that before every novel form that development discourse takes in response to the critique it resists, a number of new justifications will have been retrieved.

The most significant inspiration for the conceptualisation of development discourse as a regime of justification is the work of Luc Boltanski and Laurent Thévenot on justification. In contrast to much of critical theory, Boltanski and Thevenot's work distances itself from references to a hidden layer of reality composed of raw power and 'real' interests that are not immediately perceptible. Although this approach does not deny a materiality of reality, it is close to a phenomenological inspiration and thus accentuates the importance (the complexity and richness) of what appears before our eyes.[38]

Three central aspects of Boltanski and Thévenot's conceptualisation are of concern: justification, the orders of worth and the compromises. In a nutshell, the relation between these three aspects is the following. People, say Boltanksi and Thévenot, must be taken seriously when they justify their actions: when they act, people bear in mind that they may have to render an account of what they do, why or how.[39] Justification, arising only in situations of dispute, is one among at least three different modes of human interaction. The other two are love (where people tend to downplay possible dispute and hence, justification) and violence (where people enter into dispute without concern for a possible common understanding).[40] Locating justification in this way helps to see the importance of the concept of equivalence (or 'increase in generality'): for people to be able to justify themselves, they need to agree to shed strictly private concerns and seek common ground (which is not the case in either love or violence). In order for this common ground to be revealed, people need 'to focus on a convention of equivalence external to themselves'.[41]

This equivalence is neither universal and one nor infinitely plural: there is a 'limited plurality of principles of equivalence', located in a limited number of orders of worth. These orders of worth are constructed by Boltanski and Thévenot on the basis of philosophical texts that seemed to correspond to the types of justification given in situations of dispute that they had collected in a more directly 'empirical' way. Each of these orders of worth allows a coherent judgment and justification; a judgment and a justification that are based on a hierarchy within each order of worth. For instance, the domestic order of worth that is based on trust, tradition and hierarchical responsibility, has different beings in it – children and adults – whose 'worth' is smaller or bigger according to their placement in this hierarchy.[42] At the same time, however, next to this constraint of order (hierarchy), another constraint underlines the regime of justification: the constraint of common humanity that allows people to shift from one justification to another.

A concept of responsibility is to be found in two orders of worth according to Boltanski and Thévenot: the domestic and the industrial. In both cases, responsibility is the prerogative of the hierarchically superior *vis-à-vis* the hierarchically inferior: in both cases, responsibility is hierarchical. In the domestic case, parents are responsible for their children. Here, 'the political link between beings is seen as a generalisation of kinship and is based on face-to-face relationships and on the respect for tradition'.[43] Dependency and trust are crucial. In anticipation of Chapter 6, we may already observe that the form of 'giving' that corresponds to the domestic order of worth is the gift. The gift is the strongest sign of community, of relations that are inscribed in durability, it is the prerogative of the wealthy and it cannot be refused.

In the industrial order of worth, the people in charge (the *'responsables'*) – the managers, for instance – take care of the simple workers, or, generally, those who are less important in the hierarchy of the firm/factory etc.[44] Planning and investment are crucial. Again anticipating Chapter 6, we can observe that debt is the main form of 'giving' in the industrial order. The debt is more formal than the gift; it is inscribed in the duration of relations but frames time in a specific way.[45]

Efficiency is found in the industrial and the market orders of worth. Efficiency is the industrial world's central characteristic and it is closely related to measurability and productivity. We will call it 'productive efficiency', to distinguish it from the other sort of efficiency: 'allocative efficiency', the efficiency of the market order of worth. In the latter order of worth, the harmonious social is based on the market, which is another (second) version of 'economic relations', as stressed by Boltanski and Thévenot. Seen through market or industrial arrangements, i.e. responding to different types of uncertainty, efficiency will play different roles in, and will be differently 'compromised' by, its encounter with the different types of responsibility. The form of 'giving' that corresponds to the market order of worth is the *donnant-donnant* form (to be examined in Chapter 6).

Compromises are a way of solving a dispute, which is close to the common-sense understanding of the word. In Boltanski and Thévenot's words, 'in a compromise, people maintain an intentional proclivity towards the common good by cooperating to keep present beings relevant in different worlds, without trying to clarify the principle upon which their agreement is grounded'.[46] Given that radical criticism of (the irrationality of) development has been ineffective, and that development has continued existing without fundamental wounds, it makes sense to look at the compromises it struck with the various attacks it suffered. That the bulk of development discourse is made of compromises suggests that it constantly avoids clarifying its own principles (of agreement with its critique). This also means that when we see or hear principles of development discourse, we see or hear their compromised versions.

Development discourse's justification

Before moving on to apply this perspective, one more question needs to be answered: why does development need to justify itself?

If justification makes sense from the sociological viewpoint, can we transpose this smoothly onto the domain of discourses?[47] It certainly seems so. In development discourse, as 'mainstream science' and 'orthodoxies' appear, they clash with the preceding ones, or with enemies of the 'spirit of development'. In dispute, development needs to justify itself. As Castoriadis says that capitalism is born and develops within a society where conflict is present from the outset, so we must see in development discourse a phenomenon that advances only by stumbling onto its critique.[48]

There are additional elements in answer to this question. First, the overt moral grounding of development discourse begs justification as does any morality in a secular context, as illustrated by our discussion on development ethics. Claiming or assuming that something is inherently 'good' is a position that needs justification, at least in specific actualisations. As Ferguson puts it,

> If 'development' is today from time to time challenged, it is almost always challenged in the name of 'real development'. Like 'goodness' itself, 'development' in our time is a value so firmly entrenched that it seems almost impossible to question it, or to refer it to any standard beyond its own.[49]

But ultimately, because no overarching concept of God or Nature covers the space of doubts, development's 'goodness' is questioned and development discourse is called upon to justify it, by (often unwittingly) using standard philosophical accounts that are transformed to fit the purpose. This aspect reveals another link between capitalism and development; capitalism, too, draws on already legitimate sets of justifications and reinvents them. Those justifications change, as time passes; they lose their compellingness, or their motivational force, and then, the 'spirit' of capitalism changes too and asks for new justifications.[50] For capitalism, like development, is grounded in morality; it therefore resorts to moral, philosophical justification. Starting with Weber, going to Hirschman's 'The passions and the interests' and finishing with Boltanski and Chiapello's recent book, this is what the most innovative works on capitalism show us.

Second, the gaps in the different definitions of development demand a justification. There are at least two sorts of definitional gaps of development: the first one is that between development as an outcome and development as a process. As DuBois puts it, 'the many different meanings assigned to development in the Third World are a source of much discussion. Some of this debate concerns development as a process and some the end or goal of that process.'[51] He continues to the effect that there is a third aspect of development which is still distinct and which 'is neither debated nor discussed because it is taken for granted. Development itself – the state that certain countries find themselves struggling to attain ....' This third mysterious development looks like an instance of Foucaultian reification of the discourse and it is revealing the fundamental appeal that the existence of development has.

This definitional gap epitomises Castoriadis' discussion of the irrational rationality of development. Rather than focusing particular means on the achievement of a defined objective, development is directed towards achieving a level that will, in turn, permit the attainment of another level and so on. The most characteristic justification of this ambiguity is efficiency. The most characteristic example of this ambiguity is the opposition between 'developing' (process) and 'developed' (outcome) countries.

The second ambiguity in the definition of development is pointed out by Ferguson and it cuts across the elements of rationality/ irrationality and process/outcome.

> On the one hand, 'development' is used to mean the process of transition or transformation towards a modern, capitalist, industrial economy ... The second meaning ... defines itself in terms of 'quality of life' and 'standard of living', and refers to the reduction or amelioration of poverty and material want. The directionality implied in the word 'development' is in this usage no longer historical, but moral.[52]

This dual indeterminacy also applies, in a broader way, to 'modernity' as a temporal and substantive conception, with a certain flavour of morality. In Gasper's words, the term is simultaneously evaluative and descriptive.[53]

Finally, the 'technification' of development – to quote Escobar – 'allowed experts to remove from the political realm problems which would otherwise be political, and to recast them into the apparently more neutral realm of science'.[54] This claim is backed up by Porter: 'the hierarchy of this discourse ensures that mastery of technical metaphor paradoxically rules ...'.[55] However, this move never fully achieves the removal of development from the political realm.

In this sense, development is essentially contestable and pertains to the domain of politics.[56] Thus, the critique of development or development discourse belongs to the overt political debate. That it takes place within universities rather than in policy environments casts doubts on its effectiveness but not on the political nature of the debate. But admitting that development is contestable means conceding that the discourse that constantly reinvents it must also justify it. So the increasing technification of development discourse uncovers the fundamental paradox of development; the hiatus of the 'golden myth' offering predictability and duration and yet always needing to be 'tampered with', reminiscent of the paradoxical metaphor of the market economy working as a clock, in constant need of rewinding and yet spontaneous.[57]

Speculating on why development discourse needs justification discloses the how of a regime of justification. Escobar observed that development possesses an 'immanent adaptability to changing conditions, which allowed it to survive, indeed to thrive up to the present', but always within 'the same discursive space in which we are encapsulated'.[58] Ten years later, he asks: 'why has development been so resistant to radical critique?'[59] He answered: in its critique, development discourse finds the substance of its adaptability, like capitalism. That development has been formed out of its struggles with critique should come as a natural conclusion to those who see capitalism being reinvented through such a process.[60]

Concluding, we note that the regime of justification, which is based on a set of rules must, first, be related to 'the standard model of development'. In the light of our definition of discourse, this 'standard' is a continuous attempt at fixity. The combination of, on the one hand, the movements that are due to the tyrannical tendencies of development discourse and, on the other hand, this immobility that the 'standard model of development' tends to ascribe to the set of rules gives us a fuller picture of development discourse, whilst avoiding the dichotomy between the continuous and discontinuous views. In this scheme, the concepts of 'responsibility' and 'efficiency' are significant components of the European development discourse as a regime of justification insofar as each of them represents the main paradox of development, a process that functions automatically ('standard') while needing to be tampered with ('tyrannical movement'). Each concept serves a different type of justification; responsibility addresses the reason for aid to development, efficiency addresses the modality for aid to development. But it will become clear that efficiency has also become a reason and responsibility has also become a modality.

'Development discourse as a set of rules' points to the tyrannical tendency of development discourse, that is, its tendency to overwhelm its own borders.[61] Indeed, this set of rules corresponds to one set of boundaries. Thus, if the crossing of boundaries that development discourse performs over the decades is understood as tyranny, then the regime of justification is constantly re-imposing this renewed order. It is, for example, tyrannical to see post-Second World War economic development becoming political development, social development and lastly human development. The initial idea of development (however absurd) has crossed the boundaries of the area where it was legitimate (the economic) and imposed its logic on areas that are ruled legitimately by other principles and other sets of rules. Translated into terms of justification, this movement corresponds to a movement across different orders of justification.

Thus, a regime of justification encompasses the possibility of critique, its refutation or annexation. But both as critique and as the aim of critique, development discourse closes off possibilities. Critique attacks precisely this paradox, although it is equally vulnerable to it. Attempts at achieving closure take the form of justification that mobilises a specific framework in order to limit what can be said. Many examples of such closure can be given; for instance, avoiding expressions like 'Third World' seems difficult, even for critical writers. Similarly, it is impossible to find in the (critical) literature on development discourse texts that disengage from a directional perspective on the world. But more optimistically, it is clear that critique to a very large extent influences the ways of development discourse; even if for activists this is still too slow, too heavy, or too little.

Against tyranny

In Ancient Greek mythology, myths are never really 'golden': they are ambiguous, and their messages are unclear. The divine community is far from being perfect; theft, lying and adultery take place continuously, kindness is not a strong value and although the gods give second chances, they do not forgive. There is a simple reason for such catastrophic but interesting results; gods are understood to be close to humans. Nevertheless, the gods must not be angered, hence the myth's frequent function is to prevent humans from committing *hubris*. Hubris is arrogance towards gods and it attracts their wrath. It is the birthplace of the human ambition for autonomy and mastery, on the one hand. On the other hand, it is the doom of humanity. Emancipation is its positive equivalent, tyranny is its negative version.

European modernity has freed itself from the need for constant reminders of the results of divine wrath. But in so doing, it has opened the door to an increased threat of human tyranny. The tyrannical components of development discourse are found, for instance, in development's substantive expansionism from economic development to social development and further to human development. They are also found in the increasing tendency to mingle political elements with trade relations, or in the dominance of instrumental rationality as a way of reasoning. Tyranny is the crossing of boundaries that should not be crossed: if money, as a good to be socially distributed, permeates spheres others than its own, tyranny results. Development discourse (like capitalism) is tyrannical almost by definition;[62] it strives to cross barriers illegitimately. This certainly occurs at the discursive level; but it also has very practical daily consequences.

As this is not without struggle,[63] tyranny and resistance exist hand-in-hand. The fundamental uncertainty that Brecht's audience faces, faces us all. Not conceptualising our lives in golden myths, not seeing development as a myth, allows an unprecedented openness and is more optimistic, for it not only reminds us to look for those possibilities that lie next to the 'non-alternatives' we were facing but it urges us to act upon outcomes that may not be inevitable. That is what is offered by an approach of development as a regime of justification: a simultaneous acknowledgement of the multiplicity of areas that make up development, and the possibility to separate these areas; an understanding of development's richness and ambivalence, and a resistance to the impossibility of judging any part of development; a perception of a certain 'automatic' functioning of development, and an insistence on the fact that development is about intervention whose nature can be altered by critique; the agreement that the more economically developed and the less economically developed share a common world, and the straightforward drawing of the adequate conlusion that this then entails obligations for the more economically developed.

This means opening up more spaces for political discussions; it means finding, in the given 'common sense', themes, areas, issues that should not be 'given', which are not so 'common', and that need first to undergo debate. This brings us to scientific resistance: common sense must be denounced and the barriers that prevent questions from being asked must be breached.

4
The Vocation of Responsibility

La responsabilité exige du courage
parce qu'elle nous place à la pointe extrême
de la décision agissante,
parce qu'elle implique une vocation.[1]

Vladimir Jankélévitch says: responsibility demands courage. How paradoxical, we think at first, that something belonging to the realm of reason, that turns us into reasonable beings (how else would we live together?) should find its support in a 'passion', the feeling of courage. How paradoxical, we also think, that something which is, by definition, a response must utter a demand. Jankélévitch says that responsibility places us at the edge of the acting decision, as if it was not we who decide to be responsible; it places us at the edge of the precipice that our decision always is, as if our decision was making us, and not we our decision. To some extent this is indeed true, for at that ineffable moment of decision, of action, our decision does make us, and our responsibility has spoken for us and has done for us. It is easy to see; we need only to place ourselves in the not so improbable situation of a war, say, or a genocide. We see a man being tortured; we can cry out against the violence, the inhumanity. Indeed this does demand courage. The moment we cry out, our responsibility leads us to cross that edge on which we had been balancing. The step we had suspended has been taken. Yet, the same happens when we pass by the scene of torture in silence. Our responsibility has placed us at the edge of a decision that was taken: not to cry out.

The concept of 'responsibility', appearing in a philosophical sense in the mid-nineteenth century, 'was a new instrument for use in current and ancient controversies'; it 'made explicit an opposition which had grown up in the analysis of the imputation of actions to agents and of the accountability of acts and agents in applying penalty or punishment'.[2] Indeed, whether in strictly legal or philosophical debates, whether under this name or not, the perception of responsibility has undergone major changes. Tracing these changes unveils the ambiguities of the contemporary understanding of responsibility in development discourse and it allows the denunciation of a rhetorical usage.

From a practical or political perspective, responsibility is necessary: the most elementary relationships entail responsibility. The rules that bind two people into such relationships – love, friendship, partnership, labour contract, etc. – entail responsibility.[3] This means two things: that in creating and accepting 'the rules' implicitly or explicitly, both people take responsibility for their future actions; once such agreement is ascertained in the sphere delimited by it, both people accept to be held responsible for what they have done in what is to become their past. The important distinction here is not the difference between taking responsibility and being held responsible. The important distinction is that between a future and a past responsibility. Indeed, if 'legal' responsibility never emerges in the European development discourse, this is because of the increasing absence of references to responsibility for the past. Since the nature of responsibility is never really specified, we are thus led to look at it as moral or political responsibility.[4] The confinement of responsibility to future good intentions and its translation into 'global responsibility' are equivalent to the forgetting the colonial past and to the gradual disengagement of the Europeans *vis-à-vis* the ACP, both highly problematic perspectives.

AUTONOMY, KNOWLEDGE AND RESPONSIBILITY

Responsibility and autonomy

The ordinary image of responsibility fails to convey the historical transformations that the concept has undergone.[5] Responsibility has been conceptualised in wholly different terms by thinkers as diverse as Aristotle, Augustine and Weber. The current understanding of the concept is a relatively recent one, born in a secularised context and thus intimately bound to a characteristically secular idea of autonomy. Before the advent of 'modernity', responsibility or notions that approximate it had always been bound to a social context. For example, in the ancient Greek context, one of the most famous examples is Antigone's revolt against Kreon's interdiction to bury her brother, Polynikes. One authority, that of the moral and religious duty, that of honour and *pheme*, is stronger than the other, that of the state. The divine and the social responsibilities are mingled in Antigone's discourse in a way that renders her responsible to the gods, to the memory of her brother and to her understanding of the city's custom, and hence not responsible to the tyrant.[6]

Aristotle's views of notions that approximate moral responsibility, as they are spelled out in his *Nichomachean Ethics*,[7] paint a picture that is very different from the modern, Kantian notion of responsibility. In Aristotle, for instance, blameworthiness is separate from voluntariness, and while blameworthiness is inextricably linked to our social practices of blaming, voluntariness can be dependent on moral luck. Another major characteristic of this thought is that guilt, as 'a black spot on one's soul'[8] is absent, which is very different to the Christian concept against which Kant elaborated his own conceptualisation.

Indeed, the early Christian concept is also different from the modern one: three centuries before Kipling praised the US seizing the Philippines in his famous 'White Man's burden', the 'burden' of the first wave of colonisations was a duty dictated by God and a responsibility towards divine guidance. The metaphor of the burden has done particularly well through the centuries and we still find it in current development discourse.[9] One of its oldest and most significant instantiations is to be found in Augustine. As Arendt notes, Augustine's burden is the burden of active life imposed by the duty of charity; it would be unbearable without the possibility of philosophy.[10] Although charity roots the Augustinian human condition in action, it is neither political nor social; in Arendt's adoption of the Christian terminology, it is worldless.[11]

In this light, the 'White Man's burden' becomes typical of a religious (not only, if mainly, Christian[12]) understanding of the giver, the receiver, and the divinity in whose name the giving is done. We only need to reflect on the theological problems involved in thinking simultaneously of free will and foreknowledge, human virtue and supernatural grace, to see how different the religious and the modern understandings of responsibility are.[13] The religious understanding characterised both the domestic and the external affairs of the Europeans, and it was transformed into the welfare state and development cooperation policies that have more in common with each other than has ordinarily been supposed.

From the Enlightenment on, however, autonomy (that is one's own law) has most often been viewed as the condition *sine qua non* of responsibility in the writings of modern thinkers as important and as distant in time as Kant and Weber.[14] According to the simplest version of this relation between responsibility and autonomy, one can be held responsible only if one is autonomous. Consequently, being deprived of one's autonomy renders one incapable of being responsible. This is, for instance, the sense in which we must understand the metaphor of childhood that is very often encountered in the colonisers' discourse and has left a trace in the idea of development. Children, as the colonised are often described, are dependent on adults; lacking autonomy, they are automatically irresponsible. We must, however, underline that this is not Aristotle's view; to the contrary, he insists that 'even animals or even children are capable of acting voluntarily' and are thus endowed with responsibility.[15] Marion Smiley explains that this is valid, because Aristotle's understanding of the passage from childhood to adulthood is one of gradual transition; as a result, different levels of voluntariness (and thus appropriately different forms of blameworthiness) are ascribed to growing children at different times.[16] Here too, the Aristotelian conception of who deserves blame has nothing in common with the Kantian understanding of violation of the moral law. It is based on an understanding that A did something wrong, that this wrong can be corrected, and that it is the community who informs our understanding of what is wrong.

The non-Aristotelian argument is thought to be valid as long as the colonised countries are international legal minors, and have not yet become recognised states, before they attain the status of adulthood. Once this has happened, they become sovereign, and hence, by this logic, responsible.[17] At the same time though, if the ex-colonies are promoted to the level of the state, they remain 'backward' or 'underdeveloped' or, in the most recent version, 'developing' states. In fact, their autonomy can be questioned, and has been questioned not only by 'Third-Worldist' theories of the *dependencia* type but even, currently, by the official development discourse.[18] An asymmetry between 'developed' and 'developing', in the mildest case, is thus always present in a way that renders the connection between autonomy and responsibility a shaky one.

The idea of autonomy is part of a larger framework in which responsibility is a fact that follows the establishment of a causal link between a person and a state of affairs, as in 'A caused B'. Thus, the modern secular understanding of responsibility is based on a double assumption. The first part of this assumption is that causation equals (moral) blameworthiness and that blameworthiness equals responsibility.[19] This means that if it can be established that there is a causal link between a state of affairs and the person who brought it about, then the latter will be blamed and therefore held responsible.

However, establishing such links of causality is an endeavor that pertains more to the realm of nature and the natural sciences than to the social life of human beings. Unless the dangerous fiction of all things social taking place in a chemical bowl is adopted, we must reject the possibility of observing causal links between A and B.

The second part of the assumption on which the common-sense responsibility is based concerns the factual character of the concept. The previous equations are grounded in a belief in the non-judgmental character of responsibility. In this sense, to say that someone is responsible describes a fact not a judgment. However, despite being a secular responsibility, this common-sense responsibility pertains to a specific moral standard. This moral standard can in fact be viewed as an ideal liability that is ideal *per se*.[20] In the absence of God or Nature defining these moral standards, we must look for a different place where they are constituted; in an enriched version of the social realm.

The understanding of autonomy we have encountered up to now is based on a view of social life and of responsibility that depicts them as woven by causal ties and understandable through facts. Indeed, the extreme version of autonomy can be found in liberal individualism, where freedom of choice is understood as centrally constituting the individual and his or her actions. In this approach, the individual is autonomous and rational and, therefore, responsible for (the consequences of) the actions that s/he causes. There is an undeniably strong positive undertone in this relation between autonomy and responsibility, one that speaks of emancipation and of rendering accounts in one's own name and also, conversely, of the impossibility of escaping responsibility in the name of the supernatural or natural blamer. In this sense, although the connection between the two concepts can and should be seriously discussed, the broader emancipatory framework in which, historically at least, it made sense cannot be disregarded.[21] Grasping the historically meaningful change of these concepts allows us to question their use and misuse in the current international context.

Responsibility and knowledge

In the recent past, NATO's excuse for being sloppy in their bombings of Serbia in the Kosovo War and mistakenly targeting the Chinese embassy in Belgrade was that their maps were old and their technique inadequate, in a word they did not know or were not able to know the consequences of their raids. This points to the endorsement of the idea that it is knowledge (and by extension, intention) that determines responsibility and that ignorance excuses one from responsibility. Indeed, raising the issue of uncertainty or the unknown can offer an effective grasp on how the direct relationship between autonomy and responsibility is questionable; it is particularly relevant in the case of international politics, not least because it has been the background assumption of all theoretical endeavors in the field. More generally, it is the different answers to, precisely, the issue of uncertainty that have yielded different results in terms of social-scientific and societal arrangements.[22] In relation to responsibility, we may follow Derrida when he says that if one is in possession of full knowledge of what will happen, responsibility is not at stake.[23] Indeed, assuming responsibility means agreeing to render an account for consequences that are not fully mastered; by contrast, if one's decision was informed by full knowledge, it would only amount to the technical, as it were, application of this knowledge.

This aporetic situation of responsibility with regard to knowledge enlightens our discussion of autonomy. The part of knowledge that is necessary for a responsible decision ('knowing what one is doing') points to autonomy; this is the classical understanding of responsibility, also in the legal domain. According to this view, it is on the basis of knowledge that the free (autonomous) choice of the individual implicates responsibility. The childhood metaphor of colonial discourse is based on exactly this intimate relation between autonomy, knowledge and responsibility. To put it differently, only the adult depicted as autonomous because of her/his knowledge can be called developed. Conversely, the child – the colonised or the 'underdeveloped' – does not know what s/he does and depends, for reversing this ignorance, on the parent's intervention.[24]

On the other hand, not fully 'knowing what one is doing' – simultaneously at play in responsibility – can by extension point to the non-autonomous part of responsibility. And indeed, if we must sometimes avoid linking responsibility to full knowledge, if we must understand that the moment of the decision (or the non-decision) is a moment when there is never full knowledge, we must start to conceive of a responsibility without the necessity of full knowledge.[25] 'Not fully knowing what one is doing' ceases to view the person, and for our present purposes the EU or the state, as a fully rational individuality that masters perfectly all the relevant information and can act accordingly. It takes into account the big part of knowledge that depends on others, the other types of rationality that are expressed through actions and the fact that it is sometimes necessary to not be excused from responsibility because of the lack of full knowledge; responsibility is often at stake when (full) knowledge is not.

Thus, when we are walking past a man being tortured, we can decide whether to revolt against this or not. The full knowledge of the situation and, in particular, of the possible consequences may escape us. And (not but) at the same time, we know that this man is being tortured. To give another example: in one of Primo Levi's 'Moments of Reprieve', another Italian – but Christian, and thus, privileged in the camp – steals soup for him every day. This is an absolutely forbidden act that could result in his execution. Were he to be caught, not only would he most probably be judged responsible, but he would also have to be thought as responsible *ex ante*, that is, as *a priori* assuming responsibility. Such an endorsed responsibility is, however, wholly different from a full knowledge of what would happen to him. There remains a fundamental uncertainty, which is a necessary condition for any decision. This person knows that the Jews are hungry, he knows that offering food to them is forbidden and he does not fully or exactly know what would happen to him, if he were caught (or, more fundamentally, he does not know if he will be caught).[26]

The illustrations of this necessary uncertainty need not always be so admirable and can be found in any type of development policy, starting for instance with the international financial institutions' notorious structural adjustment programs. The ironic fact that institutions that function on the criterion of expertise, coming to realise the failure of their policies, claim that they could not have known or 'foreseen' the consequences, is regarded as irrelevant to the judgment of whether they are responsible.

RESPONSIBILITY AND THE OTHER

Autonomy and responsibility are always bound by alterity. Derrida distinguishes between three types of responses that are not 'juxtaposable; they are enveloped and implied in one another': the response 'for self', the response to the other, and the response to the institutionalised other.[27]

First, 'one answers for self, for what one is, says or does, and this holds beyond the simple present'.[28] This is the secular type of responsibility as defined by autonomy. It can be exemplified by Weber's ethic of responsibility, an ethic that is crucially turned towards its own source rather than facing the other.

As Warner has shown with regard to the 'domestic analogy' in international relations theory, Weber's charismatic leader or worthy politician is conceived as responsible towards himself; even if he is actually answering to an external calling, we will always be left out of this calling.[29] Based on such a view of Weber's responsibility, the domestic analogy leads to a realist international politics in a very straightforward way; the image of the actor conveyed here is that of the atomistic state seeking relative power, there is no external law on which action can be based or justified. But Weber's thought on this point is fundamentally ambiguous, and R. B. J. Walker, whom Warner quotes, has accurately formulated it as follows: 'the meaning of responsibility is hanging between a Kantian imperative to autonomous action in conformity with a universal law and an imperative to decide on the basis of one's own autonomous will (or in terms of international relations, on the non-rational will of one's autonomous action)'.[30] An absolutely autonomous will as the basis of responsibility is at odds with a responsibility based on autonomy in conformity with a universal law. To put it crudely, applying this in international relations yields radically different approaches: in the first case, realism, as in Warner's interpretation; in the second case, liberalism. It is this very ambiguity that has allowed a smooth passage from the era of colonialism (own will) to the era of human rights (own will according to a standard), or at a different level, to the inclusion of states in a 'civilised' international society, as Gong has shown.[31]

But this ambiguity and the chronological transformation that it accounts for is not obvious in Derrida's phrase. To the contrary, he talks of a response of one that transcends the present; a oneness (and also a uniqueness) of the person is assumed. As with the typical, as it were, secular understanding of responsibility, the ultimate necessity of this oneness that transcends time is easy to grasp. The multiplicity of the self and its chronological (if not historical) transformation cannot be excuses, in particular at the international level where the juridical fiction of the 'moral person' serves precisely the purpose of allowing legitimate action but also of rendering 'one' responsible for such action.

This first position of Derrida shifts with the second type of response: the response to the other. This type of response has two characteristics that make it more important than the other responses: first, one is not responsible in front of (or before, in Derrida's terms that point to an anteriority) oneself but responsible in front of/before the question of the other. Unless the other asks (explicitly or implicitly) for one's account, story or response, there cannot be responsibility. The second characteristic is that the very name that identifies one as responsible for oneself 'is in itself *for the other*' (that is, it exists for the purpose of its use by the other), in some cases chosen by the other and in all cases implying the other. For both of these reasons, response (and responsibility) is conditioned by the other, by alterity.[32]

This situation precedes the response for oneself or, in other words, the depiction of responsibility as stemming from autonomy. Responsibility is an interdependent condition, but an interdependence that has a limit. Indeed, contrary to Levinas' concept of the other, Derrida's other is an absolute other, an irreducible other.[33] For Derrida, confounding self and the other would be neutralising their alterity.[34]

Such an understanding of responsibility depicts people as ethically situated, as facing the other, and – to tie this with the initial, more conventional, vocabulary – adjacent to a responsibility that depends on a socially negotiated judgment rather than on a fact. Additionally, the weight of the argument is placed on responsibility as it involves oneself and the other rather than on the causal link between one's actions and their consequences.

The social and political implications of such a responsibility become clearer in the light of the third type of response that Derrida proposes, which involves 'answering *before*'. This type of response is the response to the 'institutionalised agency of alterity', one that, in some instances, 'is authorised to represent the other legitimately, in the institutional form of a moral, juridical, political community'.[35] The response *to* becomes the response *before*, the former preceding and being the reason for the latter. The novelty here is the introduction of the ideas of community and of representation; in other words, the passage to the collective level.[36] But although this touches upon a very significant issue for our purposes, namely the twin issues of collective responsibility and responsibility of representatives,[37] Derrida stops short of a fuller, and more useful, analysis of these types of responsibility. For indeed, he lightly performs an unproblematised leap from the individual to the collective level, imitating the 'domestic analogy' (that merely sees in the international situation a larger intra-state situation). Thus, for Derrida, what is crucial is the preconditioning, by the demand of the other, of one's ability, need and obligation to respond, not who this other might be.[38]

Equally significantly, in his third type of response, Derrida elevates the relation to alterity to the level of a universality: though this may be ethically laudable, it is politically too vague.

However, if the translation from an individual to a larger, state or international level seems to pose no particular problem in a (neo-) realist or liberal perspective, a look at collective responsibility and the responsibility of representatives immediately shows the specificic ways in which responsibility is constituted at that level. Instead of ethical philosophy (used by Derrida), we use here Luc Boltanski's social anthropology and Michael Walzer's political philosophy.

Thus, regarding collective responsibility, Boltanski's socio-anthropological insight stems from his investigation of the instrumentalisation of distance in a 'politics of pity': his questioning focuses on how distant suffering can be at the source of this politics of pity. This distance, the most crucial element in such a politics as far as people are concerned, is infinitely reduced when states ('legal persons') are concerned. Indeed, precisely one of the attributes of states is to reduce distance: therein lies their power.[39] Having observed this, Boltanski suggests that the transition from the level of people to the level of states be made explicit. This is all the more so, because when talking about the responsibility of a state, we almost invariably talk in systemic terms. In such systemic terms, the states ('agents') are much like the Hegelian hero who unconsciously acts out the system's own goals, says Boltanski. We can add that the observers of the system also play out a Hegelian role, one that is attributed to the philosophers, who are puppets of the system too, albeit lucid ones. The responsibility that corresponds to such thinking is collective responsibility. The evident problem is how practical such a responsibility can be, how it can still be called 'responsibility' if it is diluted among a multitude of people. The solution can be found in a hierarchisation of more or less responsible 'agents': responsibility is upheld but its collective character is diminished.[40]

Thinking about collective responsibility in political-theoretical terms, Walzer starts with the principle that 'the greater the possibility of free action in the communal sphere, the greater the degree of guilt for evil deeds done in the name of everyone'.[41] Second, Walzer's thought is based on the rejection of the argument that representatives cannot be held responsible; to the contrary, he says, they must be stringently held responsible for their actions precisely because they represent so many people and have so much power to decide 'in their name'.[42] These two premises taken together situate us in the context of representative democracy, the context of all the countries belonging to the EU. Walzer proposes that we should see democracy as 'a way of distributing responsibility' where some people can be viewed as more responsible than others, depending on their actual positions (and the consequences their actions have) in times of crisis. Thus, although Walzer is arguing from a different disciplinary and substantive perspective, reasoning on war from the viewpoint of political philosophy, he nevertheless draws the same conclusion as Boltanski: alterity remains universally significant, but differing degrees of responsibility allow a practical grasp of socio-political situations.[43]

EUROPEAN RESPONSIBILITY

The fact that responsibility is defined within the community (by the 'institutionalised agency of alterity') and *a fortiori*, within the international community, has important implications with regard to 'global responsibility'. Who is responsible in 'global responsibility'? For whom, to whom, for what? To whom is one responding and before which institutionalised version of the other? In global responsibility all are responsible for everything, responding to all and before all. The evolution of the European development discourse *vis-à-vis* the ACP countries helps us to make more sense of the issue of 'global responsibility' because the 'globality' of the EU and of the EU-ACP relationship is a good example of the ambiguities that are present in any discourse on the global, and because it underlines two observations concerning 'global responsibility'; (a) that it is rooted in a reflection on responsibility that has always been present in development, albeit in different forms and (b) that it nevertheless represents a break with the previous understandings of responsibility, in that it is a responsibility wholly turned to the future and ignoring the past.

A chronological overview, as provided below, indicates a strong movement from a hierarchical understanding of responsibility to an egalitarian one in EU development discourse. The earlier, hierarchical responsibility was rooted in a paternalistic vision of the relations between the two collectivities while the 'egalitarian' responsibility – much more ambiguous and susceptible to varying interpretations – can be seen as solidaristic or pluralist.

The issues of autonomy and community or the importance of the other in responsibility, as well as the significance, concomitantly, of uncertainty also appear in different versions. Thus, in the first chronological phase, a process of autonomisation of the EC (*vis-à-vis* mostly its member states), on the one hand, and the strong acknowledgement of the other's demands, on the other, constitute the background of a hierarchical responsibility. It is a responsibility that is strongly rooted in the past but also looks towards the future in a very open effort to reduce uncertainty through a linear vision of history.[44]

In the 1970s, the EC was portrayed as responsible for the development of the ACP; it even had a political will to promote this, an element of the political identity of the EC which interestingly later faded away, precisely as the political character of the EC was strengthened. This evolution can be encountered in the more general development discourse of the international community in the later years, when things tended to appear increasingly as inevitable and out of reach of any individual actor's will, as with globalisation. In the 1970s, however, the responsibility of the EC was still openly a matter of wanting to assume it, and it is, to a large extent, a responsibility for the future. Thus, the EC emerges as an autonomous actor through the performance of this responsibility.[45]

This responsibility of the EC for itself, as Derrida would have it, has however an easily discernible origin in the responsibility towards the less economically developed countries. The negotiating position of the ACP group is very strong, and their demands are acknowledged, praised and answered. But acknowledging the other's demands does not eliminate inequality. In some sense, it can be surmised that the other's demands are somehow always inscribed in an inequality, with the attribution of responsibility being thus the prerogative of the powerful. It is on such grounds that the powerful, in this case the EC, have a duty, as it were, to be responsible.[46] Once again, this suggests that autonomy is a prerequisite of responsibility, since autonomy (or freedom, or, in some instances independence) is generally understood to be a condition that determines power.

As time passes and we advance towards the emergence of 'global responsibility', an inverse movement takes place: autonomy becomes evident and this is the case not only for the EC/EU but also for the ACP. At the same time, however, the demand of the other – the ACP – gradually vanishes with regard to responsibility. Indeed, during the 1980s, the exercise of autonomisation of the EC was being completed and responsibility began to shift to a less hierarchical understanding. Responsibility began to be associated with notions pointing to equality, such as interdependency. If one depends on the other, then both are equally prone to ask for a response, a certain responsibility. This is best illustrated by the broader shift in the answer to the question of what can be done for less economically developed countries; from giving to sharing. Responsibility too starts to appear as something that can be shared.[47]

Sharing responsibility immediately means that both (or more) actors involved are equally autonomous. It is an attribution of autonomy onto the less economically developed countries. However, in a sense, anything else than the self-attribution of autonomy (and thus responsibility) amounts to robbing somebody of autonomy: what is given with one hand is taken with the other, autonomy should only be conceived as emanating from the autonomous. There are numerous examples in the international community of how autonomy is actually attributed, starting with the struggle for recognition of peoples, nations or territories by the international community. But if autonomy so crucially depends on others, should we not talk rather about heteronomy?

In the 1990s, the trend towards 'egalitarian' responsibility was strengthened, and the idea of shared responsibility was increasingly discussed. In a context of dismissal of Marxist claims and hesitations to wholeheartedly adopt neo-liberal approaches, it becomes difficult to decide what this responsibility of all, this shared responsibility and ultimately this global responsibility mean. There are however some indicators that help to form an overall picture.˙

The first and most straightforward element of interpretation resides in the fact that the African Renaissance is not taking place as was expected; the economic situation of the countries of the continent on the whole is in fact deteriorating. In the ACP countries, there is a multiplication of new movements and an intensification of those already existing, which criticise not only the hierarchical attribution of responsibility in the EU-ACP relations but also the lack of accountability of their governments.[48] This coincides with a wider return of 'ethics' in development studies and policies, and with an increasing sense of a theoretical and practical impasse in the area. Simultaneously, the place of ecological and environmental issues in the wider development agenda is growing, as are gender and children's issues. For the EU, in effect, equality stops being an assumption and becomes an aim to be achieved.

In this context, the 'egalitarian' responsibility that was the 1990s' trademark is a responsibility that borrows elements from conceptual frameworks that pertain to the market and to civic organisation. In the first case (the market), responsibility belongs to each person.[49] Here, one perceives the influence of liberal proceduralism which offers no legal correctives to power inequalities. In the second, wholly different case of the civic world, all are responsible for all. The world is viewed as a single entity.[50] The links binding the more economically developed and the less economically developed countries are extremely strong, and all are responsible for supporting the weak.

RESPONSIBILITY AND POWER

Apart from the narrowly conceptual level, which remains captivating in that it shows how ambiguous or equivocal 'responsibility' is, there are practical, political matters which beg the question of the concept's application. As Bauman and others have pointed out, the issue of responsibility was shockingly absent or devoid of any possibility of application in the bombings of Serbia in the Kosovo War. The Gulf War provoked the same type of questioning, as is witnessed by Walzer's or Baudrillard's writings; and although the issue of responsibility as such was not salient, the debates that immediately followed the attacks of September 2001, the launching of the 'war on terrorism' and the war in Iraq in 2003 involved issues of blameworthiness, causation, autonomy and, of course, knowledge. In such a context, it is the relationship between responsibility and power politics that is at stake, an issue that is always present in 'development discourse', and relocates it in the wider international or global framework.

How can we think of this relationship, and what does it say about development discourse? Power politics and global responsibility can be viewed both as situated in a chronological continuum (and thus one coming after the other) and as existing at the same time. On the one hand, the passage from power politics to global responsibility is characterised by a change in the justification for international intervention: from the absence of the need to justify it, via sovereignty,[51] to (global) responsibility. An increasing reluctance to admit to a world ruled by power politics and the proclaimed renaissance of morality have yielded this result. But things are more complicated; thus, the view of morality succeeding realist politics is an unacceptable reductionism, in the light of works that have shown the enormous potential for silencing alternatives that realism has had, be it in the political or the academic sphere (see Chapter 3).

On the other hand, power politics and responsibility are present at the same time, with the former being a condition of possibility of the latter. This is due to the equivocal quality of responsibility. In the context of power politics, responsibility can be either a liberal responsibility (liberal power politics corresponding to liberal responsibility because in a society of autonomous states each is responsible for itself in the name of a universal law) or a realist responsibility (each state being responsible for itself as it is characterised by an autonomous will) or an authoritarian responsibility (in an authoritarian and paternalistic version of power politics, the strongest state will dominate the weakest and endorse responsibility for it). Power politics can therefore be conceptualised as the wider framework in which responsibility is invoked.

But to think exclusively through the prism of power politics is to adopt the Hegelian position for ourselves and also for the states/institutions that act according to such power politics. Additionally, thinking about responsibility in these terms quickly encounters the problem of systemic thinking of which Boltanski warns us, namely an unavoidable dilemma between a purported, and in these terms necessary, collective responsibility and its effectiveness. But the mere evidence of *a priori* justification of different situations by means of 'responsibility' should be a sign that the Europeans are distancing themselves (at least partly) from the exercise of crude power politics. There is no reason to suppose that the EC is wholeheartedly committed to the most cynical version of this type of politics, although of course we might also find signs to the contrary in some instances, as an inevitable fall-back position.

Nevertheless, if it can be done by other means than resorting to a power-politics framework, a reflection on power is unavoidable in the context of a discussion on responsibility in development relations because of the simple question of who attributes responsibility. Indeed, answering that responsibility is (also) determined 'heteronomously' is not enough because as with any decision, the decision to attribute responsibility is ultimately taken by someone and thus, we must at least ask by whom. In other words, who is responsible for attributing responsibility? This issue is none other than that of democracy and its procedures and it amounts to asking what sort of democracy, if any, is at play in times of international relations during which intervention is as intense as it is in the cases of war, humanitarian assistance or development cooperation.

These are perennial questions of political theory. In the sense of the necessity to keep democracy as a horizon while simultaneously striving for its constant amelioration, these questions can never fully be answered. In the meantime, with changing historical contexts, the efforts to answer these questions change, as does the formulation of the questions. Thus, in our present historical period, we must for instance deal with a particular configuration of the international scene, wholly different than the one that existed before 1989 and one that is characterised by a new type of war.[52] The question of who, in this wholly new context, attributes responsibility is absolutely crucial to understanding this configuration. We can thus ask an interminable series of questions such as: who decides that there is no responsibility involved for such and such unfortunate mistakes in the war, but also who decides who is responsible, who decides that there is a responsibility of a certain part of the planet to give aid to another part of the planet, who decides that the other part of the planet is responsible for itself, perhaps more relevantly who decides that responsibility should be global?, and so on. Three issues raised by these questions are retained, to be examined below.

NGOs and IFIs

The first issue is that of the emerging 'global social movement'. The adjective 'global' has been recently added to the previous term 'civil society' that referred to the intra-state situation. If this intra-state/inter-state analogy were to be strictly maintained, then we would have to ask which is the global government to which global civil society corresponds.[53] Before attempting to answer this question, we must observe that, in terms of responsibility, one of the evolutions regarding NGOs is the crystallisation of a rupture within 'global civil society', between, to put it simply, radicals and reformists.

In relation to responsibility, and *a fortiori* 'global responsibility', two questions follow: the first one is that of a 'co-opted' civil society. Thus, the remedy to the problem of non-accountability of the international financial institutions – a pervasive feature of the politics of Structural Adjustment Programmes (SAPs) – seems fallacious. With the new discourse of participation, responsibility is conferred on those (the 'co-opted' civil society) who participate in the Poverty Reduction Strategy process, the successor of the SAP. Such a distortion of responsibility is unacceptable, not only because the actual input of 'civil society' organisations is minimal – and sometimes amounts to approving given documents – but mainly because it is always, without exception, the financial institutions that initiate such programmes. Responsibility should thus not even be shared, but fully endorsed by these institutions.

There is a second question that concerns the responsibility of non-governmental organisations (NGOs). Despite certain social and community needs which these organisations set out to give voice to, and despite their undoubted participation in rendering society more pluralistic, their lack of any sort of democratic mandate cannot be ignored. One does not need to resort to the old (party-)politics to see how, at a certain moment – precisely the moment when these organisations are deemed to 'share' responsibility for certain policies – the question of their 'representativity' or a more direct mandate for decision-making ('in the name of') is posed. Thus, although it is inevitable and right that such organisations create their own autonomy, as it were, instead of being 'robbed' of it, they are faced with a fundamental problem of responsibility.

The international community

The second important aspect of responsibility in an international context concerns the very existence of the 'international community'. In the 'globalisation era', the reality of this international community should be seriously thought through, as Zygmunt Bauman suggests in a thought-provoking paper on war.[54] This line of argument can be questioned by pointing out that the name of the international community is used every day in every 'Third World' country – and that it is attached to affairs that, though they might represent only a small part of the northern, western or more economically developed world's budget and interests, are woven into the daily practices and discourses of anyone and anything concerned with politics in a country not belonging to the 'developed' world. For politicians, academics or NGO members that live on a part of the planet that is not 'developing', it might be almost impossible to imagine how present the international community is in other settings.

Hence, the question of whether there is indeed anything like a 'real' international community becomes, to a certain extent irrelevant: the workings of 'the myth' of an international community are far too real, in terms of which policies should be followed, how democracy is to be attained, what human rights must be protected and how development should become the business (in every sense) of the people who are exposed to all of the above. Here, the question of responsibility must once again be viewed strategically: there must be an international community and there must be a responsibility that can be attributed to it by the people subjected to decisions taken in its name.

Apart from a practical and crucial concern about who (in the name of international community) should endorse responsibility in local settings, however, a widely shared view holds that the absence of a horizon of global law transforms the interventions of the international community into a mere veil under which the crudest power-politics are played out.

As Chandler shows, international law – with its cornerstone, sovereignty – is increasingly being pushed aside in the name of international justice, and its cornerstone, the 'duty' of intervention.[55] In the first case, international society (the society of nation-states) is the conceptual framework; in the second, it is the ambiguous 'global civil society'. But if sovereignty seems a rather old excuse for the absence/refusal of intervention, one might want to consider that at least when it was a valid excuse, there were no casualties without a corresponding responsibility. Now, in attributing responsibility, we must rely on those who have the prerogative and the capacity to intervene. This new 'morality', rather than a new form of solidarity, could express nothing else than unavowed (power-)politics, a view espoused on other occasions by thinkers as different as Castoriadis or Walzer.[56] But although the suspicion remains strong, our attention may once again be shifted to the exact way in which responsibility is being used. In a situation such as the bombings in the Kosovo or Iraq Wars, is there a serious basis for an argument of 'global' responsibility? Isn't it rather the case that the designation of the enemy, an exclusion, in fact erases such a globality?

Responsibility in time

The third question on responsibility in the international context concerns the affinity between war, humanitarian assistance and development. Indeed, war, humanitarian assistance and development – in the guise of time parenthesis, urgency and stages, respectively – are interventions on time and memory.

The conception of war as a parenthesis stems from the opposite tradition than the one we may call 'Hobbesian'. 'War as a parenthesis' is a view frequently held in current liberal thinking. But it supposes deluding oneself into thinking that somehow after the bombings and after all the atrocities that are committed during war, things will come back to normality. Perhaps more perversely, it sticks to the legalistic view of 'civilizing' the war, which was precisely the object that Grotius, 'father of international law', had given to his *De Jure Belli ac Pacis* of 1625. Finally, again following the mainstream legalistic view, it endorses an understanding of war that covers with shadow other, non-metaphorical types of war that are constantly present in people's lives, more far-reaching in terms of the lives they claim and of the possible changes they can operate on a world scale. This 'war as parenthesis' view boils down to facing war as a necessary evil but also as an unavoidable regulation of disturbed international relations; this is not far from a downright realist understanding of war as the continuation of politics by other means.[57] Having to choose between the realist, 'community of anarchy'[58] view that holds war to be normal and the 'parenthesis' view of war as an abnormal episode of an equilibrium that is indefinitely maintained thanks to the right ingredients (republics in Kant's words, liberal democracies in current European discourse) is as unacceptable as having to choose between a deontological and a consequentialist position *vis-à-vis* the US attack on Afghanistan.

Humanitarianism is another, similar intervention on time: things, in humanitarian parlance, are urgent because they are exceptional. The fact that no debacle followed television images of politicians unloading rice sacks on Somalian beaches shows how deeply such an understanding of urgency is rooted. Not only in situations of drought and famine, but also in genocides as in Rwanda, and in the case of HIV/AIDS retroviral medicine, 'urgency' only serves to cover 'trained incapacity'[59] to prevent catastrophes.

The most telling case is that of development, not least because its 'time' lies at the heart of the concept and because it has been much theorised about, by any social and political theorist who was preoccupied with social changes outside the 'North'. For our purposes, the way that responsibility has participated in this intervention on time is interesting. There are two separate aspects to this issue. As such, they face resistance.

The first, to which we alluded at the beginning of this chapter, is that responsibility has increasingly been divided between responsibility *ex ante* and responsibility *ex post*. If it is analytically possible to distinguish between these two times (i.e. I accept to be held responsible in the future *or* I am judged responsible for the past), it is practically impossible to do so, on the basis of the common autonomy-based understanding of responsibility. Indeed, responsibility *ex ante*, as, for example, in Weber's ethics of responsibility, takes into account a responsibility *ex post*. In other words, a politician who adopts an ethics of responsibility now in fact accepts the possibility of being held responsible for his or her actions later. This double understanding has prevailed in development discourse.

However, with the introduction of global responsibility these two times of responsibility do as a rule become separable. Indeed, global responsibility can only be a responsibility *ex ante*; one can hardly see how everyone and everything would be held responsible on a global scale, in contrast to the case of a government that is democratically accountable. It is a responsibility for the future rather than the past. This raises a question on the practical application of accountability 'in the name of'. The cases of 'wars in the era of globalisation', as well as ongoing development practices, reveal the *lacunae* of this global reasoning.

The second aspect of this question concerns the tendency of global responsibility to produce a radical rupture with the previous era; it is closely linked to its facing only the future. In this sense, it is a responsibility that works against memory, too, and in particular, in the European development discourse, against the (post-)colonial memory. To use our initial vocabulary of power in relation to responsibility, the question of power (and power politics) does not cease to be posed once the (dubious) end of realism is decreed. In contrast, it is perhaps more intensely present in locations such as that of memory and, more precisely, when there is a certain imposition of forgetting. If the past is deemed irrelevant, if it is forgotten, *that* decision which would express responsibility has been erased. But this asks for more than a mere passive stance: irresponsibility must indeed be talked about as 'disengagement' because such a formulation points to the present call (of the past). Forgetting can thus be seen as an active erasure of what has been done, but in failing. It is that ultimate failure which creates another precipice, another decision to be taken. This observation is closely related to Arendt's reflection on forgiving: 'the possible redemption from the predicament of irreversibility – of being unable to undo what one has done though one did not, and could not, have known what he was doing – is the faculty of forgiving'.[60] If forgiving is geared towards reversing what is irreversible, so is forgetting in a complementary way. Indeed, we must see how, in Arendt's words, 'men are unable to forgive what they cannot punish and ... they are unable to punish what has turned out to be unforgivable'.[61] That is precisely what makes the punishment (down to the very practical question of trials) of genocides painful;

that is what renders the reparations for colonialism difficult; and that is what obstructs the non-violent redistribution of land that has been 'stolen' by the colonisers from the colonised. This extreme difficulty is the birthplace of resistance to the imposition of forgetting;[62] it is in this resistance that we must look for the emergence of a more precise meaning of 'global responsibility' or for its substitution by more precise 'responsibilities'. It is in this resistance that we may find the courage of responsibility, and its vocation.

5
The Passion of Efficiency

> Mind, none of us would feel exactly like this.
> What saves us is efficiency – the devotion to efficiency.
> But these chaps were not much account really.
> They were no colonists; their administration was merely a squeeze,
> and nothing more, I suspect.[1]

The criterion used by Marlow, the narrator of Conrad's *Heart of Darkness*, for distinguishing between the Roman conquest of Britain and British colonialism in Africa is efficiency, which justifies 'the taking [the earth] away from those who have a different complexion or slightly flatter noses than ourselves', as he later says.[2] We must be attentive to the religious undertones ('what saves us', 'the devotion'); it is the blind faith in efficiency, still with us today, that prevents us from questioning the uses and misuses of a concept whose technicality should have confined it to a limited domain. Unveiling that, in efficiency, we are dealing with a concept that has grown out of its legitimate sphere to ultimately become an imperative, is necessary to resist some parts of development discourse that do not usually pose a problem.

Consider another story. It tells of a playground built on a hill. Every so often, children swing so strongly on their swings that they fall down the hill. After having experienced such accidents repeatedly, the community decides that these accidents must end. There is however disagreement on the solution to adopt. Some think that the best solution is to place ambulances at the bottom of the hill, thus, the wounded would be taken care of immediately. Others think that prevention is best; build a fence around the playground, they say.[3]

The developmentalist undertones are easy to grasp for those familiar with the metaphors of childhood or 'helping the weaker', which are woven into any development discourse. What we have here is a metaphor of the international community *qua* more economically developed countries (the adults) trying to solve the technical problem (falling down the hill) of the less economically developed countries (the children). From a different, more critical viewpoint, we can discern elements such as the assignment of a very defined activity to the children, as well as a very defined space where they can exercise it and, most significantly, the damages created by this enclosure.

To return to a developmentalist version of the story, if the common-sense understanding of efficiency is 'to do better what we now do',[4] then in our story, efficiency (in the form of the fence and the ambulances) allows the playground to function more smoothly (with fewer accidents). Between these different types of efficiencies, however, there is competition: one is 'more efficient' or 'better' than the other. Advocates of the fence could say that the ambulance solution intervenes too late in the process, when community children have already suffered wounds, and that the costs of public health would inevitably increase. Supporters of the ambulance might say that the fence turns the place into an ugly, prison-like environment, and deprives the children of their sense of measure and responsibility.

Returning to the critical perspective, we may realise that neither in the story as such nor when it was narrated, did anybody imagine relocating the playground onto a flatter terrain, or abolishing it altogether. Nobody thought that common sense could be distorted in these ways, or thought of asking: 'Is what we do now good?' or 'Why should we do this better?' This chapter, as a result, is concerned with the particular kind of epistemic blindness[5] that renders the mere thought of relocating the playground (in other words, radically changing things) unthinkable: that of economic efficiency. Uncovering the economistic[6] 'common sense' that presides over efficiency is the first task; showing how the artificial dichotomies of efficiency actually render things 'natural' is a second; and looking at the dangers this hides is a third.

ECONOMICS, POLITICS AND MORALITY

Efficiency is usually referred to in two ways: the first is the straightforward, common-sense understanding of 'how to do better what we now do'. The second is more indirect: efficiency is weighed against something else, such as justice or fairness.[7]

Efficiency and instrumental rationality

'Do better what we do now' covers the two fundamental components of the concept of efficiency: the means and the ends. If 'better' refers to a desirable result, the gap between the current situation and what is desired calls for the means to bridge it. Although such a statement may be a generalisation that leads to a loss of operationality for an economist, it nevertheless indicates something important: that the concept of efficiency epitomises instrumental rationality. 'Instrumental rationality' is at work, according to Max Weber who famously invented the term, when an '[a]ction is rationally oriented to a system of discrete individual ends (*zweckrational*) when the ends, the means, and the secondary results are all rationally taken into account and weighed'.[8] For Weber, this type of rationality is one among others, value-rationality, affectual rationality and traditional rationality. Value-rationality is the closest to the opposite of instrumental rationality since an action driven by it focuses exclusively on an absolute value 'for its own sake and independently of any prospects of external success'.[9]

But such a strict distinction between forms of rationality cannot be upheld. One of the most enticing critiques of the concept of instrumental rationality is the one proposed by Castoriadis.[10] He shows how two central aspects of Weber's thought, namely methodological individualism and the issue of the origins of society, work closely together to reduce Weber's own initial openings; one of these openings concerns instrumental rationality. Given how influential this reductionism has been, particularly in political science dealing with development issues, a closer look is warranted. While instrumental rationality was initially seen as one of the rationalities guiding an action whose meaning can be understood, 'the "understanding" is reduced more and more to the understanding of instrumentally rational action'.[11] Although Weber gives numerous examples where other rationalities are at play and admits that action driven by instrumental rationality is marginal in social life,[12] he thinks it is easier to understand someone whose rationality is instrumental. It is also easier because the different 'ultimate values' engendered by value-rationality are mutually irreducible (or, in other words, do not have a common denominator).

Weber is, therefore, obliged to conclude that the limits of sociological understanding are restricted to instrumental rationality. In Castoriadis' words, Weber 'establish[es] instrumental rationality as the horizon of intelligibility of the social'.[13] However, and this is crucial for our concerns, there is a further consequence of this operation and Castoriadis points it out. As instrumental rationality becomes the most plausible horizon of intelligibility, so do other 'values' (embedded in value-rationality) become less intelligible. If such operation is accepted, it can, as it does nowadays in a conservative guise, give rise to arguments of the 'clash of civilisations' type.

Acknowledging the problems that surround instrumental rationality – the collapse of other rationalities that it operates, despite its being empirically marginal – is crucial to understand the pitfalls of efficiency. Efficiency is nothing but an example of instrumental rationality. The similarity in the pattern ends-means is observable in any more detailed definition of efficiency, be it 'productive' or 'allocative', that is, within the frame of an industrial order or a market order. It is, for instance, discernible in 'the conventional sense' (productive), which is 'the maximisation of current output of goods and services with the available factors of production and with adequate provisions of resources for future growth'.[14] 'Do better what we now do' is to keep the factors stable while enhancing their productivity. Similarly, in terms of the Paretian sense of (allocative) efficiency, 'do better what we now do' entails a reallocation of inputs (means) for a production level where more for someone will not mean less for anybody else; this is the location of the 'better'.[15]

But instrumental rationality is a sociological concept whereas efficiency is nowadays used predominantly in economics. The big difference between the two concepts is that, unlike the initial (at least under the form of Weberian hesitations and prudence) and the most recent currents of sociology, economics has been built exclusively on the assumption of notions like efficiency, notions that assume economic behaviour to be founded on such rationality. In this context, efficiency has been conceived not only as a certain type of rational calculation but as the only type of rational calculation.[16] 'Doing better what we now do' is doing it (more) rationally. That which is not included in this understanding of the rational becomes by extension irrational and ultimately unintelligible.

The economic and the political

The second type of (references to) efficiency contrasts it to other concepts, such as justice, fairness or equity. In such contrasts, efficiency divides the economic, as the major category of representation of individual behaviour (Dumont), from the political, as the ever renewed questioning on the fate of the collectivity or, in Castoriadis' words, its 'institution'.

The kinship between efficiency and 'economic' interest[17] points to apprehending efficiency as something more than a calculation that is 'inject[ed] into human behaviour';[18] efficiency becomes the epitome of a specific type of human behaviour; the economic. Indeed, the concept ascertains the existence of a separable and separate social domain, the economic (as opposed to, say 'the social' or 'the political') as economy. As Dumont says, the historical emergence of a separate domain of the economic supposed a raw material that was recognised as having specific qualities relative to the rest of the social.[19] This also means that in order for this raw material to be recognised, a certain type of thought (that sees things economically) emerges. It is the second component of the emergence of the economic, 'economics'.[20]

Dumont's raw material refers us directly to the natural sciences, whose example economics attempts to follow. Indeed, the possibility of cutting up the social, as it were, into economic, political or religious parts, presupposes an organic view of the world as a whole that can be accurately dissected (which is in accordance with the view of the natural sciences). Lefort has warned against such a tendency with special regard to the political: 'The criterion of what is political is supplied by what is non-political, by the criterion of what is economic, social, juridical, aesthetic, or religious. This operation is not innocent; it hides behind a truism borrowed from the domain constituted as that of exact knowledge: science deals only with particulars.'[21] The same operation takes place with regard to the economic. In other words, caught between philosophy and the natural sciences, economic science opts for a method that overwhelmingly emulates that of the natural sciences while occluding its philosophical presuppositions.

Efficiency is, originally, a perfect illustration of this separateness of the economic domain as well as the specific mode of apprehending it, economic science or economics. The concept (while being irrelevant in Marxist economics) plays a central role in neo-classical theory where the entire economy is geared towards an efficient use of scarce resources. Since the economy is synonymous with the market, the market is also perceived to be directed towards greatest efficiency; according to this logic, the most spontaneous functioning of the market is in principle the most efficient. It follows that the 'logic of neo-classical theory ... tends to equate state intervention with economic inefficiencies and predatory policies regardless of the historical, institutional and political context'.[22] However, in theoretical terms, there is one possibility open for intervention in the market; if, and only if, it increases efficiency.[23]

In this context of the autonomisation of the economic, efficiency is a limit of the possible in the domain of actors and their actions, and in the mode of thinking this domain.[24] As a concept of rational calculation, it centrally constitutes the main actors in the neo-classical economy or the market; they cannot possibly act in any other way than the one required by efficiency. Indeed, '[e]conomically rational man ... desires to accumulate capital in the most efficient way'.[25] And since '[t]he insatiable quest for wealth and profit is seen as one of the major motives for economic and social development',[26] the economic actors cannot want to be inefficient. Efficiency also constitutes the economic domain as such; economic activity, as a result and as a process, in sum as a market, cannot exist outside efficiency. Thus, in terms of economic efficiency, the economic always strives to use its available resources for more gains.

In a slightly subtler version, it is unthinkable that economic activity in general is just or fair but inefficient. Two alternative trends of thought derive from this postulate of the 'unthinkable'. The first follows the argument according to which justice/fairness is precisely the result of efficiency, thus, the remuneration of factors of production according to their contribution to the overall production is fair, an argument whose highly problematic nature is evident if one thinks about the labour factor. According to the second trend of thought, questions of justice or fairness are not economic, rather, they belong to the political or the moral realms. They concern debates about how the affairs of the collectivity should be negotiated, not the very possibility of these affairs taking place. Consequently, the economic does not deal with these questions but it promises that they will be resolved if economic activity is left to function unhindered. This is how the political is initially separated from the economic; in this understanding, the latter cannot be thought through political terms precisely because it is ruled by laws such as efficiency.[27]

Efficiency and the morality of capitalism

The 'rules of the economic' have been (and to some degree still are) an era's and an area's morality; European capitalism. In this context, efficiency does more than delimit the possible; it also defines the content of the desirable, how things should be under European capitalistic conditions. Originally, the concept is an offspring of consequentialism/utilitarianism – and by extension pragmatism, as we saw in Chapter 2 – whereby actions are judged according to their consequences and inputs according to outputs. The philosophical opposite of consequentialism is constituted by deontological approaches that are concerned with the principles that guide actions, rather than their consequences. It is a matter of fact that most current political issues are still framed in either of these two ways. The debate on the adequate response of the US and their allies to the terrorist attacks of 9/11 is an example of these two tendencies; and the actual solution that followed is a case of infelicitous compromise between the two.

In the guise of efficiency as instrumental rationality, consequentialism/utilitarianism has thrived because of the rest of the arsenal put in place by economic thinking; while utilitarianism has operated a major cut in the previous morality by propelling individualism to the fore, its central justification has been the idea that individual interest promotes the general welfare. As Polanyi says: 'To the typical utilitarian, economic liberalism was a social project which should be put into effect for the greatest happiness of the greatest number; *laissez-faire* was not a method to achieve a thing, it was the thing to be achieved.'[28] The reduction that this operates is clear; the public welfare is thereby equated strictly with economic development.

The evolution that has led to these two equations (individual interest promotes public welfare and public welfare is economic development) must be traced back to Adam Smith's early contribution to economics and its morality, that is, to the morality of a then emerging capitalism. For justification, the capitalistic 'demand for accumulation of capital by formally pacific means'[29] has turned primarily to neo-classical economics: efficiency is one of capitalism's justificatory pillars that have been detected by Boltanski and Chiapello.[30] There is a paradox, here, that has been pointed out by many critics of capitalism. The market economy cannot be equated with capitalism in the sense that while a market economy entails (some level of) competition which reduces costs for the consumer, capitalism attempts by definition to curtail anything that minimises capital accumulation. But in order for accumulation of capital to occur, consumers must buy what is produced (which is transformed into money, which becomes investment, which becomes production, which is then consumed, etc.) and therefore, although capitalism is impeded by the market, it can nevertheless not do without it.

Commenting on the uneasy alliance between market economy and capitalism, Polanyi, too, observes that the capitalistic market economy implied a double movement, namely, of expansion of its own principle and activity, and of restriction, because its very principle could engender 'society's ruin'; historically, liberalism and interventionism struggled for the theoretical but also practical domination of the market system.[31] This is of crucial importance for us, because it largely explains the presence of efficiency both in the industrial and in the market worlds, if these are conceptualised as distinct entities.[32] Indeed, these are two different types of efficiency, the market efficiency and the industrial efficiency, both offsprings of European capitalism, both representing a 'basis' for understanding though in different, albeit capitalistic, ways. However, the religious references in Weber or Polanyi as well as in Hirschman[33] always reconnect these efficiencies to morality.

The practical consequence of the morality of efficiency is spelled out by Bourdieu in the following manner:

> [T]here is a need to radically question the economic view which individualises everything ... and which forgets that efficiency, which it defines in narrow, abstract terms, tacitly identifying it with financial profitability, clearly depends on the outcomes by which it is measured, financial profitability for shareholders and investors, as at present, or satisfaction of consumers and, more generally, satisfaction and well-being of producers, consumers, and ultimately, the largest possible number.[34]

This extract unveils efficiency's set objectives, in the common use of the concept. The fact that 'what we now do better' is thus generally equated with 'financial profitability' confirms the moral underpinnings of efficiency as a participant of a capitalistic system. 'Better' means 'more profit'.[35] But from a second point of view, this extract draws our attention onto Bourdieu's self-made ambush: the mere mention of efficiency collapses the critique that intends to be most radical into a utilitarian frame of thought that can ultimately not transcend its own components.[36]

Two ways of mastering uncertainty

By limiting the economically possible and the capitalistically desirable, efficiency acts as a foil against uncertainty, as an attempt to secure the relation between actions and consequences, or inputs and outputs, in certain cases, or as an attempt to chase away insecurity about the future. This uncertainty has been theorised as one of the main questions posed by the modern condition, modern social life: the question was how to reduce uncertainty and the answer was mastery. The 'self-harmonisation of social life' that economic mastery promises, claims to impose order where there is disorder and positive laws where complexity would otherwise reign.[37] In this context, efficiency paradigmatically fulfils this central objective of mastery by making the future understandable in the present or, simply, by erasing time.

In *The Secret Miracle* by Borges, a poet is arrested and condemned to death. The night before his execution, he prays God to be given another year during which he will write the epic poem of his dreams. God grants him the wish, but a whole year elapses in the poet's mind within some hours of 'real' time. When the moment of the execution comes, the poet has had the chance to compose his huge poem in his memory. Efficiency is godlike; it shrinks years to seconds. In its very definition, time is domesticated and brought to the present.[38] This is done either by reference to the market or by reference to industrial intervention. Post-Second World War development theory has proposed both types of answer to the uncertain condition of modernity: expertise, planning and industrialisation, on the one hand, trust in the spontaneous (self-)regulation of the market, on the other. The 'planned' spontaneity of the market favours the immediate exchange, when time is brought to its infinitesimal possibility. By contrast, the originally 'spontaneous' striving for the regulation of, and intervention in, the industrial production prefers the subdivision of time into successive periods (since the industrial process functions through careful planning of stages of production). Yet, the centrality of efficiency is not affected; as far as capitalistic uncertainty is concerned, efficiency sings two different but equally pervasive songs.

In the first case, market arrangements have been deemed as the most efficient mode of allocation and distribution of all resources (this is allocative or market efficiency). The spontaneity of the market implies an easy job for efficiency; whatever the outcome of the process, it will be the most efficient. The calculation is done by an invisible hand; this is particularly evident in economic knowledge where there is a gap between what economics advocates and what 'actually happens'.[39] Going back to the idea of time held in market efficiency, the possibility of calculating efficiency rests both on an assumption of a perfect market and on an assumption of imperfect markets that have preceded it. In other words, on the one hand, the unhindered, perfect market is the market that functions most efficiently; on the other hand, to know this, one must have a preceding measure of comparison, the perfect market must and can only be compared to the imperfect market that preceded it. Efficiency's situation is thus one where there must be a lapse of time (where two different markets exist) and one where there is none (the 'shrinking' of time).[40] The trap that efficiency attempts to set for uncertainty turns against efficiency itself. It is easy to see that any such suppression of time inevitably renders any such calculation hypothetical, hence, by definition, potential and never actual. Ultimately, uncertain.

In the second case, productive or industrial efficiency emerged in the same context of capitalism and under the same hegemony of neo-classical economics, but, here, economic things are viewed as needing a helping hand. Productive or technical efficiency is industrial efficiency par excellence; it has been described as the central criterion of the industrial world.[41] Here too, the rational calculation of the best attainable result given the available means cannot, as a matter of fact, take into account future conditions and will not, as a principle, take into account future means, but it envisages a future brought towards what exists in the present. Here too, the incorporation of the future into the present overwhelms the calculation of efficiency.

Finally, the closure on uncertainty that efficiency attempts links things causally, not contingently and not reciprocally. Such preference for causality may be accounted for by the origins of the meaning of efficiency. In the Oxford English Dictionary, the first meaning is located in the positive sciences and denotes something that brings about something else, an 'operative agent', an 'efficient cause'. Consequently, the current causality in efficiency is a sign of the economic constituted as a science, between emulated natural sciences and unavowed philosophy. Economic causality has then spread to the other social sciences under the guise of positivism, historically the only social-scientific school that has ever advocated that causality of relations in the social world can be established.[42] It is in the form of rational choice that such claims have developed in the current social sciences: but rational choice has been found wanting in terms of empirical adequacy.[43] The same assurance that is perhaps made by economists in relation to efficiency might also be made for causality: that it is only a 'standard' according to which existing relations are evaluated. This is not convincing. Although models have for a long time been striving to match reality, reality is increasingly made to fit the models. Additionally, exactly as in mainstream economics, 'rational choice' theory tends to give an impoverished picture of social life, in which humans interact in an exclusively rational and individualistic way. This severe impoverishment of the functioning of the social world renders the account that produces it undesirable, since it fails to accomplish its initial goal; to give a more extensive account of human interaction.

As with metaphysics and capitalism, rational choice economics and rational choice social science's 'eternal attempt to profit from its ventures is based upon an irreducible loss, an "expenditure without reserve", without which there could be no idea of profit'.[44] The loss is the loss of the other. As Colin Leys summarises, '[i]t remains one of the bitterer ironies of the last two decades that so many of the poorest people in the world were forced to become even poorer, and in many cases to endure unspeakable suffering, through the imposition of Structural Adjustment Programmes justified in terms of "rational choice"'.[45] This is how epistemic blindness works; with repeated assertions of blind faith[46] in its own assumptions.

EUROPEAN EFFICIENCY

The divisions of efficiency

The different ways in which efficiency is a modality, reflect each other as if they were multiple mirrors. The concept justifies how development should function through three main oppositions. The rational, prudent calculation is opposed to the irrational. This opposition bears its imprint on the second division, the one between the modern and the traditional; this, in turn, refers to a third division, between politics and economics.

First of all, efficiency in the European development discourse is the rational, the epitome of instrumental rationality. When there is talk of 'rationalisation', 'rational cooperation', 'more rational utilisation of means', this always points to a certain way of relating the available resources to a better outcome.[47] What is left behind by efficiency – a calculated past or an unsatisfactory present – is less rational or irrational. In this context, efficiency is a certain quantity, rather than a quality, that must be injected into development practices, the quantity of 'reason'. It is reason through the usage of 'reasonableness' and its opposition to 'excess', milder if not different variants of 'rational/irrational', that transform efficiency into the criterion of the correct weight of things; resources and results. In phrases which praise 'reasonably high standards of living and education' and 'reasonably high standards of development and industrialisation' and others which deplore 'excessively protectionist measures' or 'excessive regulation', we find an echo of the same correct quantity of rationality and efficiency.[48]

Is 'reasonable' an improvement over 'rational'? 'Reasonableness', it has been argued, actually includes the idea of rationality as involved in the reasons that people give for their actions or the reason guiding their rational decisions; further, the idea is that the 'good reasons' that people offer to others must be understandable, acceptable, objectifiable and justifiable.[49] However useful, such a conceptualisation accepts the concept as an improvement over rationality and thus does not emphasise the opposition between reasonable and excessive that illustrates the economic correctness of the discourse.[50] In contrast, it can serve to undermine proposals for alternative reasons that have been put forward, in particular by East Asian scholars.[51] Additionally, this conceptualisation refers to another contestable aspect of efficiency, objectivity. Indeed, objectivity often seems to be another word for efficiency.[52] However, particularly in the context of knowledge, Weber has long ago warned against an unreflexive belief in objectivity.[53] To endow things with such a quality is, in the European development discourse, a unidirectional process, most often going from the EU towards the ACP states or, as in the example in note 52, towards the member states of the EU.

The deployment of the rationalising/objectifying tendency of efficiency can also be observed in the second dichotomy between modern and traditional. Efficiency belongs to a modernist discourse, that is, to a discourse that works with assumptions such as human mastery over the world. This discourse is naturally centred around the concepts of modernisation, of technological innovation and, generally, of novelty.[54] Time is handled in a particular way: efficiency is associated with speed, in particular after 1980.[55] This is not surprising when it is read in the light of the suppression of time that efficiency and neo-classical economics tend to cause. If time cannot disappear altogether, let it at least run quickly. The capitalist underpinnings are evident. In few words, time is money.

The dichotomy between traditional and modern in the European development discourse appears on the repeated occasions when the inefficiency of traditional techniques is deplored.[56] Indeed, technological innovation is highly praised in development discourse, both by neo-classical and by structuralist economics. In international relations, this is translated into both liberalism's and socialism's belief that 'developments in the sphere of technical rationality would provide the impetus for progress in the domain of morality and politics'.[57] In this sense, 'development certainly constitutes an expression of modernity ... essentially this is through its techno-economic side'.[58] Banal as it may seem, the European development discourse counts as modern that which is not traditional (old and no longer valid). The function of efficiency is clear here; tradition is inefficient.

On the whole, however, a certain chronological evolution in the pair modernity/tradition has occurred: at the beginning of the 1990s, such 'traditional' ways were not readily dismissed. On the contrary, their value and importance were upheld in a committed way.[59] Moments such as this have the potential to make a difference between the development discourse of the international financial institutions or of the US and the European development discourse: they are significant both because they say something about the autonomisation of the EU and its identity-building, and because they are more open to contestation. Lodged in moments like this is not only a double resistance of the EU to its member states and to the international community but also a space left open for resistance by the EU's own interlocutors.

Thirdly, efficiency divides the economic from the political. Contrary to the other pairs (rational/irrational and modern/traditional), this is characterised by major upheavals in the European development discourse during the period of the 1970s–1990s. Two main movements are discernible: the first is the growing importance of the economic mode of thought in the discourse, the second concerns the spreading of efficiency over to the political field. How can efficiency divide the two, strengthen one and spill over to the other at the same time? This is not a paradox, it is the evolution of efficiency towards a diktat.

The double movement of European efficiency

Early in the European development discourse, the economic is subordinated to the political. In the early 1970s, free exchange between the partners is hailed by reference to its economic efficiency and, 'mostly', that is principally, to its political significance.[60] In various instances when the two elements are mentioned together, it is clearly stated that the economic (rational, efficient) aspect is at the operational level while the political one precedes it at the stage of the decision.[61] In this case, the economic endorses the neutral role, governed as it is by immutable laws, whereas the possible choices and decisions are left to the political. In the 1970s, the EU insisted on its own political will, despite Lomé's political neutrality, consequently, efficiency was firmly maintained at the position of a means with the objective of improvement of morality and politics. Of course, there are radically different strands of the development discipline informed by neo-classical, structuralist or (neo-)Marxist and dependency theories, but during that period, development studies were equated with structuralist economics.[62] Therefore, the political had the upper hand, also because the mainstream economics of the time allowed this. It is clear that when economics becomes predominant, it is because state intervention, or political will, is less crucial in the re-emerging neo-classical economics.

Hirschman sees in the overriding concern with efficiency, at the end of that period, the reason for 'the decline of development economics'. For him, 'development economics' was the only reasonable alternative to the neo-classical and Marxist 'monoeconomics'. But when efficiency becomes the objective to be attained, neo-classical economics becomes predominant over 'development economics': 'Economic development policy was here in effect downgraded to a technical task exclusively involved with efficiency improvements.'[63]

In the European development discourse, however, this shift takes more than a decade. Meanwhile, what has been advocated by economists earlier has already driven the development discourse of other international institutions in that direction and has allowed big changes in the international scene to happen. This explains a more substantive neo-liberal discourse emanating from the Europeans but also an incorporation of the rising resistance to it. Typical of this movement in the European development discourse, for instance, are statements concerning a changed world where geopolitics becomes less important, and where, consequently, concern about the efficiency of aid or cooperation increases.[64] Similarly, economic efficiency is accompanied by neo-liberal methods; indeed, the concept is increasingly associated with flexibility and adaptability, qualities that must characterise the partners of the Europeans.[65] The belief in the free market has repercussions on the division of labour between private and public sectors, and on these occasions, classic Smithian vocabulary such as 'sympathy' is retrieved.[66] This shows that the old aporia between the *Wealth of Nations* and the *Theory of Moral Sentiments* may still be haunting advocates of the market. And we are still in the realm of the carefully wound up watch that the economy is, according to Sir James Stewart, even though this winding up might concern only technical aspects, 'plumbing repairs or improvements in traffic control'.[67] It points to the more general paradox of the European development discourse; the urge addressed to the less economically developed countries to be efficient, and so, to intervene, as they face what is supposed to be an unavoidable phenomenon, namely globalisation.

Mapping the 'free market versus interventionism' debate onto the previously identified pairs of opposites of efficiency (rational/ irrational and modern/traditional), shows ambiguity too. In the excess/reason version of rationality, only interventionist measures are characterised as excessive. But when intervention encounters the modern, the result is not always similar. Indeed, there are positive references to intervention in the context of modernisation; in the 1970s particularly, intervention is not always related to the 'traditional past' but to modernity. Thus, we can conclude that productive efficiency is preponderant, in such cases, and that the industrial world retains a value over the market world and its corresponding allocative efficiency.

Relevant to this context is the fact that efficiency promotes performance.[68] Thus, very recently, one of the criteria of evaluating aid cooperation seems to have changed, as the ACP countries' needs start mattering less than their performance. Simultaneously, the criticisms of the ACP countries are also brought to the fore. This must be related to the more general movement that transforms efficiency from a means to an end. The previous end, 'needs', was a synecdoche of 'satisfaction of needs', the typical collective objective of the market in neo-classical economics. By contrast, 'performance' has an individualising quality, even when it refers to a market.[69] Not only does such a concept have the potential of breaking up the bulk of the EU's partners according to the question who performed better, but it also unambiguously places the ability to decide this on the promoter of this objective (who decides what performance is). The connotations of 'deserving poor' are too loud not to raise dissent.[70]

While this was taking place in the 1990s, efficiency was also spilling over to the political. This second, general movement of the European development discourse suggests that the economic is eating up the political: the space of the political is increasingly reduced, particularly with respect to issues such as globalisation, which tend to emphasise inevitability and powerlessness.

However, if the political becomes characterised by efficiency, then efficiency no longer divides the political and the economic, and therefore, the separation of the economic from the political is contested. Indeed, the introduction in the European development discourse, since the mid-1980s, of 'political' themes like governance, democracy, human rights, the rule of law has meant that Europeans are no longer distancing themselves from these issues. Efficiency becomes not only a condition for their success, but also an objective as such.[71] Finally, efficiency literally becomes a diktat, in such a way that any other objective of development policy and action becomes secondary relative to the concept.[72] But while any conception of the political and the economic being strictly separated belongs to historically recognisable discourses such as those of neo-classical economics, modernisation or (neo-)Marxism, blending them into each other also poses the problem of tyranny or the confusion of orders.[73] In both cases, therefore, efficiency runs into problems.

EFFICIENCY AS A PASSION

Gauchet has seen in development the desire 'to deal differently with everything, in order to do better and to gain more, and constantly to transform nature for the sake of efficiency'.[74]

Jeopardising democracy

Are the political and the economic divided and should the political regain primacy? Is interventionism in the economy necessary to enhance justice or is the efficiency of *laissez-faire* eventually conducive to increased general welfare? Does a moral statement underlie the transformation of efficiency into an end in itself, or does morality have nothing to do with economics? All these questions to which we have alluded have already been raised in the recurrent debates about the disengagement of European states from the welfare state.

Schematically, a right and a left attack of the welfare state on the grounds of inefficiency are discernible.[75] The right's efficiency-centred argument claims that instead of helping to harmonise the conflicts arising from the market (i.e. market failures), the welfare state actually exacerbates them (as it creates a disincentive to both investment and labour). This amounts to saying that the only possibly acceptable intervention in the market, that which is done in the name of efficiency, is in principle inefficient. The efficiency-centred argument of the socialist left similarly asserts that instead of eliminating the causes of the creation of needs, the redistribution of the welfare state merely compensates for its consequences; it is thus inefficient. Neither of these approaches is prepared to do away with the welfare state, precisely because of the intimacy between market or capitalism and welfare state.[76]

However, the two arguments outlined above use the concept differently: the first is more consistent with the common understanding of efficiency ('do better what we now do'). By contrast, the second argument looks for the 'causes' of phenomena instead of their consequences, and, in this sense, its use of efficiency is less conventional. If neither of these arguments challenges the ultimate compatibility between the notions of justice and efficiency, it is because efficiency and justice mean something different and take a different order of precedence in each case. The right-wing argument claims that efficiency makes fairness come about spontaneously. The two concepts are not opposites, but justice follows efficiency. It is the other way around for the left-wing argument; efficiency is at the service of justice and present arrangements are inefficient because they do not challenge injustice.

In such debates, efficiency is considered an ideal standard that serves to criticise results arising not from less-than-ideal applications of the same standard but from decisions made in the name of other standards, such as justice.[77] This is a recognisable case of a dispute which either remains unresolved or ends up in a compromise.[78] But this issue also has a substantive political aspect: efficiency becomes a threat to democracy.

The argument that democratic procedures are not efficient belongs to an old reactionary rhetoric of order. But its periodical excavation makes it as dangerous today as it was in earlier times.[79] The danger lies in two aspects: the first is its advocacy of less democracy for more efficiency, applying the opposition between the economic and the political in favour of undebatable economic laws. This argument is an extension of the 'right-wing' argument that we saw and according to which 'economic' efficiency will eventually bring about democracy or social justice. Here too, the procedure is mechanistic, placing infinite trust in the laws of the economy. In such a view, 'decision-taking' (as opposed to decision-making) is reduced to a tool that allows the desired outcome to come about. The moment of decision loses its ethical, critical and disruptive endowment and is reduced to that point of the procedure when the calculation is made. In fact, decision is transformed into a non-moment: this is the story of efficiency that suppresses time. Hence, to be efficient is also to defy time and since this is impossible, to be rapid. But democracy takes time, because plurality, dialogue, debate and contest take time; in this sense, democracy is more about the long drawn-out process of making the decision than taking it.[80] 'Losing (the resource of) time' is what efficient thinking must avoid.

The second, dangerous aspect of this argument is its assumption that the existing democratic procedures are those of an actually existing standard of democracy. Indeed, the conflation between admittedly existing flaws of democracies and their ideal permits this dangerous conclusion. It has been forcefully objected, however, that democracy must remain unattainable, for reasons that pertain to the very understanding of democracy or its spirit. As Judith Butler points out, the insistence on the 'unrealisability' of democracy serves to underline that this democratic ideal is indeed an ideal while its 'modes of instantiation' are here, with us, and not to maintain a distance between an ideality of philosophy and an actuality of the world.[81]

The 'chronopolitics' of efficiency

That development discourse is a Eurocentric discourse with universalistic references and universalising tendencies is an argument that is at least 30 years old. Its recent invigoration is due to two very interesting currents of thought: first, the 'periphery', 'subaltern', 'southern' writers and, second, those who would like to match a critical view with post-structuralist insights. Although the potential for resistance to development is both uncovered and advocated, the image that these writings convey is that development, both as discourses and as practices, has effectively silenced possible alternatives of seeing the social world and human beings in it.

Efficiency is one of those developmentalist devices that seem hard to resist yet have an insidious effect not only on what can or cannot be said and thought but also, significantly, on how Europe's 'other' is depicted. It is a matter of empirical observation that admonitions for things to be more efficient are, as a rule, addressed to the less economically developed countries.[82] Through the divisions that efficiency operates, it becomes evident that, on the one hand, a picture of the purveyor of such admonitions as efficient, modern and rational is drawn. In other words, it is always the EU that emerges as a subject when these qualities are mentioned. On the other hand, damage is done to those to whom paternalistic or disengaged suggestions are addressed: the 'other' is implicitly or explicitly taken to be 'irrational', 'traditional', and of course inefficient. The less economically developed partners of the EU are thought to be lacking in technical merit, and are depicted as emotional.[83] These traits validate a picture of others who are simultaneously hailed as equals, which is radically flawed when judged against the standard of instrumental rationality.

There are a few albeit exceptional cases when emotions seem to be accepted, and even sought, in the relations between the EU and the ACP. In fact, the Europeans reinforce the previous picture of the ACP and manage to incorporate some resistance in their discourse, by admitting that relations of interest are also about passions. In no case, however, does this render the ACP more 'rational', 'modern' or efficient. Indeed, less economically developed states' interventions are in good neo-classical fashion considered 'totally impotent and incapable of acting in an economically rational and efficient way'.[84] However, the same policies that apply this type of logic typically see in less economically developed states omnipotent actors who can freely and influentially decide their macro-economic policies.[85] While the states are pictured as rational actors in the second case, they are considered politically impotent in the first.[86]

Fabian's concept of 'chronopolitics' is at work here. Chronopolitics 'consisted in casting the lateral, contemporaneous diversity upon the timescale, and so representing the different as obsolete, a relic of the past that outlived its time and now exists on a borrowed one, carrying a no-appeal death verdict carved all over its body'.[87] In the 'applied' social sciences that take development as their object of study, efficiency is the device of chronopolitics par excellence, as it renders all who are without it irrelevant for the present.

Fabian analyses anthropology as denying coevalness, that is as involving 'a persistent and systematic tendency to place the referent(s) of anthropology in a Time other than the present of the producer of anthropological discourse':[88] despite being contradicted by anthropologists' personal perceptions, this tendency was nevertheless always followed. Things are not different for development 'sciences', whose very definition owes a lot to colonialism and anthropology. In the economics and the sociology of development, the assumption has always been that less economically developed countries will eventually 'catch up'.[89] Less economically developed and more economically developed countries are thought to be on a strictly defined chronological continuum, some in the front (modern), the others in the back (traditional). Santos' observation of the 'fallacy of false contemporaneity' refers to the same issue. It centres on the different perceptions of time that people from the two sides of development have when meeting each other. Thus, he tells us, '[when World] Bank officials meet with African peasants (...), the peasants' present reality is conceived by them as a past present and by the World Bank as a present past'.[90] The World Bank officials deny coevalness, in Fabian's terms, whereas the peasants conceive of their own reality as what we can call, for want of better words, a 'tradition' that is alive.

The twin assumptions on which chronopolitics is based, namely that history is a 'process of gradual but relentless universalisation' and that western rule is extended so that it becomes universal, might be slowly eroding,[91] although chronopolitics has not yet loosened its grip on development entirely. On neither side of the 'partnership' between Europeans and mainly Africans, has any voice been raised against efficiency, the current understanding of it, or its spilling over into political discourse. If efficiency is gained, as a profit, if 'we have not lost time', it is accepted that politics, governance and respect for human rights must become efficient and their 'technification' is not contested. Thus, a certain understanding of the political, as the possibility of having a discussion on substantive matters of the polity, is lost.

Also lost are the people who are denied the mere possibility of needing time, or expressing it. Seeing in Africa – whatever complex realities this term might actually cover – a 'forgotten continent' unequivocally speaks of a loss of peoples in time.[92] It is not only that Africa is left aside, it is that it is left behind, as a thing of the past. But here is the ambiguity; remembering that Africa is left behind (by forgetting it altogether) leads to the interpretation of this forgetting as the 'backwardness' of Africa. Thus, forgetting and assigning to the past and to backwardness, feed each other. Responsibility is disengaged and the burden of the proof unloaded on the 'backward'; after all, the argument goes, it is normal to forget what cannot keep up with the pace, what is not in time. As Ezra Pound says:

The age demanded an image
Of its accelerated grimace
(...)
The 'age demanded' chiefly a mould in plaster,
Made with no loss of time (...).[93]

6
Pandora's Box: Giving Development

The Greek gods were furious when, despite their interdiction, Prometheus stole fire for the humans. In addition to punishing the titan, they decided to create Pandora, a woman who possessed all the gifts, but also one evil; curiosity. She was sent to the humans, carrying a poisonous gift; a box that she was forbidden to open. However, as soon as she had descended from Mount Olympus, Pandora opened the box, and every imaginable evil was unleashed to haunt the humans forever. As quickly as she could, she closed the box and trapped one thing only; hope.[1]

The wealth of canonical anthropological discussions of the enigma of the gift first reveals to us that the *gift* is equivalent to the creation of the community. Conversely, a poisonous gift has the capacity to destroy the community. Among various forms of giving, it is the 'free' economic exchange that has the most hazardous consequences for the community. In economic exchange, things can become acquired (and resold), a quality that attacks the durability of people's relations and of people's relations to things, since the exchange does not bear a long-term significance. At the other extreme, the gift is about things and relations enduring over time, which moves it closer to the debt that inevitably sustains a duty and thus a community link.

A critical look at the parents-children metaphor of the more economically developed-less economically developed countries (a metaphor that has been incessantly used in colonial and development discourses) clarifies the phenomenon. In most uses of the metaphor, children/the colonies/the less economically developed countries must accept their parents'/metropolis'/the more economically developed countries' supervision up to a point of their 'evolution'. This period of supervision is the time of the gift, when children accept gifts from their parents. Later, revolt[2] or disengagement brings about the period where market-exchange (exchange between equals) becomes the main functioning mode of giving. An intermediary form, the debt, is always present in failing in the other two forms of giving. Thus, giving in development relations is not as innocent or as homogeneous as it may look at first sight.[3]

In this chapter, giving is conceptualised as the articulation of responsibility and efficiency. Articulation is viewed as 'a practice that establishes a relation among elements such that their identity is modified as a result of the articulatory practice'.[4] Giving articulates the concepts of responsibility and efficiency in such a way that their original meaning changes. Having criticised the conceptions of responsibility and efficiency, we now turn to the different times and forms of giving. Giving in one or another of its three main forms, gift, debt or exchange, is permanently, overtly and dynamically present in the justification of development; it is a fruitful way of raising the most crucial political questions of redistribution, debt forgiveness and reparations.

This articulation is crucial, as there seems to be an original dilemma between the two concepts: which should be preferred (as a guiding principle) and which should be sacrificed, responsibility or efficiency? Indeed, responsibility and efficiency seem to belong to wholly different ways of thinking. If responsibility is understood in terms of an 'ethics of responsibility' (Chapter 4) and efficiency is formulated in terms of 'instrumental rationality' (Chapter 5), Weberian analysis – from which this vocabulary is retrieved – concludes that there is an equivalence between the two concepts; there is thus no dilemma. A well established critique of Weber's position by various scholars, however, quickly uncovers the commonality underlying both concepts: 'conviction' – the purported opposite of 'responsibility' – is to be found in both, and they become comparable. Thus, of two convictions, one is predominant. In practical discursive terms, this corresponds to the separation of the economic and the political, and to the predominance of one over the other. Among the dividing performances of efficiency we have observed the division between the economic and the political that resolutely places efficiency on the side of the economic. By contrast, responsibility insists on social and political grounding. The result is an imposition of terms (of action, of discourse) by efficiency on responsibility, by the economic on the political.[5]

THE ENIGMATIC GIFT OF DEVELOPMENT

Giving in the community

Any community, including the Convention that has brought together the EU and the ACP countries, is created by a commitment to superseding the problem of uncertainty. Giving constitutes this commitment insofar as it serves primordially to create bonds, be they political or not. Thus, according to Arendt's account of Augustine, the community-creating component of Christian charity contributes to a community that attempts to escape the political or public realm (not necessarily successfully).

From the eighteenth century onwards, however, giving has been regarded as the epitome of the political act, because it centrally involves a decision about whom to give to and from whom to take, and because it is explicitly introduced in the public realm. Yet, giving can also be, and has been conceptualised as, a commercial exchange; as such, it involves a strongly economic logic. The consequences are clear; in the first case, giving is primarily a matter of responsibility, in the second case, it is primarily a matter of efficiency. In other words, in an ideal-typical situation where giving is thought to be a purely political gesture, economic or technical efficiency will not be relevant. By contrast, in a situation where giving is expressed in terms of an economic exchange between individuals, responsibility will not play a part; we can say that the latter economic exchanges do not answer a 'call' but obey an 'imperative'.

The theme of giving with respect to social questions is an old one. Epigrammatically, one can say that 'foreign assistance does at the global level what welfare institutions do at the domestic level'.[6] More radically, Lumsdaine sees the development of cooperation aid as rooted in the rise of the western welfare states. In this vein, Lumsdaine quotes Myrdal who attributes the growth of foreign assistance to 'the misery of those far away [having] been brought home to the peoples of the richer countries'.[7] That this 'distant suffering' is gradually brought home results in the deployment of these policies that have covered a 'politics of pity', be it development cooperation or humanitarian assistance.[8]

An overview of different authors who have looked at the history of the practices of giving suggests three major historical-conceptual changes: first, the entrance of giving into the political domain (the political), second, its reappropriation by a newly invented 'social economy' (and thus, a conceptualisation in terms of the social); and third, its return to political economy (the economic). So the first change is that compassion/charity/pity[9] – the 'reason' for giving – slipped into the political domain only in the eighteenth century; before that, it was 'frequently outside the established hierarchy of the Church'.[10] A century after having entered the public realm, charity became contestable through that which can be interpreted as the first historical articulation of responsibility and efficiency. The nineteenth-century liberals spoke out against the inefficiency of the juridification of charity (its legal 'codification'), since the attribution of rights to the poor legalised the obligation of the wealthy and, thus encouraged the institutionalisation of the poor: 'donnez des droits aux pauvres et vous aurez des pauvres' ('give rights to the poor and you will have poor'), as Ewald puts it.[11] In other words, if you want to be efficient in poverty administration you need to be freely responsible, not obliged to give.[12] From a conservative rhetoric perspective, this is a typical case for Hirschman's 'perversity thesis', as it sees in what could otherwise be construed as progress, a mere re-creation of what was initially opposed; hence, inefficiency *par excellence*.[13] From a philosophical viewpoint, it is reminiscent of the Kantian positioning of the law in oneself, and of Mill's anti-paternalistic utilitarianism. If, here, the responsibility belongs to the free and autonomous individual, and if autonomy places the law in oneself, the position of the law protecting the weaker (necessarily external) becomes fragile. In other words, to give or not remains an arbitrary decision, to which the poor is subjected without possibility of invoking regulations.

A similar conclusion is reached by the contemporary 'socialist left' when it criticises the welfare state's 'inefficiency', on the grounds that it merely compensates for the consequences of incidents rather than eliminating their causes.[14] Both these versions of the argument (propagated during the nineteenth and twentieth centuries) put efficiency and responsibility in the same Weberian basket of a means-ends rationality. In the European development discourse of the late twentieth century, the gradual detachment from the European states' colonial ties – and the accompanying erosion of the naturalness of less economically developed countries' demands – resulted in the 'trade not aid' motto of the 1980s that, while never wholeheartedly adopted by this particular discourse, was nevertheless a perfect example of its articulation. More generally, the movement from a hierarchical to an egalitarian responsibility, and the increased occurrences of efficiency in the European discourse participated in that tendency.

The second important historical change that took place in the welfare discourse with regard to giving is, according to Procacci, that 'the new philanthropy' of the industrial era brings to the fore a new '*savoir*', social economy, that is a critique of and, to a large extent, a substitute for classical political economy. While political economy was a science and, as such, invented its own scientific object abstracting from the real (the economic, as we saw in Chapter 5), social economy was a *savoir* and therefore defined by its use of the previously invented scientific object for interventions in the real world.[15] Thus, political economy's object – eliminating the poor – was transformed into the aim of administrating the poor.

One would need to expand on the colonial vision of the other to understand in which way 'the colonised' is different from 'the poor': for the moment, it is important to remember that there is no systematic vision of 'eliminating the colonised' before their administration (as 'poor') becomes the prime target. This phenomenon was institutionalised through the establishment of development cooperation. Indeed, the colonised are 'edified', a process that implies that they are ultimately needed by the coloniser.[16] Thus, this movement from elimination to administration is very strong in development discourse, although it actually operates the other way around; the administration of the poor is supposed to lead to the target of eliminating poverty.

Finally, the third big historical change was the reintroduction of political economy as a remedy for the poor's ignorance of their duties as these were understood by the wealthy,[17] which is similar to the edification of the colonised. Its purpose is the inclusion of the poor in the existing order, a means by which to enlarge the middle classes. The accent is put on giving education (training) and offering participation (legitimacy). The creation of community through giving is salient. It brings to mind Walzer's conceptualisation of the community as a good that can be distributed. Although its distribution depends on those who are already in it, community also entails giving mutual aid or, when the inequalities in economic terms are significant, redistributing income. In such a context, it would be scandalous not to give, which amounts to saying, as Walzer does, 'that every political community is in principle a "welfare state"'.[18] In this context, questions of merit or deserving are better left unasked and giving is a regular communal provision. Boltanski makes a similar observation with regard to the merit of those stricken by catastrophe and to whom pity is addressed: it would be scandalous to consider their merit ('do they deserve pity or not?').[19] Although obstacles to the process of development can hardly be compared to a catastrophe, the European development discourse is less lenient and does take the merit of less economically developed countries into consideration, particularly with regard to order, rule of law and democracy. Even nineteenth-century liberals such as Mill refused to consider merit as a criterion for distribution.[20]

In fact, in development discourse, giving has been channelled through both political economy and social economy. As such, it has been the object of both the 'science' of political economy – and this is exemplified by the economistic extreme of efficiency – and the *savoir* of social economy, as it is pushed to its limit by responsibility.[21] From a scientific perspective, giving must be done efficiently, whereas from the perspective of a *savoir* – that of 'development studies' or 'development strategies' (Brohman) – giving is a 'know-how' bestowed from the responsible giver, the more economically developed countries, on to the recipient, the less economically developed countries. But a closer look reveals that efficiency – as 'knowing how to do better' – is also a *savoir*, and thus that development is ineluctably geared towards intervention. The double quality of efficiency (science and *savoir*) mirrors its two versions (allocative and productive), which involve development both in the spontaneity of the market and in the interventionism of the industrial world.

The gap between theory and reality that neo-classical economics creates to a degree unprecedented by other scientific endeavours can be bridged by a *savoir*. In fact, that is the special task of a *savoir*, to bridge that gap. It is the simultaneous belief in efficiency's pure scientificity, and in its qualities as a *savoir* that render the concept tyrannical and produce the fallacy that it calculates, after all, what is happening in reality. The obsession with that type of calculating knowledge also invades responsibility, which instead of being seen as a decision taken without full knowledge, is viewed as the logical conclusion of full mastery over facts.[22] This hesitation between science and *savoir* is another mirroring instance of the paradox of development assistance that cannot sustain at the limit its ultimate goal lest it should announce its own elimination.

The forms of giving

Bourdieu's work on different forms of giving has the advantage of introducing time, and thus more substance, into this ideal-typical fight between responsibility and efficiency over giving. His forms of giving are the gift, the debt and the *donnant-donnant* (market exchange).[23] This conceptualisation – used here as an inspiration[24] – renders a mapping of the different chronological orientations of the development discourse between the 1970s and 1990s possible, as the understanding of responsibility, of efficiency and of their articulation change. Thus, the forms of giving have distinct temporalities. In the *donnant-donnant* situation, the giving comes from both sides (A gives to B and B gives to A) simultaneously. By contrast, between the gift and the countergift, there must intervene a certain time (A gives to B and then, B gives back to A). Finally, the situation of the loan (or debt) is a hybrid between the two, since A gives to B while, simultaneously, B agrees to give back to A later.[25]

The European development discourse from the 1970s up to the 1990s has moved from a conception of giving centrally involving the gift to a conception of giving as market exchange.[26] Following an understanding of responsibility as related more to the gift, and a conception of efficiency as increasingly related to the market exchange (rather than to the industrial world), the reduced significance of responsibility in giving is matched by an ascendant efficiency. Although the observation of this movement rests on premises that undo the complexities woven into both of these concepts, it signals a fundamental change in European development discourse; while responsibility was originally the condition of possibility of efficiency, the roles have now been reversed so that efficiency becomes an overriding goal and, hence, the condition of possibility of responsibility.[27] Efficiency dominates responsibility, while being rooted in the latter.

First, the 1970s discourse is constructed around a notion of giving as gift, where the expectation of a counter-gift speaks of duration and where responsibility prevails over efficiency. Indeed, '*[t]here where there is gift, there is time* ... The gift gives, demands and takes time.'[28] Numerous examples of the development discourse of the 1970s attest to the prevalence of this concept of giving.[29] The distinct national development traditions are obvious when the ex-colonial countries privilege gifts rather than loans (as opposed to the newcomers in development cooperation). Ex-metropoles and new aid-givers perceive different kinds of responsibility in the gift. In the 1970s context, when the former (particularly the French) dominated European development policy, responsibility was a hierarchical paternalistic responsibility. In the 1970s, it was indeed the responsibility of the giver that was emphasised. Giving was performed (under the sign of 'dons', i.e. gifts) but always justified, accounted for, as a response to the weaker, the less economically developed countries. It was a practical application of the saying '*noblesse oblige*'[30] (nobility obliges).

The precise link between responsibility and giving is exposed by Derrida:

> [I]t is also necessary to render an account, it is also necessary to give consciously and conscientiously. It is necessary to answer for [répondre] the gift, the given, and the call to giving. It is necessary to answer it and answer for it. *One must be responsible for what one gives* ...[31]

Responsibility is involved in this limiting of generosity, in avoiding excess through reason. In the frame of hierarchical responsibility, limiting excess occurs from the side of the donor.[32]

Efficiency, however, is not absent; it is at the same time an alternative (albeit passive) mode of limiting the generosity of the gift and a condition for responsibility to fulfil its function with regard to giving.[33] It ensures that responsibility and giving are framed in a means-ends relation. If responsibility is an account for the gift, it is not only an account *post hoc* but also an *a priori* justification for 'the call to giving'.[34] It allows the gift-form to operate smoothly; only once out of the situation of the gift can it be contested. That is the moment when the situation of the loan/debt reveals the presence of the gift within it.

Indeed, the loan is a second fold of Bourdieu's triptych.[35] From an anthropological perspective, it can be viewed as the legalisation of the exchange (gift) framework. For Bourdieu, it is characterised by the time involved in its restitution. But restitution has already taken place at the moment when the contract stipulating the predictability and calculability of its prescriptions has been established.[36] We see the paradox of a situation that can only be enacted via a contract in vigour at the precise moment it is 'signed', but dealing with a type of giving that obliges the recipient in the future. Conversely, this is the logic of the debt, since the recipient finds him- or herself obliged towards the giver. On a global scale, the 1980s were characterised by the growing importance of the issue of forgiving the 'Third World's debt'.

In the nineteenth-century welfare debates, the problématique of debt – as in *'les secours publics sont une dette sacrée'* (public aid is a sacred debt *vis-à-vis* the poor) – posed the question of a corresponding right of the poor,[37] a question also present in the earlier wave of colonisation. The roles of the lender and the debtor were reversed when, in the 1980s, the debt raised the issue of the lender's rights. It seems a more straightforward question than the one posed in the case of welfare which involved three subjects (the rich, the poor and the state), it only involves the more economically developed and the less economically developed countries. But it is more complicated; for we are not talking here about the right to be reimbursed, an obvious right, however open to criticism it might be in desperate situations of insolvency.[38] We are talking about the right to impose another debt on the debt; the conditionalities. The principle of the conditionalities is reminiscent of the *'aides liées'* of the 1960s and 1970s, which bound aid to the obligation of using it in the donor's country. It did so with an extra twist; the recipient was obliged to contract a debt in order to contract another debt. The promise of fulfilment of one debt is what enables the indebted to promise the fulfilment of a second debt: one conditions the other.

The content of conditionalities – and in the case of the Lomé Convention, the usual combination of human rights, democracy and rule of law is, later, ambivalently called *'acquis'*[39] – sheds light on responsibility in this form of giving, debt.[40] The superiority of the more economically developed countries' political systems that renders them responsible for bestowing these practices and knowledge upon the indebted ones, is an element that the debt has in common with the gift of the 1970s. That which changes is the universality of the more economically developed countries' distinct superiority, giving rise to an oxymoron. The right to doubly in-debt the less economically developed countries is self-attributed by the more economically developed countries in the name of a universal responsibility. This reveals both an external standard against which responsibility is judged (and which becomes problematic with the introduction of 'global responsibility') and an explicit construction of a common universe between the more economically developed and the less economically developed countries.[41]

The distinctive feature of giving in the 1980s was the equal role of efficiency in the construction of debt. As a key element of industrial economics, efficiency is central to investment, and in development cooperation, investment (including foreign direct investment) relies heavily on loans. Not only is the recipient required to use the loan efficiently, but the actual act of contracting a loan or, better, of the more economically developed countries *in-debting* the less economically developed countries must also occur efficiently. Here, then, it is time – in Bourdieu's element of delay – that binds efficiency and debt.

There is a certain ambiguity concerning efficiency's times, turning towards the future in consequentialist fashion, but also looking at the past in *post hoc* evaluations. Inherent in both temporal directions is the calculation now of the optimal way to attain a future result. In Chapter 5, we called this efficiency's effect of 'time shrinking'. It gains a new significance now; the difference in time of the means and the ends (the delay) brings out the element of debt in efficiency. If we view the debt as a means for something – which is its most common understanding – it becomes evident that an optimal debt is an efficient debt. But then what is an optimal debt? In the light of aid conditionalities, an optimal debt is paradoxically one that allows a further debt to be contracted.

Additionally, efficiency and debt are brought together by the notion of interest. On the one hand, the use of loan interest is condemned in a line of tradition that dates back to Aristotle, to the Old Testament[42] and to Christianity.[43] The interpretations of this tradition vary greatly, and the most distinctive feature is the size of the community. Thus, Aristotle did simply not consider life outside the community when he denounced *tokos*, which is the Greek word for offspring. Indeed, says Aristotle, the interest of a loan is the same thing as its 'parent'; money. At the opposite pole, the Christian brotherhood is universal and thus, the condemnation of interest is applied to all, which explains much of the controversy surrounding usury and the Jews' position in medieval Europe. On the other hand, efficiency is a calculating device, a 'disciplined understanding of what it takes to advance one's goals'. Efficiency answers: it takes *time* and knowing how to manage time. In the framework of development cooperation (a capitalistic community) the debt (and the profit made out of its delayed repayment by the debtor, through charging him or her interest) is the perfect example.

Third, the significant changes in these two concepts during the 1990s demonstrated the preponderance of the market exchange. Responsibility took on an egalitarian flavour; it became 'shared' and can be called liberal since individual responsibility is one of the two main principles of liberalism.[44] Efficiency spread from a strictly economic domain into other areas, such as the political. Its significance increased.[45] Thus, the combined picture is one where responsibility is divided among all while efficiency is gaining momentum. Bourdieu's *donnant-donnant* form of giving clarifies this third articulation of responsibility and efficiency: through the form of *economic – market*

– *exchange*, giving keeps its central place in the justification of the discourse and brings responsibility and efficiency together.

The ratio of responsibility to efficiency diminishes since a responsibility that is shared amounts to disengagement. If the more economically developed countries are responsible for the less economically developed countries at the same time as the latter are responsible for themselves (and through the interdependence argument, the less economically developed countries are portrayed by the more economically developed countries as also being responsible for them), then the burden of responsibility of the more economically developed countries is undeniably diminished. This shared responsibility brings about a market exchange between equals.

The predominance of allocative efficiency in a market type of giving is self-evident. Here, the time of the giving is squeezed to the minimum; its ideal condition is simultaneity. This is radically different from the gift form of giving. The market type of giving expresses 'the cold economic rationality, (...) capitalism, and mercantilism'.[46] The similarity of the histories of the welfare state and of development cooperation, regarding this market type of giving is important; this type of development discourse corresponds to the discourse of Esping-Andersen's contemporary 'liberal' welfare regime or Ewald's picture of the original liberal welfare discourse.[47]

Nevertheless, this hailing of the immediacy of market exchange provokes resistance. In the 1990s, the demands of the less economically developed countries for restitution and compensation for what was taken in colonialism (both land, the space, and in a developmental logic, time) were becoming an irritation to the metropoles. The argumentative give and take continues.

INNER AND OUTER CALLINGS

Why are responsibility and efficiency such strong requirements? Are they hidden values of those who (re-)create the European development discourse; are they special callings? In short, are they vocations? Or are they what their interlocutors demand of them, what the other participants of development discourses call for when they ask for cooperation? Are they not rather always situated in different contexts determined by different interlocutors?

Both Weber's predominant understanding of responsibility as an ethics that is opposed to an ethics of conviction, and the usual perception of efficiency point to a self-contained vocation (in politics) or imperative, and not to any kind of grounding or contextualisation of the concepts. Vocation is rooted in the Christian tradition and imperative springs from the effort to overcome this tradition. But in both cases, the Weberian vocation and the Kantian categorical imperative refuse to consider a source of wisdom and law external to people. A transcendental trace remains, though, in that vocation and imperative maintain a supernatural power, now expressed through a certain devotion to science (that, incidentally, neither Kant nor Weber shared). But vocation and imperative can be turned away from these understandings and made to reverberate to another source of the call: the other. Vocation then means grounding.

What does grounding stand for? It presupposes, first, a certain temporal interactivity, and, second, a spatial response to the problem of being together (the question of co-existence in a common world). This double understanding of grounding embodies the concepts of efficiency and responsibility in that which, originally, is a Hegelian answer to the abstraction in Kant.

In temporal terms, giving always begs the issue of a rhythmically determined counter-gift, the due repayment of the debt or a more immediate return. The articulation between efficiency and responsibility can be summarised as an encounter of (internally changing) approaches to time. If, for example, the most recent version of efficiency has the tendency to 'shrink' time also in politics, so too does the most recent version of responsibility tend to forget the long time of the colonial past. Thus, a strong emphasis on permanence, solidity and engagement was characteristic of the 1970s. The 1980s discourse, in contrast, used temporisation, praising the maturity and permanence of the EU-ACP relations but also introduced rapidity and flexibility of rhythm. The 1990s, furthermore, saw the culmination of an uncontrollable acceleration, of a *laissez-faire* and *laissez-passer* that are allegedly beyond mastery.[48]

The second type of grounding – a response to being together – expresses responsibility more than efficiency. The centrality of collective responsibility in being together is evident in development where the problem is how to preserve a coherence, or minimally a being-together, between poor and rich nation-states; or how to avoid a disruption of the international system due to the purported underdevelopment of some.[49] However, given that efficiency is a concept-remedy, and that the question of grounding is conceptualised as a problem, efficiency always sustains, *sotto voce*, all possible solutions to it.

The issue of dependencies and interdependence focuses explicitly on this problem of the coherence of an international society where 'North' and 'South' co-exist: the transformations in the spatial dimensions of the discourse are particularly relevant illustrations. In the 1970s, when (post-)colonial relations were relevant, special responsibilities existed for particular regions, and, at the same time, internationalisation, which brings the different parts of the world together was considered necessary, whereas *dependencia* arguments argued the opposite.[50] To summarise, the coherence of the world was either sought or avoided. The incoherence of the world gained momentum up to the 1990s when putting an ever-shrinking world in order emerged as the main theme of the European development discourse. The interdependence created by globalisation generated new duties and the necessity for an increased efficiency in all matters of development. Hence, both responsibility and efficiency adapted to the demands of the moment, to each period's understanding of how big the world is and who depends on whom.[51]

These temporal and spatial responses to the problem of being together, and the substance of these responses – the giving – form the frame in which responsibility and efficiency are invoked. Depending on the different analogies of the frame, as they were just mentioned, the two concepts are depicted either as self-imposed imperatives or as external callings. However, in the European development discourse, there is an ultimately undecidable step between inner vocation and outer calling, exactly as a responsible and efficient decision is ultimately taken with no full knowledge (of what the exact stakes and consequences are). But the 'undecidability' of this step is the precondition for decision; at the moment where we interrogate the origins of the calling for the gift,[52] the articulation of responsibility and efficiency is always normatively overwhelmed by responsibility.

An external calling can only come from few sources: the less economically developed countries, the more economically developed countries, or a collectively shared belief in the goodness of responsibility. Each calling is not exclusive of the others, but each has different consequences for our understanding of the articulation of responsibility and efficiency as well as for the wider implications for development discourse. Thus, for example, the responsibility of the EU that is called for by the less economically developed countries – and which was very present in the 1970s – is one that is polemically political since a public dispute takes place around it. Responsibility as an inner calling is the exact opposite; it is the self-attribution of responsibility where the stakes are apparently low and the tones understandably consensual. Things are not debatable when good intentions are declared.[53]

Similar hesitations regarding the responsibility of the less economically developed countries are revealing. The mere fact that, in the discourse, there is no instance of inner calling of responsibility of the less economically developed countries shows that the ACP's responsibility is always externally attributed. The subtle transformation of a responsibility called for by the more economically developed countries of the EU into a responsibility that is a collectively shared belief (and that can still be called external) is a characteristic of the present era of development discourse.[54]

In a parallel way, the oscillation of efficiency between an absolute standard, representative of the absolute economic rationality, and a pragmatic standard, accommodating political considerations and therefore expanding efficiency's range of application, express the same uncertainty in the definition of efficiency as a self-imposed imperative or as an outward necessity. Once again, the consequences of a self-imposed efficiency differ from an efficiency that is called for by external sources in that, for instance, the first can usefully resist imposition of external, developmentalist standards whilst the second cannot.[55] But more often than not it is the inner calling of efficiency that accredits it with naturalness. Conversely, criticisms of the imposition of a 'western' rationality model on 'Third World' countries are a good example of the negativity with which an external calling for efficiency of the less economically developed countries is perceived.

Different answers to the question of the outward/inward source of development ascribe different roles of responsibility and efficiency to the (re-)creators of the discourse. Ultimately, they allow different spaces for those who are held by the strongest obligation in the giving: its recipients. The solution to the enigmatic 'giving development' lies in acknowledging that both extremes (vocation and grounding) inhabit the space of development discourse; thus, the political transformation of giving needs to take both in account.

COMPROMISED GIVING

Even though each decade can be broadly characterised by a specific form of giving, it must be remembered that this form never appears entirely separated from the others, both because such forms of giving are ideal-typical and because of the ambiguities of the discourse itself (its dilemmas between concepts or their origins). This richness is expressed by the compromises between the different forms of giving, that is, their encounters and mutual influences. Below, three significant compromises are traced, which will allow us to look at a reconstructed, enriched version of the European development discourse.

Tradition, good habits and experience

The first compromise to be examined is that between the debt defined by productive efficiency and the gift defined by hierarchical responsibility. The debt and the gift share the features of an extended period of time, a constrained space and the fact that the recipient owes something to the giver.

The debt and the gift involve the industrial and the domestic worlds respectively. In Boltanski and Thévenot's conceptualisation of the compromise between the industrial and the domestic world, the points of compromise are numerous. Four of them are particularly relevant to the European development discourse: the embeddedness (of new methods, products, etc.) in a traditional environment, the use of modernisation to conserve traditional quality, the efficiency of good habits and the issue of professional experience.

The *embeddedness* (of new methods and products) in a traditional environment is present at the most detailed level of development discourse, most particularly in specific industrial techniques that must respect the ones that already exist in the developing economy; and in a renewed emphasis on agriculture in the 1980s.[56] More abstractly, the first occurrence of this embeddedness, salient in the 1970s, concerned the EC's preferential attitude towards particular areas of the world. The new methods, products, etc. constructed the European Community's new policy, after the age of colonisation, which is the traditional ground in which this policy is embedded. The numerous references to the 'traditional relations, ties, links, past' between the Community and its counterparts may be shocking to today's reader, as they justify a 'preferential' development policy.[57]

With the birth of the Lomé system, it is not merely the memory of the colonial past that is expressed, but the rooting of a particular relationship in zones of colonial domination.[58] The future politics of regionalisation stem from these premises and show the role of efficiency in the construction of a policy that constantly rearranges the means for the end. The hierarchical responsibility that is involved is clearly the Community's; because of the shared traditional past, because of a common geography and a common history, the Community is responsible for the ACP countries. The constrained space and the extended period of time justify something of a gift, or, in other words, the preference given to these countries as they are placed in an environment of their own, distinct from the rest of the world, in a very domestic fashion. See how swiftly the purported obligation of the Community is turned into a debt that burdens the less economically developed countries; for such is the fate of the 'privileged' that they are always indebted towards those that are less privileged (as is, more evidently, the case the other way around).[59]

The second more abstract instance of this point of compromise between debt and gift is the issue of *conditionalities*. The background of conditionalities in the 1990s was considered to be tradition; it must be taken into account. It was perceived as being adversely predisposed to the necessary changes that the conditionalities demand. In the late 1980s, such an embeddedness was not considered; the deterioration of most African countries' situation may be one explanation for a turn towards the existing 'traditional' institutions; the academic strengthening of 'cultural studies', another. In the 1990s, the rule of law, democracy and good governance were assumed to be non-existent in most countries, but their planned imposition without paying heed to the existing culture was also thought to be counter-productive.[60]

Expanding on this view, the EU also envisages 'global governance' with the same impetus of intervention in the internal affairs of states.[61] Although such 'good governance' involves public accountability and a responsibility that is shared among all participants of such processes,[62] we will insist on the hierarchical facet of responsibility; despite disclaimers, the imposition of conditionalities involves authority and the roles of responsible for, and responsible in front of, that are consequently assigned to the EU and its partners.[63] But the counter-productivity of not taking into account cultural and traditional backgrounds alludes directly to productive efficiency; traditional environment then becomes one way of achieving sound economic and political development.[64] The aspect of the debt involved in this issue is quite evident; the debts contracted by the less economically developed countries permit the more economically developed ones to impose conditionalities, as we have seen above. But the involvement of the traditional background – a given – highlights that the transmission of the western institutions is thought to be a gift.

The *use of modernisation for the conserved traditional quality* is the second point of compromise between the debt and the gift. Here, again, the most interesting example concerns the whole Lomé relationship. The argument is that the past relationship between less economically developed and more economically developed countries is valuable, and that for this reason it should become more adapted to reality (i.e. the actual needs of the less economically developed countries, sustainable development or international pressure). The hierarchical responsibility of Europe is the result of historical links (an argument which is reminiscent of the 1970s discourse on preferential treatment). Yet, it is also a question of power: Europe is perceived as the only actor that has the power to modernise the traditional policy that exists between the more economically developed countries and the less economically developed countries.[65] This new policy arising from the modernisation of the traditional relations is thus a gift made by the responsible Europeans to the Africans. The negative aspects of the traditional policy are dismissed as colonising and infantilising, 'efficiency' is often mentioned to mark the advent of a modernised policy where things are more flexible, adaptable and geared to what really matters; where, in other words, the relation of means to ends is fully calculated. The product – the outcome – which this efficiency calculation addresses, is a 'true' policy. The debt is present both in the sense of the investment that such a modernisation represents and in the future debt that less economically developed countries will contract to solve the problem of their externally defined 'wounds' and 'needs'.

The third point of this compromise is *the efficiency of good habits or rather the inefficiency of bad ones*. It focuses mainly on the issue of dependence between Europe and Africa, on its negative and positive sides.[66] The most obvious negative side of this dependence is exposed as the contracting of debts by the less economically developed countries. It is deemed inefficient both for the latter's growth and the relations with the EU. The issue of space is central since the establishment of a code of good habits presupposes a limitation of space. This is particularly clear in the case of international treaties of conduct (in times of war, for instance) that delimit the imaginary space within which such 'good habits' apply. At a more general level, we can observe that an increased emphasis is placed on the inefficiency of the past. On the positive side, however, interdependence is praised. Although this ostensibly points to an egalitarian responsibility, one must also acknowledge the hierarchical responsibility involved, as it is the EU which is, first of all, in charge of cultivating this much-needed good habit of interdependence. The 'special relations' that are part of these good habits also specifically contribute to the efficiency of the EU's external policy, notably *vis-à-vis* others in the international arena. These 'special relations' constitute an undeniable gift but, at the same time, the interdependence that they create is in fact a debt. The more general theme of interdependency is the only occurrence of the EU acknowledging a debt towards its ACP partners and, as such, it is exceptional. In the example given, it is remarkable to note that this had been admitted in the 1980s, in an era where few concessions were readily made to the EU's African counterparts. In the 1990s, however, the issue of interdependence became broadened, justifying an egalitarian responsibility.

The theme of *professional (in)experience* is a generalised theme in the development discourse, particularly with regard to human resources.[67] The acquisition of skills and techniques has always been regarded as paramount to the development process because it enables the people of the less economically developed countries to rise to the level of the more economically developed countries, and because it allows them to attain a greater technical mastery of the imported machines. These technological or technical transfers assume a lack of experience in these domains; such an assumption can be extrapolated to everything 'modern' that is happening to the economies or the politics of less economically developed countries and which is faced with professional inexperience. The transmission of experience is, on the one hand, a gift made to the inexperienced, and it comes with the whole apparatus of what is relevant knowledge. The exercise is aimed at achieving a more efficient development process, at maximising (the quality of) the means for the given purpose. In the most recent but equally telling development vocabulary this takes the name of 'capacity building' and, following the shift in focus from industrialisation to political institutions, it concerns the professional aspects of public administration and the rule of law.[68] However, the transmission of experience also involves the creation of a debt: indeed, professionalising the unprofessional is an investment for the future. Moreover, becoming professional requires the loan (of skills and knowledge), in a more matter-of-fact sense, acquiring the infrastructure that allows professionalism to come about in the first place.

Property, trust, memory

The second compromise is the one between the market exchange as defined by allocative efficiency, and the gift as determined by hierarchical responsibility. Those two are antithetical: one is immediate whereas the other has a long time span; one defies space while the other always posits an exterior. However, they seem to have something in common; the recipient does not apparently owe anything to the 'giver'. But this is only apparent. The gift always calls for the countergift, which thus brings it close to the debt. This apparent similarity between gift and market exchange is very important in that it traces the continuity of the European development discourse that we have described as starting with the gift and ending in the market exchange. A pending obligation of the less economically developed countries is denied in both cases. In this, we can also perceive the workings of an egalitarian individual responsibility, connected to the market exchange.

The market exchange can be connected to Boltanksi and Thévenot's concept of the market world, whereas the gift is relevant in the domestic world. Among the points of compromise identified by Boltanski and Thévenot, two are closely related to the specific compromise we find in the European development discourse between the market exchange and the gift: *property* and the intervention of *trust and memory* in a market exchange.

Property answers to the uncertainty generated by a pure market exchange by bestowing something forever, even though this property might then 'change hands', it bears the mark of an extended time. Two issues in the European development discourse involve property: the '*acquis* Lomé' and the most recent theme of 'ownership'.

The issue of the *acquis* Lomé is a fascinating one in the history of the EU-ACP relationship. Following pressure from both NGOs and donors, the EU gradually introduced a clause on human rights, the rule of law and good governance, called '*acquis*' after the first time it was used. At issue is the progressive presentation of these principles as something traditionally belonging to the field of the EU-ACP relationship. But not only was the Lomé relationship highly acclaimed as being non-political (meaning non-interventionist on these issues); it was also supposed to be exceptional for exactly this reason. The current hesitations on whether the Lomé Convention is or is not political after all, are significant.[69] This ambiguity is expressed by the term *acquis* which is now used for the clause on which conditionalities can be based. Even when the documents' language is English, this word remains in French because it is not easily translatable. It means something acquired, gained, but also carries strong connotations of stability, permanence and victory following a struggle (in this, it is reminiscent of civic expressions). The Green Paper speaks of an 'acquired culture'.[70] If this clause and the principles it stipulates have been 'gained', it is quite unclear who gained them. The ambiguity persists if we ask who fought for these stipulations to be included in the Convention. The *acquis* encompasses the ACP countries' existence in these 30 years in a linear view of history, whereby stage after stage common things and principles are accumulated. The clause – and its ambiguity – is the translation of the more general malaise of the EU *vis-à-vis* its ACP partners on the one hand, and the international community on the other hand. Striving to present the inclusion of this clause as a joint result when it is actually the sole initiative of the EU, the latter actually engages in an external compromise with other donors.

As we saw in the compromise between debt and gift, conditionalities occur in-between gift and debt. However, the *acquis* does not clearly have the quality of 'conditions' imposed on receiving aid, precisely because of this connotation of joint struggle. The stability of this result expresses the longer period in which the 'property' of these principles is valid, the influence of the gift. Responsibility hesitates between its hierarchical and egalitarian aspects: if this *acquis* is collective, we are facing a collective egalitarian responsibility, proper to a civic exchange. But from the viewpoint of the source of the *acquis*, hierarchical responsibility pushes the EU to make the gift of these principles to the ACP countries. Yet a third interpretation is that responsibility becomes egalitarian in the sense that each is responsible for oneself, nobody owes anything, leaning rather towards the aspect of the market exchange in property: the property of these principles has been achieved, they have changed hands, and there are no issues pending on any side. This then is closer to conditionalities, although it still differs from them in that the *acquis* does not involve a debt. Allocative efficiency calculates the value of gaining these principles.

The theme of *ownership* is a second, and very recent, version of property, as it provokes the encounter of the market exchange and the gift.[71] Insistence on ownership of development projects or programmes of the less economically developed countries is ambiguous. On the one hand, ownership comes from participation and involvement in the development process, a shared egalitarian individual responsibility, which is characteristic of the market exchange.[72] On the other hand, if ownership is due to EU initiative, hierarchical responsibility becomes prominent, gracefully conceding the property of projects etc. to the less economically developed countries as in the gift.

The second compromise point regards *trust and memory*, which share the same characteristic between them and with 'property': they extend the time span of the market exchange by meeting the gift. Trust and memory pertain to Boltanski and Thévenot's concept of a domestic world in which the gift establishes one or more of these qualities between people. In a business relation characterised by the market exchange, however, such trust, reputation and memory are also essential components. This is the same dilemma facing 'capacity building'.

The memory of the past, as the bearer of reputation, is a theme that tends to fade away since it concerns colonial ties.[73] When the memory of the colonial past emerged in the 1970s, it invariably did so with regard to a hierarchical responsibility that tied the more economically developed countries to the less economically developed ones. The exchange that took place between them is inexorably sealed by this past and the Europeans' inescapable position is to accept responsibility. By contrast, in the 1990s, this past became irrelevant, being not only an insufficient explanation of the problems of the less economically developed countries, but actually portrayed as an excuse for receiving without giving back.[74] This past almost vanishes from the discourse in the 1980s. Thus, we discern a passage from a past involving the gift to a past that involves the market exchange. As far as efficiency is concerned, in the 1990s the relevant past became that of the European development discourse as such, no longer that of the colonial period; European development cooperation has acquired a past, and it is proclaimed unambiguously to be a failure.[75] Based on such an estimation, the future allocation of resources and methods in order to achieve development must change.

The changes that are based on the lessons of the past also change the meaning of trust.[76] In the early European development discourse, trust is something asked for the sake of the gift. In other words, the Europeans, aware of the distrust created by colonial times, asked the less economically developed countries to trust them. In this context, the 'humanity' of the relationship was insisted upon, although it was not necessarily a common humanity.[77] By contrast, in the 'new contractual' approach of the gift, trust appears as the quintessence of the compromise between gift and market exchange. It results in a contract with equal obligations between true partners and responding to reciprocal interests; we have here the armature of the individual egalitarian responsibility that characterises market exchanges. 'Contractuality' has always been one of the principles of Lomé, and its equivocal meaning accompanies the change of the meaning of trust. However, the unresolved question of 'whether to place more trust in the partners' re-establishes a hierarchical responsibility by letting the EU decide whether the ACP are worthy of the EU's trust: can they be trusted to be responsible? This is again the scheme of hierarchical responsibility permitting egalitarian responsibility.

Partnership, sustainability and liberalism

A compromise between market exchange and civic exchange, characterised by egalitarian collective responsibility, is improbable. Boltanski and Thévenot did not find any compromise between the market and the civic worlds in the documents they examined. The ideal-typical attitudes – and the corresponding types of giving – entailed by these worlds seem incompatible; thus 'too often a radical choice is posed between individual freedom and collective solidarity'.[78] The historical emergence of the welfare state, however, is an answer to this dilemma; organised collective responsibility (the welfare state) rose on the foundations of the market economy. The variety of welfare states in Europe is a further witness to different versions of the compromise between market and civic worlds. Given the strong affinities between the welfare and the development discourses, one might be inclined to search for such a compromise in the latter too.

In the European development discourse, the dichotomy is both sustained and blurred. When the compromise does not take place, it is acknowledged that both components are significant; this often takes the form of simultaneous references to solidarity and mutual interests, in formulations that remain quasi-identical.[79] But the compromise is sought: market and civic exchange are valued in a way that makes the European discourse more ambiguous, and this opens up different alternatives for it, not least for a constructive critical discourse. However, such a situation leaves the issue of responsibility undecided. Is the EU responsible in an individual or a collective way, and what does it expect from its partners? There is no ambiguity in efficiency, since both civic and market exchanges are characterised by allocative efficiency; but are the resources, goods, and means to be allocated common or not? The problem between types of giving can ultimately be solved by responsibility and not by efficiency.

The theme of *partnership* sketches this compromise. It suggests a relationship based on the solidarity of those involved in it *vis-à-vis* the rest of the world and, increasingly, a reciprocal exchange.[80] The political and economic components are chronologically entangled, a political partnership was acclaimed earlier in the European development policy at the same time as political neutrality was advertised, whereas an explicit economic turn comes later when a political dialogue is instituted. Despite this, the concept of partnership constantly aims to convey strong links, a sense of equality and mutual obligations. This theme is closely related to the interdependence between the less economically developed and the more economically developed countries, also arising in the compromise between the debt and the gift. The civic exchange pulls the compromise towards the inclusion of an egalitarian-collective responsibility of the partners towards each other, while the market exchange instils rationality by means of allocative efficiency. In this case, the partnership is based on a rational calculation according to which the optimal state of affairs involves solidarity.

The theme of *sustainable development*, also sketching this compromise, is by definition tied to an extended period of time; it is the time of the intergenerational debt, i.e. the people of today, more economically developed and less economically developed, owe it to the people of tomorrow. This intergenerational debt is related to the debt of the civic exchange in that it places a very strong emphasis on collective well-being. At the same time, the more economically developed countries owe it today to the less economically developed countries and vice versa, stipulating now a debt to come later.[81] Which is the dominant form of responsibility? The ambiguity is only answered by reference to market exchange. In all cases, responsibility will be egalitarian, the problem lies in choosing between an individual egalitarian responsibility and a collective egalitarian responsibility. If market exchange is prominent in the idea of sustainable development – and it often is, in the tendency of the discourse to emphasise the need for market liberalisation and efficient allocation of (common) resources – then responsibility will take on an individual egalitarian aspect, i.e. each is individually responsible for sustainable development. If market exchange is less prominent, trade liberalisation less of a priority and efficient allocation of the resources between the EU and the ACP not a stronger concern than redistribution, then sustainable development involves a responsibility that is collective egalitarian, i.e. we are all collectively responsible.

Finally, in the belief that the liberalisation of the economy favours representative political structures another point of compromise between market and civic exchanges takes shape.[82] This is an abstract version of the debate raging in the late 1980s on the links between democracy, development and trade liberalisation, of which the 'conditionalities' were an application. This logic is based on the calculation of the efficient allocation of resources, the possibility of solidarity and the acknowledgement of collective debts by less economically developed countries. But the richness and interest of the European development discourse consists of the fact that this instance of the discourse is also contradicted, not only by statements seeing the relationship as invalid but also through destroying the very plausibility of such a compromise.[83]

7
Europe's Quest

Europe was in my head crammed together with Africa, Asia and America. Squashed and jammed together in my dustbin head. There is no rubbish dump big enough to relieve me of my load. Swinging upside down, threatening to burst the thin roof of my experience. Those years of my travels. Years of innocence and experience. Motherfucking months of twiddling my thumbs with insecurity. In search of my true people. Yes, in search of my true people. But wherever I went I did not find people but caricatures of people who insisted on being taken seriously as people. Perhaps I was on the wrong planet.
In the wrong skin.
Sometimes.
And sometimes all the time. You know. In the wrong skin. This black skin.
My thoughts swung gently like an uncertain breeze. Swung towards that unsuspecting female anthropologist who was bathing at Blunt Rock Falls. She had a certain renown in her own country. This intrepid seeker after the ideal human society. Blanche Goodfather, that was her name. I had avidly read her books. On life among headhunters. Life among skinheads, screwballs, dossers, downs and outs, tarts, the shitheads of skidrow. Life among cannibals. She was a moth fiercely attracted to the lights of the savage, the earthy, the primitive. And how she roamed the earth – how she too searched – ferreted out the few bits and pieces of authentic people reducing them to meticulous combinations of the English alphabet. Those books.[1]

THE QUEST FOR EUROPE

From the extract above, we may immediately surmise the complex relationship Marechera had with Europe and, here, with its personification, the 'unsuspecting female anthropologist'. The facts of his life tell us that, an exceptionally talented *poète maudit*, Marechera only came to terms with his blackness, in an experience similar to Fanon's, when faced with Europe's whiteness in London and in Oxford, from where he was eventually thrown out. His anti-colonialism was virulent, but neither a straightforward follower of Fanonism nor a rhapsode of the joys of hybridity, Marechera nurtured a less unambiguous thought; though profoundly aware of his own half-diasporic condition (evident in the first lines of the extract), he was also deeply grounded in the urban setting of Salisbury/Harare, a colonial and then post-colonial 'African' capital. At the same time, despite his acute awareness of the hybridity in his own life, in particular through white friends and lovers, he violently denounced the 'white man's' devastating influence in Africa.

Because of an interpretation of this last trait as being preponderant in Marechera's work, his writings are nowadays taught at school in Zimbabwe while he remained a very poor man during his life, even after 1980. The material conditions of Marechera's life explain perhaps why he was less able than others to enthuse in (Bhabha's) hybridity, in having 'family in Europe and in Africa', as Appiah somewhere writes, or in any other type of joyous affirmation of the 'black man's' condition between Europe and Africa. To take the point further, there is an often strong material difference between those 'Africans' who belong to the diaspora and those 'Africans' who are in 'Africa'. They are not only subjected in very different ways to Europe, America, the West, or the North, ways that vary in their spatial characteristics and in time, but they are also facing very different material conditions of living on the whole. In Africa, people still have to bear the signs of the colonial past everywhere, even on the land; and under conditions of extremely unequal income distribution.

Thus, the Europe of the African diaspora may be very different from the non-diasporic Africans' Europe, and while the first understanding of Europe may have incorporated the lessons of PanAfricanism and the independences in a distanced but joyful way, the second Europe may have emerged from the lessons of such movements with less irony, particularly when this Europe is thought as an object against which struggle continues. In Zimbabwe, where the first version of this text was written, European and non-European mean two very different things. One understanding of 'European' is very recent and it relates to the EU, the instigator, according to the official governmental discourse, of all evils currently befalling Zimbabwe. This understanding, however, would not have the rhetorical political power it has, in the hands of the governmental press, were it not related to a second older one, much more firmly entrenched in the divided self-understanding of Zimbabweans:[2] a divide between Europeans and non-Europeans that is mapped on a divide between white colonisers and black colonised. 'Europeans' are thus all the white people in Zimbabwe, irrespective of how many generations their family has spent living in the African continent and of whether they originally come from Europe, Australia or the US. Non-Europeans include black 'Africans', 'coloureds', 'Indians', 'Chinese', etc.[3] If the historical origins of such appellations are obviously found in the colonial past of Zimbabwe, it is none the less significant that these names have persisted 20 years after the country's independence in 1980.

The survival of these names is due both to black Zimbabweans (for example, to the government's rhetoric) and to white Zimbabweans. In fact, originally, as we know, for instance, from Said's accounts, the divide between Europeans and non-Europeans is cultivated by the white settlers.[4] In the 1960s, when the Civil Rights and the PanAfricanist movements took shape and black became beautiful, the 'African' identity was endorsed affirmatively, and the 'European' one viewed with anger or irony or other feelings of resistance.

To go back to today's Zimbabwe, and following what Blair Rutherford writes in his recent anthropological study on black workers and white farmers in the country,[5] the 'European' identity is upheld by the white farmers on two axes: the spatial one that defines paternalistic authority *vis-à-vis* the African who must be edified; and 'the axis of "modernity" which informs contemporary distinctions between farmers and farm workers'.[6] This second axis is more relevant to our general discussion, and in Rutherford's account, it encompasses echoes of discussions held in the different milieus with which he is familiar in North America. 'But', he says, 'a difference of this discourse of modernity amongst white farmers compared to what I knew in Canada was that it carried an *immediate* sense of mission, an undercurrent that served as a support to the frontier milieu it assisted in creating ... The target of this edification was always Africans.'[7] To be European in Zimbabwe's commercial farms is thus to endorse the modern mission of edification of the traditional African. This points both to the neat divide between modernity and tradition that the European 'developmentalist efficiency' operates, and to the paternalistic/hierarchical responsibility that was prominent in the first period of the European development discourse examined here.[8]

We now see how far-reaching and entrenched in local post-colonial settings bureaucratic development discourse can be. In the same way, we see how the unreflexively used notion of 'Europe' carries a very precise significance in the geography of the ACP countries, a significance that is to be found right on the soil of these countries and not (only) in a collective bureaucratic interlocutor in Brussels.

One may object that there is a difference between the meaning of 'Europe' and 'European' in rural areas and in urban areas.[9] Thus, for instance, the paternalism present in 'European' white farmers (some of whom know, for instance, how to speak Shona or, rarely, Ndebele) is absent in the relations between urban 'Europeans' and urban 'Africans'. How relevant is this to the way 'Europe' may be understood in Africa? If the component of modernity in 'Europe' as it is used in the farmlands is taken into account, then there is an evident difference between the urban and the rural settings, in terms of the access one has to this 'European' modernity. The myth of the frontier, of the 'heart of darkness' that is illuminated by the 'white man's' advance into the wilderness breaks down. In Harare of 2002, 'African' executives wake up at 5 o'clock in the morning to go to their gym club, drive their Mercedes to the office lodged in a skyscraper and have two cellular telephones to arrange their multiple meetings. To this division between urban and rural, we could add numerous others. Living in the high density suburbs of Harare does not necessarily give access to this lifestyle, for instance; being a woman – even an intellectual – still supposes that the *lobola* (bride-price) be paid to one's parents at the marriage; being a 'coloured' or an 'Indian' possibly excludes from activities other than commercial or, for a very small but dynamic minority, working at the university.

How crude is this Europe!, we Europeans[10] think. How utterly misunderstood! Generations of the most serious, self-reflexive European thinkers have thought through the paradoxes of Old Europe, about striving for universality hand-in-hand with the admission of (at least Europe's own) particularity; about belief in reason and the monstrous passions it has unleashed; about hailing of freedom and the nightmarish disciplines that it has imposed on its peoples. Europe is 'the historical teleology of the infinite goals of reason' and if it falls into barbarity, it can also be reborn 'from the spirit of philosophy through the heroism of reason' because it has 'a mission for humanity';[11] Europe has a 'psyche' whose most important characteristics – those that render it superior – are 'burning desire, ardent and disinterested curiosity, a happy blend of imagination and logical precision, a scepticism that is not pessimistic and a mysticism that is not resigned'.[12] Europe has a real 'intellectual unity';[13] indeed Europe is above all a spirit and 'what threatens European identity would not essentially threaten Europe but, in Spirit, the universality for which Europe is responsible (...)'.[14] There is a mystery of the spirit of Europe and it may be useful to think it over when envisaging an enhanced political existence of Europe, but Europe has also been plainly un-mysterious in the oppression and the tyranny it has exercised over its peoples and over other peoples. This tension certainly needs to be thought through in face of the future political union. As Gadamer notes – one would say prophetically, had this not already been evident quite some time before 1983 – 'sooner or later, the disparity between their own being and that of the Europeans will arise in the consciousness of the people of the Third World; and then, all new efforts which we are presently pursuing could prove to be just subtle forms of colonisation and likewise fail'.[15]

THE GIFT OF EUROPEAN KNOWLEDGE

This phrase by Gadamer comes in an essay that he devotes to 'the future of the European humanities'. Exactly before the above phrase, he asks a question that we have been posing in various ways throughout the preceding pages: 'is what we have to offer, what we control, scientific-technological perfection, really always a gift?'.[16] Gadamer is being rhetorical and that is why he assumes that 'we control' the scientific-technological tool and that we have brought it to perfection. We must disregard these points to focus on the question of the gift; the question of responsibility as it faces technical and economic efficiency; and the question of Gadamer's more general concern, the humanities, as they face the ascendancy of 'science'.

Europe, if there is such a thing, has for a long time been offering knowledge and development as a gift. This has been its rhetoric, this has been its politics and sometimes it might even have been its intention. When this 'free' gift (on which we played the different tunes of gift of life, gift of death or poisonous gift, seeing that it never is free) was exhausted as a motivational theme and, as a historic inheritance, it was slowly replaced by debt and eventually economic exchange.[17] A first look at the European development discourse told us that the unambiguous 'trade not aid' motto had overwhelmed domestic and industrial forms of exchange.[18] A second look revealed that things of the past cling to the present more stubbornly than developmentalists would like to think. There are indeed, within the European development discourse, next to the increasingly hailed market exchange, aspects of the gift that go with a slow and extended understanding of time and a domestic conception of the relations between more economically developed and less economically developed countries, not unlike those very contemporary white farmers in Zimbabwe who wholly belong to today. The technological-scientific-economic transfer of development – the gift of how to think, work and live *efficiently* – is still often thought as a gift, and as a gift it cannot be refused.

The same stubbornness, in a more accusatory mood, is displayed by the debt. But there is an 'innocence' in the gift (in giving the gift and bearing a hierarchical responsibility for doing so), there is a naivety – unforgivable as it may be – that cannot be found in the debt. The debt states bluntly the powers at play, it frames the time of the exchange and the deadline of repayment in a precise manner. What happens when debts exceed every such limit (that it is their role to impose), when they 'explode' as they say, is the ongoing story of the relations between more economically developed and less economically developed countries. The renegotiation and the *forgiveness* of the debts are among the most significant adventures of the contemporary world. Until when can the debts be forgiven, what is the threshold of forgiveness, the *seuil de tolérance*? And what if the more economically developed countries just decided to drop the debts, to put the counter back to zero, to 'forgive' the debts, what would that mean? These are of course hypothetical questions, but the wild guesses they push us to make, reveal something about our understanding of the past. Will it be erased if debts are 'forgiven'; will then the less economically developed countries have to drop their own demands for colonial reparations? And of the future; how effective is the promise of forgiving the debts? Most importantly, the guesses they push us to make reveal the limits of the international imagination in the present, that is, the limits of the self-creating imagination of this international system that resolutely sticks to its past mode of functioning, a functioning that includes colonialism and development, except when, shaken by a new catastrophe, it seeks to mend its wounds.

It becomes evident that the question of giving is a burning one in development. For once we have decided – and this must always undoubtedly be thought as a decision and a responsibility – that we Europeans can no longer give, and once we have become situated in the potentially explosive situation of the debt, is the market exchange the only alternative we are left with? Can we face the less economically developed countries by limiting our give-and-take to the 'neutral' immediacy of that exchange which will annihilate, as it happens and happens again, both the past and the possibility of a durable common future? In a world certainly resisted, full of hybridity, *métissage* and revolted 'others' and 'subalterns', but still very much painted in the colours of the powers that be, where are the less economically developed countries to go, once we have decided to avoid to face them? To put it more practically; as long as we are politically indifferent to the plight of AIDS in SubSaharan Africa, for instance; as long as we do not practically demand the free distribution of anti-retroviral medicine; as long as we have not heard that the EU can impose sanctions in countries where people are dying of hunger because it happens to think that 'governance' and 'human rights' are more important than drought; as long as we Europeans are not even aware that we can say something against this because these policies are being applied in our name; as long as British firms are packing up and going from an ex-colony only to be replaced by French ones that benefit as much as their predecessors from 'European' development 'investments to the ACP countries'; as long as all this is happening literally in front of our eyes without us saying anything, we are not facing the less economically developed countries.

The European role in the less economically developed countries has increasingly been to denounce the corruption in them, the 'bad governance', the oppression of the minorities. But isn't it true that Greece, Italy or Belgium ranks very high on the list of the world's most corrupt countries? Isn't it true that only a few decades have gone by since the last military putsch in Europe? And isn't it true that minorities all over Europe are still suffering from various political and sometimes even legal forms of discrimination? So emphasising those elements in the less economically developed countries, while we understate them in the European case, serves a purpose: to constitute them as economic reservoirs of raw materials, or objects of study. In this respect, the contempt towards 'developing countries' that Hirschman had observed in development economics can be said to characterise both applied economics or the market exchange and a disciplinary understanding of the rationale of the social sciences. From the preceding pages, it is clear that such attitudes towards the 'developing' countries and their people do not amount to properly facing them.

As the beginning of a remedy to such ways of thinking, an alternative understanding of solidarity (as opposed to mechanic or organic solidarity) must be retrieved, which eliminates the contempt that is displayed by the mainstream social sciences *vis-à-vis* the less economically developed countries. This solidarity is enriched; to a solidarity traditionally promoting redistribution in the community, an understanding based on claims of recognition is added that extends our knowledge to areas (and others) previously not considered inter-esting.

There are four central elements in this conceptualisation. The first is that the sovereignty-solidarity debate, when transposed to the international level, points to the shared world that is between us.[19] Group- or state-terrorist attacks, dropping bombs somewhere or occupying a country, cannot be understood as happening in a world separate from the one where the attacks 'originate' or the bombs are fabricated. Such an observation both denounces a geographical fallacy according to which people imagine that 'evil deeds' are always prepared and mostly happen far away (rudely interrupted by the shock of the US population after 9/11); and proposes that the world that separates us is also the world that unites us – and that by virtue of this space at once uncrossable and inhabited (by us and the other), we have interests in common, at least as humans.

The second consequence of the alternative solidarity is its promotion of an understanding of the social movements, and by extension the 'global social movement', that focuses on recognition. Fighting and attempting to supersede social inequality becomes a matter of recognising differences too. But these movements present the specificity of resisting 'the social' since they address categories that have been ignored by it. For them, solidarity is as much an internal objective as an attitude towards the outside. In two words, this alternative solidarity is both universalistic and particularistic.[20]

Such an understanding of solidarity encompasses and uses the social-scientific knowledge as much as the social-scientific knowledge uses it; the social-scientist becomes relevant to the activist not only as a source of information, but also as a participant in solidarity. It is thus an answer to the dichotomy of 'critical' or emancipatory knowledge and 'scientific' or regulatory knowledge. In this perspective, the scientist and the activist do not belong to different 'fields' but to a common world to which they relate differently, with different insights. This marks a two-way flow of knowledge, a knowledge that can be political or 'scientific' coming from either side.[21]

Finally, and perhaps most significantly, the alternative understanding of solidarity includes the possibility of disagreement or dispute. The one-sided emphasis on the separateness of the elements of older, commoner understandings of solidarity is overcome. The world is not only divided, it is also common to all; the solution to inequality is not only redistribution, but also recognition; although some principles have universal validity, acknowledgement of particular identities and situations is necessary; and if the political is expressed in areas other than that of knowledge, the social sciences can nevertheless not forego political thought. The tensions created between the separateness and the community of the world, redistribution and recognition, universality and particularity, the political and knowledge are fruitful: they allow for conceptual dispute in the very formulation of an alternative understanding of solidarity; and practically, they allow the self-creation of a global social movement.[22]

The seeds of this conceptualisation of solidarity were, however, sewn earlier than it may seem at first glance.[23] We can see some aspects of it, and in particular the relation between solidarity and knowledge in Marechera's text. Here, the similarity of the quest of the anthropologist and her object of study ('in *search* of my *true* people', 'how she too *searched*', 'the bits and pieces of *authentic* people'); and also the similarity of the subjects of study (since, ultimately, Marechera is the anthropologist's 'subject' as much as she is the author's 'subject') are emblematic of this, even if, in the 1970s when he writes, it is impregnated with the quest for authenticity.[24] The issues of gender and race that are evident both through the explicit discussion of the 'black skin', 'the authentic people' and through the 'unsuspecting female' anthropologist's name cannot be discussed at length here but are also expressions of the same interweaving that takes place between, in this case, solidaristic politics and yet another form of knowledge, literature.

TYRANNY AND PLURALISM

Humanities, says Gadamer, are asked to face 'the task of the human future which has truly gained global significance': 'human coexistence'.[25] It is this task with which the humanities must engage; it is in this sense that the production of social scientific knowledge plays a political role. If indeed the issue is how humans can and will co-exist, showing, first, that this is desirable, inventing, second, how this is possible and insisting, third, on the discussion and dispute that this always entails is the task of 'humanities', whose concern lies with human lives.

Unless social scientists and social and political theorists passively resign themselves to this task being taken up in their name by others, explicitness in reclaiming such a task and boldness in assuming a scientific as well as a political responsibility are required. The hegemony of some weak but widespread methodological version of positivism in the social sciences has been so powerful, that it is forgotten that such a stance as we just described above is the oldest understanding of philosophy; in the broad sense, a sense that encompasses social sciences.

This issue has been touched upon at various points, mostly in Chapters 3, 4 and 5, that of the polarity between ethics and economics, or the dichotomy between ethics and development studies. It invites a reflection on the lack of historicity that abstract philosophical discussions can present, as well as on the lack of meaningful interpretation that technical uses of knowledge often have. This issue also begs the question of the separability of disciplines, whose well traceable historical origins and laudable reasons should not protect these disciplines forever from, precisely, interdisciplinarity. Additionally, this issue has oriented the construction of all chapters, by demanding that the theoretical and historical (also in the history of the social sciences) presuppositions of the concepts used are shown before seeing how these melt into the development discourse's contemporary but changing uses of the same concepts, and by demanding that these concepts are always examined in their broader political context. Finally, it is this same issue which asks of the students of development discourse to denounce its tyrannical potential and restore pluralism.

Tyranny – the tyranny of the European development discourse – has been a guiding concern of this book. The definition of tyranny we used, we borrowed from Walzer: it is the illegitimate crossing of borders between 'spheres of justice'. Development is tyrannical almost by definition (as is capitalism), because of its tendency to take over other domains than the domain originally ascribed to it, the economic.[26] The study of the use of efficiency in the European development discourse is a good case in point, as it shows how efficiency (an originally economic and technical concept) is becoming 'political'. We have seen that this has more practical consequences than such a conceptual and discursive argument may seem, at first sight, to allow for. In 'developing' countries, in particular, the practice and the discourse of development are everywhere, from the power exhibited by the institutions of the more economically developed international community to the local politics objective of 'developing' (and this, even when 'official' development strategies are rejected), to the individual entrepreneurs' reappropriation of the vocabulary of development.[27]

Tyranny is omnipresent and faces little resistance; it is the disappearance of criteria of justice other than those condoned, created or co-opted by development discourse. We could say, in yet different words, that what is external to development discourse (what permits us to see that it is only one discourse among others) is being conquered, and thus, the people touched most by development lose the possibility of taking refuge from the development discourse that often subjugates them. Working with social- and political-theoretical approaches that insist on pluralism effectively undermines the tyrannical potential of development discourse, both because these approaches reveal the ambivalence of the concepts used by development discourse (Chapters 4 and 5) and because they open up the multiplicity of outcomes of the development discourse as it exists and as it could exist (Chapter 6). Putting the accent on the changing understandings of responsibility and efficiency, showing that 'giving' has at least four forms, and that the combinations of the latter with the different understandings of our two central concepts (stemming, as they do, from a variety of 'worlds') gives us a wealth of compromises. All this bears a certain spirit of opposition, an opposition to accounts of development that see no future against its hegemonic power and take no account of the creativity of 'the oppressed'; and a resistance to development discourse itself as it tends to appear, at a first glance, monolithically a-political.

In the event, two more steps were taken that try to circumscribe the problem of the tyranny of development discourse and it must be clear that they pertain to the same problem: the first step was to define the relation between more economically developed and less economically developed countries as a community; the second was to distinguish between different levels of domestic, national, international, social and political affairs.

Describing the development relation between the EU and the ACP as a community had a political purpose in the face of the current European disengagement; a community entails mutual aid and obligation. The idea of this community can be encountered in the earlier European development discourse, even if its full consequences are never spelled out; it is therefore shocking that it was so easily made to fade away without this being at least presented as a political decision. Instead, we hear discussions about the inevitable forces of globalisation and the responsibility of the ACP. Furthermore, from a quasi-technical but concomitant viewpoint, envisaging the EU-ACP relationship as a community helped to pinpoint more accurately the elements involved in maintaining engagement and obligations (the exceptionality of the relationship, the common past, efficiency subordinated to responsibility) and the elements involved in disengagement (global responsibility and global relations, irrelevance of the colonial past, responsibility subordinated to efficiency). In the aftermath of the analysis, these elements may seem as obvious as the conclusions drawn from them, but a critique of development discourse can only be taken seriously after such detailed empirical examination. Finally, and most significantly, envisaging the relationship as a community points very directly to the equal right of the ACP and their peoples to address issues politically.

The second move to deal with the problem of tyranny was to attempt a distinction between the levels of discussion about the national, the European (international) and the global, a strategy followed mainly in Chapter 2, in the discussion of global responsibility in Chapter 4, as well as in Chapter 6. Thinking along the lines of such a separation is attributable to two personal experiences. The first returns us to Zimbabwe, and it has again to do with domesticity as it is created by the paternalism of the white farmers that we saw, but also by the urban domestic workers and wives (involving, more generally, issues of gender). Running the eco-nomy of a farm can be related to running any household in urban areas in Zimbabwe, and in the current political circumstances, compared to running the state.

The second experience that urged a separation between such levels was the anti-globalisation meetings held in Europe over the past few years. The debates that preceded and followed these meetings related to 'globality', but also to the *national* environments as well as to the European one, not to mention that the demonstrations were addressed against the international financial institutions. That participants may not have seen this as problematic says a lot about the emerging global movement, its force and its weakness; untangling those levels is necessary for the resistance it expresses to be heard by those it addresses. More generally, concerning development, the separation of such levels seems important at times where conventional international relations analyses, for instance, treat land redistribution as an irrelevant domestic matter, or where sociological/economic/anthropological studies interested in the national level fail to see how international interference is a factor not to be left out. As another way of addressing the tyrannical potential of development discourse, this strategy enabled us to see both how development encroaches on a multiplicity of levels, but also that one level X will always maintain some exteriority *vis-à-vis* level Y, and thus will be able to resist tyranny. Finally, bringing these separated levels close to the idea of the community between the more economically developed and the less economically developed shows how pervasive development discourse is; how it is impossible, as much as the EU may have wanted it, to consider the Lomé Conventions an exclusively 'domestic matter'; and how it is impossible, now that the community is wished away, to consider that these relations are prey exclusively to uncontrollable global forces.

Ultimately, however, denouncing the irrationality of development seems to be the only conceptually convincing critique of development discourse. Too little effort has been made to read again authors of the 1970s when imagination was not afraid of speaking its name in scientific fora. Conservatism is not only 'being right wing', although the left-right distinction retains a meaning; conservatism is shunning away from imagination because of scientific standards or development standards that we have not participated in making. Challenging them has consequences in terms of what one would call responsibility; a stance that has far-reaching implications for what can be done to change conditions of suffering elsewhere than in Europe and European awareness of them. In a nutshell, this means that we can simultaneously keep on asking the practical questions we have been asking with regard to the ACP countries while refusing to see them through the prism of development. It means that efficiency needs to be put back where it belongs, or else undergo systematic political criticism for turning consequentialism into our dominant mode of thought. It means that responsibility needs to be understood as solidarity, a solidarity that takes into account a divided past but is the present, self-reflexive creation of the world we have in common.

Notes

1 EUROPE AND DEVELOPMENT REVISITED

1. We could add a gendered reading of the play: Madam Zachanassian became pregnant by a man who disavowed her. She then had to 'hide her shame' from the morality of her village, and sought revenge by becoming a woman who despises men and is surrounded by eunuchs: she has become a castrator and her last act will bring this to its limit, murder. Dürrenmatt himself warned against the 'moralisation' of the play; 'Claire Zachanassian', he said, 'doesn't represent Justice or the Marshall Plan or even the Apocalypse, she's purely and simply what she is, namely the richest woman in the world and, thanks to her finances, in a position to act as the Greek tragic heroines acted, absolutely, terribly, something like Medea.' In Friedrich Dürrenmatt (trans. Peter Bowles), *The Visit (a tragi-comedy)* (London: Jonathan Cape, 1962) Postscript, p. 106. In fact, the heroine is compared to Medea in the play itself; it is not explained, but we can see the point: she had an abortion (Medea killed her children) and she seeks revenge from the man who wronged her (again like Medea). But there is one major difference, in the face of the division Europe/Barbarians; Medea is herself a Barbarian (and as such is always the absolute stranger in her husband's country, even when on the throne), whilst Zachanassian is the child of the soil, although her name suggests the contrary.
2. Derrida's call in Jacques Derrida (trans. Pascale-Anne Brault and Michael B. Naas), *The Other Heading. Reflections on Today's Europe* (Bloomington: Indiana University Press, 1992). Here, the use of Derrida's injunction is both a reminder of responsibility and a question on 'Europe' (which will be asked again in the conclusion).
3. See for instance Alain Touraine, *Pourrons-nous vivre ensemble? Egaux et différents* (Paris: Fayard, 1997), in particular pp. 219–26; Zygmunt Bauman, 'On universal morality and the morality of universalism', *European Journal of Development Research (EJDR)*, Vol. 10, No. 2, Dec. 1998; Cornelius Castoriadis, 'Réflexions sur le "développement" et la "rationalité"', *Esprit*, No. 5, May 1976.
4. Castoriadis, 'Reflexions'.
5. Jonathan Crush (ed.), *Power of Development* (London: Routledge, 1995). M. P. Cowen and R. W. Shenton, *Doctrines of Development* (London: Routledge, 1996). David B. Moore and Gerald J. Schmitz (eds), *Debating Development Discourse: Institutional and Popular Perspectives* (London: Macmillan, 1994). Arturo Escobar, 'Discourse and power in development: Michel Foucault and the relevance of his work to the Third World', *Alternatives X*, winter 1984–85.
6. Des Gasper, 'Essentialism in and about development discourse' in Raymond Apthorpe and Des Gasper (guest editors), 'Arguing development

policy: frames and discourse', *EJDR*, Vol. 8, No. 1, June 1996, for example, p. 170.

7. Peter Wagner, 'Certainty and order, liberty and contingency. The birth of social science as empirical political philosophy' in Johan Heilbron, Lars Magnusson and Björn Wittrock (eds), *The Rise of the Social Sciences and the Formation of Modernity* (Dordrecht: Kluwer, 1998).

8. Luc Boltanski and Eve Chiapello, *Le nouvel esprit du capitalisme* (Paris: Gallimard, 1999). They see this 'new spirit' emerging after the '*Trente Glorieuses*' period at the end of the 1960s. Moore's development periods correspond to this description since he describes the period stretching from the 1970s to now as the second phase of development (the first starting with the active interest of the US in the 'Third World' in the immediate post-Second World War years). David B. Moore, 'Development discourse as hegemony: towards an ideological history – 1945–1995', in Moore and Schmitz (eds), *Debating Development Discourse: Institutional and Popular Perspectives* (London: Macmillan, 1994).

9. It has been suggested that instead of talking about 'poor', we should talk about 'impoverished', instead of marginal, about 'marginalised', etc., formulations that point to responsibility. See Boaventura de Sousa Santos, *Toward a New Common Sense: Law, Science and Politics in the Paradigmatic Transition* (NY: Routledge, 1995), p. 353; and Rajeev Patel, 'Resistance in a time of fascism: solidarity, feminism and global capital from Zimbabwe' (PhD dissertation: Cornell University, 2002).

10. This 'we' is the pronoun of collective-egalitarian responsibility, that is, the pronoun of anybody whose voice can be heard.

11. Michael Walzer, *Spheres of Justice* (Oxford: Martin Robertson, 1983), p. 29. Emphasis added.

12. We may reflect on this division between domestic and external (or insider/outsider) at both the global 'social' level and at the international 'political' level. In the first case, Zygmunt Bauman's writings are interesting, as they deal with the abandonment of the old type of community. The new, 'post-modern' community that Bauman describes is a community of the thinnest efforts, of the lowest engagement, and of the fewest long-term commitments, in fact, it is a community where 'ethical responsibilities' do not have a place. Such a thin community is possible because of the likeness of its members. Those who do not belong to these like-minded, who happen to be the most flexible and the best endowed in financial and educational terms, are left behind in a community of their own, the community of the weak. The main problem of such conceptualisation is the 'victimisation' of the weak and, equally importantly, the refusal to conceive of a common world. But it offers a clear picture of what exclusionary politics can be. See Zygmunt Bauman, *Community, Seeking Safety in an Insecure World* (Cambridge: Polity Press, 2001).

To Zygmunt Bauman's foreboding (that concerns a global 'social' level) can be added R. B. J. Walker's groundbreaking reading of international relations theory. According to the latter, development can be seen as one of the consequences of the relaxation of an exclusionist logic within the state sovereignty framework. To make this clearer, we must first note that 'the principle of state sovereignty did not appear out of thin air. It embodies a historically specific account of ethical possibility in the form of an answer to questions about the nature and location of political community'. R. B. J. Walker, *Inside/Outside: International Relations as Political Theory* (Cambridge: Cambridge University Press, 1993), p. 62. In the discipline of international relations, the object of Walker's study, 'state sovereignty' serves as that principle which makes international relations, precisely just relations between states (anarchy) and not a community between states, a community being equivalent to politics (the space and time where they can be discussed): in other words, sovereignty serves to establish an outside and an inside (also in 'disciplinary' terms). But if this division of inside/outside or inclusion/exclusion is relaxed, there appears the reverse temptation of moving from anarchy (a division exists) to community (no division), from particularistic (the nation-state claim to sovereignty) to universalistic. This second temptation often takes a temporal form: development for instance, or a linear history, or progress.

13. Later on, Walzer says: '[W]e who are already members do the choosing, in accordance with our own understanding of what membership means in our community and of what sort of a community we want to have … But we don't distribute [membership] among ourselves; it is already ours. We give it out to strangers. Hence, the choice is also governed by our relationships with strangers – not only by our understanding of those relationships but also by the actual contracts, connections, alliances we have established and the effects we have had beyond our borders.' Walzer, *Spheres of Justice*, p. 32.

14. Recognition/redistribution (mutual aid/membership) can be thought of as different forms of exchange that are criteria of intensity of the community in terms of solidarity; then the community created by development is of low intensity. For central references on these issues, see: Axel Honneth, *The Struggle for Recognition. The Moral Grammar of Social Conflicts* (Cambridge: Polity Press, 1995) and Nancy Fraser, *Justice Interruptus, Critical Reflections on the 'PostSocialist' Condition* (New York: Routledge, 1997).

15. The religious connotation of Hegel's understanding of work must be noted, in particular as he relates it to the universal spirit become substance. It reminds us of the constellation of religious interpretations underlying basic ideas of capitalism, development and colonialism. See Hegel, 'Independence and dependence of self-consciousness: Lordship and Bondage' in G. W. F. Hegel, *Phenomenology of Spirit* (trans. A. V. Miller) (Oxford: Oxford University Press, 1977 [1807]).

16. For Marx, see Shlomo Avineri (ed.), *Karl Marx on Colonialism and Modernization* (NY: Doubleday & Company, 1968).

17. See, for a precise typology of development discourse, Des Gasper, 'Essentialism in and about development discourse' in *European Journal of Development Research*, Vol. 8, 1996. Des Gasper suggests that there are at least five different understandings of the expression: (i) discourse that centrally uses the term (social/economic/political) development; (ii) discourse in development studies; (iii) discourse that uses 'developmentalist' presumptions; (iv) discourse of development

policy; (v) discourse of leading international donors. The first and third definitions are related to what development discourse says, the second and the fourth to the setting of the discourse, and the last to the agent using it.

18. And politically, as it warns of the dangers of consensus politics.

19. See Ernesto Laclau and Chantal Mouffe, *Hegemony and Socialist Strategy: Towards a Radical Democratic Politics* (London: Verso, 1985) and Jacob Torfing, *New Theories of Discourse* (Oxford: Blackwell, 1999), Chapter 1.

20. See, for the clearest texts: Michel Foucault, *L'ordre du discourse* (Paris: Gallimard, 1971); *The History of Sexuality. An Introduction* (London: Penguin, 1988 [1976]); and 'Politics and the Study of Discourse' in Graham Burchell, Colin Gordon and Peter Miller (eds), *The Foucault Effect: Studies in Governmentality* (London: Harvester Wheatsheaf, 1991).

21. The way of quoting that I have chosen is the following: for articles of the *ACP-EU Courier*, three numbers appear. The first is the number of the issue, the second is the year of publication, and the third is the page number. Thus, 41 1977 45 corresponds to: Issue 41 of the journal, published in 1977; and page 45. For the five larger documents (reports) that I used, the first number corresponds to the year and the second to the page, as in 1997 15. These latter documents are the following: *Mémorandum sur une politique communautaire de coopération au développement*. Communications de la Commission présentées au Conseil le 27 juillet 1971 et le 2 février 1972, Commission of the European Communities, 1972; *Europe and the Third World, A study on interdependence*, Commission of the European Communities, 1979; *Ten years of Lome. A Record of ACP-EEC Partnership 1976–85. Report on the implementation of financial and technical cooperation under the first two Lomé Conventions*, Commission of the European Communities, 1986; *The Europe-South dialogue*, Commission of the European Communities, 1988; *The Future of North-South Relations. Towards Sustainable Economic and Social development*, Commission of the European Communities, 1997. Finally, for texts emanating from think-tanks, NGOs etc., the normal quotation system is adopted.

22. Hannah Arendt, *The Human Condition* (Chicago: University of Chicago Press, 1998 [1958]), p. 237.

23. See Armin Rabitsch, 'Die EU – Förderer und Beispiel von regionaler Integration?', PhD dissertation, University of Innsbruck, in preparation. Also see this in the light of the US debt relative to the European trade surplus: Philip McMichael, *Development and Global Change, A Global Perspective* (Thousand Oaks: Pine Forge Press, 2000), p. 184.

24. This is shaped to a great extent by the French Union (1946) and by the Belgians who support it.

25. See Andrea Koulaimah-Gabriel, *The Geographic Scope of EC Aid: One or Several Development Policies?* (Maastricht: ECDPM 1997), p. 3/17.

26. Ibid.

27. Quoted in Marjorie Lister, *The European Community and the Developing World* (Brookfield USA: Avebury, 1988), p. 59.

28. Ibid., pp. 103–4.

29. The Commission comprised until recently 25 Directorates General (DG), each of which had competences for a specific area/theme. DG VIII was

responsible for the implementation of the Lomé Convention. DG REL. EX. stands for Direction Generale des Relations Exterieures.

30. The role of the European non-governmental organisations (NGOs) cannot be neglected, all the more so due to the close links they have with Brussels through institutional lobbying.

31. Lister, *The European Community and the Developing World*, p. 215.

32. J. G. de Matos Ferreira, *EC Development Policy* (Brussels: European Commission, March 1997), p. 4.

33. Joseph A. McMahon, *The Development Co-operation Policy of the EC* (The Hague: Kluwer, 1998), p. 40.

34. Lister, *The European Community and the Developing World*, p. 154.

35. Koulaimah-Gabriel, *The Geographic Scope*, p. 3/15.

36. Ferreira, *EC Development Policy*, p. 7.

37. McMichael, *Development and Global Change*, p. 49.

38. Koulaimah-Gabriel, *The Geographic Scope*, p. 3/15.

39. *Europeanisation* means the dynamics leading to an empowerment of the Community institutions, and particularly of the Commission, relative to the member states' role in this policy-making. The Treaty of Rome did not give 'exclusive competence' to the Community institutions for treating this policy, since the member states considered it to be part of foreign policy. As there was no such a thing as a Europeanised foreign policy, development policy was logically considered as part of each member state's own foreign policy. In the long run, however, development policy was an area increasingly dealt with by the European institutions: and as such it started to become 'Europeanised'. Indeed, today the Commission has increased autonomy since it has been given the right of initiative and responsibility for elaborating strategies and implementing EU development policy (A. Koning, *Strengths and Weaknesses in the Management of the European Development Fund*, Maastricht: ECDPM, Working Paper No. 8, 1995, p. 3) although 'most states have been opposed to relinquishing complete control of such a major instrument of their bilateral relations with the developing world' (K. Arts and J. Byron, 'The mid-term review of the Lomé IV Convention: heralding the future?' in *Thirld World Quarterly*, Vol. 18, 1997, p. 76). As far as legislative competence is concerned, the principle currently ruling development policy is that of subsidiarity: this entails that the EU is allowed to intervene in a legislative manner in this policy area only if the aims of this policy cannot be successfully realised by the states. The principle, introduced at the request of the UK during the negotiations of the Treaty of Maastricht, generates constant conflicts between the Commission and the member states.

40. The first and second pillars refer to two of the three big areas of the TEU construction: the first embraces the dispositions concerning the EC, the European Coal and Steel Community (ECSC) and the Euratom Treaty. Here, community integration procedures are applied, i.e. decisions are taken directly through the EU institutions. The European development policy is part of it. The second pillar comprises the burgeoning Common Foreign and Security Policy (CFSP) and, here, the methods of decision-making are intergovernmental. Yves Doutriaux and Christian Lequesne,

Les institutions de l'Union européenne (Paris: Documentation Française, 2000), p. 7.

41. But the not highly successful coordination of the member states on the CFSP, however, seemed to condemn the possibility of a coherent European development policy conducted as part of a European foreign policy. This possibility would have brought Europe closer to the American model.

42. See, among others, Dieter Frisch, *The Future of the Lomé Convention: Initial Reflections on Europe's Africa Policy after the Year 2000* (Maastricht: ECDPM, 1996).

43. *Cotonou Infokit. The Reform of the EC External Assistance* (22) (Maastricht: ECDPM, 2001).

44. Arts and Byron, 'The mid-term review', p. 86.

45. Jean-Jacques Gabas, 'L'Europe et les pays ACP: comment envisager une convention de Lome?' in GEMDEV, *La Convention de Lomé en questions: les relations entre les pays d'Afrique, des Caraïbes et du Pacifique (ACP) et l'Union européenne après l'an 2000* (Paris: Karthala, 1998), p. 24.

46. Jean Coussy, 'L'appui de l'Union européenne aux ajustements structurels' in GEMDEV, *La Convention de Lomé,* p. 318.

47. The concept is here not examined from a legal perspective, a third strand.

48. Pierre Bourdieu, *Esquisse d'une théorie de la pratique* (Paris: Seuil, 1972).

49. See Chapter 3 for a brief presentation of 'worlds' and 'compromises'. The move is somehow iconoclastical, given Boltanski and Thévenot's disagreement with critical sociology.

2 OUT OF AMERICA

1. The idea of suppression of ambiguity in the US emerged in a discussion with Peter Wagner.

2. Gustavo Esteva, 'Development' in Wolfgang Sachs (ed.), *The Development Dictionary* (London: Zed Books, 1992). Truman's Fourth Point reads: 'Fourth. We must embark on a bold new program for making the benefits of our scientific advances and industrial progress available for the improvement and growth of underdeveloped areas.'

3. Cowen and Shenton, *Doctrines of Development* (London: Routledge, 1996).

4. The use of 'America' instead of the 'United States' in this chapter emphasises its invention and the imaginary signification of what the country represents.

5. Louis Hartz, *The Liberal Tradition in America* (NY: Harcourt, Brace and World, 1991), p. 10. John Dewey would have perhaps agreed with the phrase, but not without underlining that 'American thought continues European thought ... For long years our philosophical thought was merely an echo of European thought.' Dewey, 'The development of American pragmatism' in H. S. Thayer, *Pragmatism: The Classic Writings* (Indianapolis: Hackett Publishing Company, 1982), p. 38.

6. Jean-Philippe Mathy, *Extrême Occident* (Chicago: The University of Chicago Press, 1993). Richard Rorty, *Achieving our Country. Leftist Thought in Twentieth Century America* (Cambridge: Harvard University Press, 1998). Richard Rorty, *Contingency, Irony, Solidarity* (Cambridge: Cambridge University Press, 1989). Richard Rorty, *Consequences of Pragmatism* (Brighton: The Harvester Press, 1982).

7. The link with empiricism is similar and is best explained by Dewey: 'Pragmatism, thus, presents itself as an extension of historical empiricism, but with this fundamental difference, that it does not insist upon antecedent phenomena but upon consequent phenomena; not upon the precedents but upon the possibilities of action.' Dewey, 'The development of American pragmatism', pp. 32–3.

8. H. S. Thayer, 'Introduction' in Thayer, *Pragmatism*, p. 12: 'It used to be said by its critics that pragmatism was a peculiarly American turn of thought, a glorification of action and the useful, an idealisation of American Big Business ...'; Mathy, *Extrême Occident*, pp. 241–50.

9. See Eric M. Gander, *The Last Conceptual Revolution. A Critique of Richard Rorty's Political Philosophy* (Albany: State University of New York, 1999), pp. 9–14.

10. Cited in Hartz, *The Liberal Tradition*, p. 50.

11. One should not forget not only the historical ambiguity of the American stance between their principled support of freedom and their support of European metropoles, but also that the US possessed and still possesses dependent territories, like Guam, American Samoa or the Virgin Islands, for instance, whose status is close to that of colonies.

12. René Schwok, *US-EC Relations in the Post-Cold War Era* (Boulder: Westview Press, 1991), p. 19.

13. Task Force on International Development, *US Foreign Assistance in the 70s: A New Approach. Report to the President from the Task Force* (Peterson Report) (Washington DC, 4 March 1970), p. 14.

14. On page 37 of the same document: 'On evidence of good performance and of demonstrated need by the developing countries, the industrial countries should be prepared to make available the necessary amount of development assistance.' One could see a contradiction here, but the ambiguity is not visible to the eyes of American developmentalists: if indeed economics is not ideological, it seems the most natural thing to equate efficiency of aid with a preceding burden of proof of good performance.

15. Ibid., p. 13.

16. Nicholas Eberstadt, *Foreign Aid and American Purpose* (Washington: American Enterprise Institute for Public Policy Research, 1988), p. 36.

17. The differences in the understanding of left and right between the US and Europe and across the US (broadly, on a North-South axis) are well–known.

18. David A. Baldwin, *Foreign Aid and American Foreign Policy* (NY: Praeger, 1966), p. 241.

19. Ibid.

20. Commission on Security and Economic Assistance (Carlucci Commission), *Report to the Secretary of State* (Washington DC, November 1983) p. 2.

21. Ibid., p. 8.
22. Constant preoccupation with efficiency, and the same suppression of the ambiguity that the concept holds in its oscillation between principle and application, can be found in documents of, or on, USAID, the United States Agency for International Development, but also in documents and research on non-governmental organisations, such as CARE. See D. R. Mickelwait, C. F. Sweet and E. P. Morss, *New Directions in Development: A Study of USAID* (Boulder, Colorado: Westview, 1979), p. 213; Eugene Linden, *The Alms Race* (NY: Random House, 1976); Eberstadt, *Foreign Aid and American Purpose*, p. 143.
23. Irene L. Gendzier, *Managing Political Change: Social Scientists and the Third World*, (Boulder: Westview Press, 1985).
24. John Palmer, *Europe without America? The Crisis in Atlantic Relations* (Oxford: Oxford University Press), 1987, p. 37.
25. Baldwin, *Foreign Aid*, p. 63.
26. Eberstadt, *Foreign Aid and American Purpose*, p. 33.
27. Peterson Report, 1970.
28. Commission on Security and Economic Assistance, *Report*, p. 42.
29. David Campbell, *Writing Security, United States Foreign Policy and the Politics of Identity* (Minneapolis: University of Minnesota Press, 1992), p. 154.
30. Nathan Glazer, 'American epic: then and now', *The Public Interest*, No. 130, 1998, p. 7.
31. B. Honig, 'Declarations of independence: Arendt and Derrida on the problem of founding a republic', *American Political Science Review*, LXXXV, 1991, pp. 97–113.
32. John van Oudenaren, 'Europe as Partner' in David C. Gombert and F. Stephen Larrabee (eds), *America and Europe, A Partnership for a New Era* (Cambridge: Cambridge University Press), 1997, p. 114. It is interesting to read John Dewey's attempt to distanciate American pragmatism from a crude overarching emphasis on action. See, respectively, the first chapter of Rorty's *Achieving our Country*, and Dewey, 'The development of American pragmatism', pp. 25 and 38.
33. Baldwin, *Foreign Aid*, p. 61.
34. Peterson Report, p. 7.
35. Eberstadt, *Foreign Aid and American Purpose*, p. 39.
36. Ibid.
37. Schwok, *US-EC Relations*, p. 31.
38. Commission on Security and Economic Assistance, *Report*, pp. 8 and 25.
39. Van Oudenaren, 'Europe as partner'; David C. Gombert, 'America as partner', pp. 110 and 157.
40. Palmer, *Europe without America?*, p. 47.
41. Ibid., p. 5.
42. Michael Walzer, 'What does it mean to be an "American"?', *Social Research*, Vol. 57, No. 3, 1990.
43. Hartz, *The Liberal Tradition*, pp. 59–63. This is the well-known view of Hannah Arendt ('The social question' in Arendt, *On Revolution* [NY: The Viking Press, 1963]) who, comparing the French and American revolution, starts out by claiming that 'the prejudice of the nineteenth

century that all revolutions are social in origin was still quite absent from eighteenth-century theory or experience' (p. 61), to render clear that 'The problem [the laborious poor in America] posed was not social but political, it concerned not the order of society but the form of government' (p. 63). On these grounds, Arendt sees in the American Revolution an overarchingly political revolution and in the French one, a revolution that turned social, by necessity: 'The direction of the American Revolution remained committed to the foundation of freedom and the establishment of lasting institutions, and to those who acted in this direction nothing was permitted that would have been outside the range of civil law. The direction of the French Revolution was deflected almost from its beginning from this course of foundation through the immediacy of suffering; it was determined by the exigencies of liberation not from tyranny but from necessity, and it was actuated by the limitless immensity of both the people's misery and the pity this misery inspired' (p. 78). The argument of this chapter is an indirect critique of the Arendtian view, first because it claims that the American Revolution mainly 'leapt over' the social question that it could have faced; it ignored or neglected it, postponing thus a serious generalised thinking about it to almost two centuries later. And second, because the general point of this chapter is that one cannot usefully distinguish between 'tyranny' and 'necessity', at least not in any other way than the analytical; and that, therefore, 'the social' and 'the political' must be viewed as intimately linked.

44. Michael Zuckerman cited in Campbell, *Writing Security*, p. 136.
45. Ibid., p. 139.
46. Cited in Gendzier, *Managing Political Change*, p. 27.
47. Max F. Millikan and W. W. Rostow, *A Proposal, Key to an Effective Foreign Policy* (NY: Harper and Brothers, 1957), p. 40.
48. Commission on Security and Economic Assistance, *Report*, p. 40.
49. As in the following: 'Neither can [the United States] assume that development will necessarily bring political stability. Development implies change – political and social, as well as economic – and such change, for a time, may be disruptive. What the United States should expect from participation in international development is steady progress towards its long-term goals: the building of self-reliant and healthy societies ... .' *US Foreign Assistance in the 1970s*, p. 2. Stability is thus synonymous with health, but in an admittedly long-term perspective.
50. Gendzier, *Managing Political Change*, chapter 6.
51. The quote is from Millikan and Rostow, *A Proposal*, p. 151.
52. Ibid., pp. 145 and 181.
53. Eberstadt, *Foreign Aid and American Purpose*, p. 13.
54. Campbell, *Writing Security*, p. 105. The expression 'imagined community' in Benedict Anderson, *Imagined Communities. Reflections on the Origin and Spread of Nationalism* (London: Verso, 1991).
55. Diana Schaub, 'Patriotic political science', *The Public Interest*, No. 131, Spring 1998, p. 112.
56. Hartz, *The Liberal Tradition*, p. 55.
57. Walzer, 'What does it mean to be an "American"?', p. 594.
58. Hartz, *The Liberal Tradition*, p. 286.

59. Campbell, *Writing Security*, p. 250.
60. Baldwin, *Foreign Aid*, pp. 64 and 65.
61. 'Among intellectuals in many Asia countries, the term "socialism" has become synonymous with values to which we are also dedicated: equality of opportunities, the public welfare as the test of economic performance, equitable distribution of income ... .' Millikan and Rostow, *A Proposal*, p. 15.
62. Ibid., p. 240.
63. Commission on Security and Economic Assistance, *Report*, p. 3.
64. But it is ultimately easy to understand through the arrogance of statements, such as: 'As our emergence into national maturity lifts our horizons beyond our shores, and as we come to agree as a people how to manage democratically our mature capitalist economy, we need the challenge of world development to keep us from the stagnation of smug prosperity.' Millikan and Rostow, *A Proposal*, p. 8.
65. Baldwin, *Foreign Aid*, p. 65.
66. Ibid., p. 254.
67. Commission on Security and Economic Assistance, *Report*, p. 34.
68. Walzer is wrong in saying that Americans don't refer to America as 'home'. In my experience they are those, among expatriates, who do so more often than anyone else.
69. Hartz, *The Liberal Tradition*, p. 309.
70. Ibid., p. 58.
71. Rabitsch, 'Die EU – Förderer und Beispiel von regionaler Integration', PhD dissertation, University of Innsbruck, in preparation 2004.

3 THE FAILED MYTH OF DEVELOPMENT

1. Bertolt Brecht, *The Good Person of Szechwan* (trans. John Willett) (London: Methuen, 1987 [1962]).
2. Gilbert Rist, '"Development" as part of the modern myth: The western "socio-cultural dimension" of "development"', *EJDR*, Vol. 2, 1 June 1990.
3. Ibid., p. 18. Charles Taylor makes the same observation: '... even societies which seem to be founded on the utilitarian tradition, or an earlier Lockeian variant, like the United States, in fact have recourse to "myth", for example the myth of the frontier, of the perpetual new beginning, the future as boundlessly open to self-creation. This last is the greatest irony of all, in that the utilitarian theory itself leaves no place for myth of this kind, for speculative interpretation of the ends of human life in their relation to society, nature and history as part of the justifying beliefs of a mature society. These are thought to belong to earlier, less evolved ages. Mature men (sic) are attached to their society because of what it produces for them. As recently as a decade ago this perspective was widely believed in by the liberal intelligentsia of America and the Western world, who announced an imminent "end of ideology". But they turned out to be latter-day, inverted variants of Monsieur Jourdain, who were speaking not prose but myth without knowing it.' Charles Taylor,

Hegel and Modern Society (Cambridge: Cambridge University Press, 1979), pp. 112–13.

4. As Castoriadis does: 'Myth is essentially a way for society to vest with meaning both the world and its own life within the world – a world and a life that, otherwise, are obviously meaningless.' Cornelius Castoriadis, 'The imaginary: creation in the social historical domain' in *A World in Fragments* (trans. David Ames Curtis) (Stanford: Stanford University Press, 1997). This point is also one that can be made regarding the 'cultural' or the 'social' whose creativity always supersedes any attempt at these worlds' interpretation: 'Culture always requires interpretation (which, in a sense, is a political act); but it is also in excess of any given interpretation – with the result that interpretations (and political "uses") remain contestable.' In Fred Dallmayr, 'Global development? alternative voices from Delhi', *Alternatives* 21 (1996), p. 278.

5. Cornelius Castoriadis , 'La "rationalité" du capitalisme', in Cornelius Castoriadis, *Figures du pensable, Les carrefours du labyrinthe* VI (Paris: Seuil, 1997), p. 66. 'Capitalism is the first social regime that produces an ideology according to which capitalism is "rational". The legitimation of other types of institution of society were mythical, religious or traditional.'

6. R. B. J. Walker, *Inside/Outside: International Relations as Political Theory* (Cambridge: Cambridge University Press, 1993).

7. Ibid., p. 55.

8. Ibid., p. 5.

9. Cornelius Castoriadis, 'Le cache-misère de l'éthique' in *La montée de l'insignifiance, Les carrefours du labyrinthe IV* (Paris: Seuil, 1996).

10. An important symbolical date is the 1884–85 Berlin Conference that formalised the second European descent on Africa into a neat territorial division – still visible on the map. On the impression that Africa was a vast blank territory both then for Europeans (for an example, see Conrad's *Heart of Darkness*) and later, for Africans at the moment of decolonisation, see Said, *Culture and Imperialism*. 'Berlin' produced less homogeneous a result than was often presented – there were very distinct British, say, or French or German commercial strategies; and the agreements signed there were altered after some years. For the commercial aspect, see Hélène d'Almeida-Topor and Monique Lakroum, *L'Europe et l'Afrique. Un siècle d'échanges économiques* (Paris: Armand Colin, 1994).

11. See Chapter 2 on that period. The latest Anglo-American 'war on terrorism' can be read as a dramatic effort to re-shape the international world in terms of allies and adversaries, à la Huntington.

12. This is the period from which Gasper starts and identifies three conceptual 'stages' of development ethics: the first focuses on the concepts of development discourse; the second, 'tries to refine and relate different principles and build systematic theoretical alternatives'; and the third stage – partly existent – looks at 'the real worlds of practice and compromise'. Des Gasper, 'Culture and development ethics: needs, women's rights, and Western theories', *Development and Change*, Vol. 27, 1996, p. 629.

13. On the relation between crisis and criticism and its importance for the social sciences, see Reinhart Koselleck, *Critique and Crisis* (Oxford: Berg, 1988), in particular the introduction pp. 5–12; and for an application

to the critique of capitalism, Peter Wagner, 'Modernity, capitalism and critique', *Thesis Eleven*, No. 66, August 2001, pp. 1–31. In an earlier text, Wagner discerns two crises of modernity – one at the end of the nineteenth century and the other starting from roughly the end of the 'Trente Glorieuses' (end 1960s). See Peter Wagner, *A Sociology of Modernity. Liberty and Discipline* (London: Routledge, 1994), Chapters 4 and 8. Boltanski and Chiapello see two such moments: end of the nineteenth century (that they explicitly relate to Wagner's observation on 'modernity's first crisis', p. 242), and post-1968 that is leading, according to them, to a connexionist type of capitalism (p. 28). Luc Boltanski and Eve Chiapello, *Le nouvel esprit du capitalisme* (Paris: Gallimard, 1999).

14. G. B. Mathur underlines this in a quite vivid manner: See G.B. Mathur, 'The current impasse in development thinking: the metaphysic of power' in *Alternatives*, 1989, Vol. XVI, No. 4, Oct. 1989, p. 469. See also Peter Dale Scott, 'Peace, power, and revolution: peace studies, Marxism and the academy', *Alternatives*, IX, Winter 1983–84, pp. 351–72: in particular the stress on production and productivity common to capitalism and Marxism that has been criticised by very different theorists, e.g. Benjamin, Horkheimer, Castoriadis and Baudrillard. Also, concerning the assumptions of the economics of Marxism and neo-classical economics, see the 'monoeconomics claim' of Hirschman, in 'The rise and decline of development economics' in Albert O. Hirschman, *Essays in Tresspassing, Economics to Politics and Beyond*, (Cambridge: Cambridge University Press, 1981). See also Ronaldo Munck, 'Deconstructing development discourses: of impasses, alternatives and politics', in Ronaldo Munck and Denis O'Hearn, *Critical Development Theory: Contributions to a New Paradigm* (London: Zed, 1999).

15. The expression is Cameron's in John Cameron, 'Kant's categorical imperative as a foundation for development studies and action' , *EJDR*, Vol. 11, No. 2, December 1999, pp. 23–43.

16. Colin Leys, however, sees a renaissance of dependency theory in the 1990s. See Colin Leys, *The Rise and Fall of Development Theory* (Bloomington: Indiana University Press, 1996), Chapter 2.

17. Albert O. Hirschman, 'The rise and decline of development economics'.

18. Ibid., p. 24.

19. Des Gasper, 'Violence and suffering, responsibility and choice: issues in ethics and development', *EJDR*, Vol. 11, No. 2, December 1999, pp. 1–22. But less economically developed countries were often portrayed as overwhelmed by their emotions. The ambiguity of the concept of interest, its historically shifting understanding, must be kept in mind throughout the following chapters.

20. As Leys points out, the most virulent critiques of neo-Marxists were Marxists *tout court*; and the current debate within institutionalism speaks of a more complicated picture than the one painted above. Leys, *The Rise and Fall of Development Theory*.

21. See David Booth, 'Marxism and development sociology: interpreting the impasse', *World Development*, Vol. 13, No. 7, July 1985. For a somewhat more mellow view, see the first chapter of David Booth (ed.), *Rethinking*

Social Development, Theory, Research and Practice (Essex: Longman, 1994).

Munck pinpoints how this 'impasse' was nothing else than the discrediting of neo-Marxism and the retreat towards the old modernisation paradigm, due to the confusion of 'radicalism' and 'Marxism' (hence dependency was understood as being firmly placed in a Marxist lineage) and to the belief that Marxism was absolutely opposable to the modernisation paradigm. Munck, 'Deconstructing development discourses', p. 197. For similar views on the 'impasse' see Leys, *The Rise and Fall of Development Theory* and Moore, 'Development discourse as hegemony'.

22. Björn Hettne saw this result as the combination of 'two rather questionable retreats: back to the disciplines and back to the conventional development paradigm'; quoted in Munck, 'Deconstructing development discourses', p. 197. However, younger academic branches that correspond to 'issue politics', such as gender studies and ecology considerably enriched debates about development. If examined through the prism of the relation between recognition and redistribution, it becomes clear that such areas make the strongest and most interesting claims for a left agenda in academia. For an explanation of such continuous aversion, from a gender studies viewpoint, see Shereen Essof, 'Preliminary thoughts on gender, politics and power in African contexts' (draft paper, Cape Town: Cape Town University, 2003).

23. Leys identifies five main theoretical responses to the problem of development theory facing a changed world, 'apart from neo-liberalism': the theoretical impasse, to be overcome by better concepts, eclecticism as usual, further evolutions of dependency theory, neo-institutionalism, and renunciation of commitment to development. But it could be observed that 'eclecticism as usual' constitutes a mainstream thinking, and this mainstream has been the revival of neo-institutionalism (and within it, rational choice theory dominated). Secondly, this neo-institutionalism, purportedly often coming from the left (following Myrdal), is neo-liberal in its presuppositions (in this sense neo-classical economics – where rational choice finds its root – must be understood as going hand in hand with neo-liberalism. On this, see John Brohman, 'Economism and critical silences in development studies: a theoretical critique of neoliberalism', *Third World Quarterly*, Vol. 16, No. 2, 1995). Finally, the 'de-linking' advocated by some currents of 'dependency theorists' is quite close to the rejection of development, it is the rejection of a certain development: it is not a coincidence that 'post-development' advocates came from Latin America (see, for example, Arturo Escobar, 'Beyond the search for a paradigm? Post-development and beyond', *Development* [online pub.], London: Sage, 2000) as did 'dependentistas'.

24. Bob Sutcliffe, 'The place of development in theories of imperialism and globalisation' in Munck and O'Hearn, *Critical Development Theory*, p. 136.

25. For central uses of these metaphors, see James Ferguson, *The Anti-politics Machine: 'Development', Depoliticisation, and Bureaucratic Power in Lesotho* (Cambridge: Cambridge University Press, 1990).

26. See, for the passage from market to Fordist to network/connectionist capitalism, Boltanski and Chiapello, *Le nouvel esprit du capitalisme*.

27. Castoriadis, 'La "rationalité" du capitalisme'.

28. Sutcliffe, 'The place of development'. See also Jan Nederveen Pieterse, 'After post-development', *Third World Quarterly*, Vol. 21, 2000, pp. 175–191. In Pieterse's terms, desirability corresponds to 'alternatives to development', while polarisation and attainability point to 'alternative developments'.

29. Sutcliffe, 'The place of development', p. 150.

30. What he calls 'a politics of conduct rather than of class' or 'dependency politics'. See Lawrence M. Mead, 'The new politics of the new poverty' in Christopher Pierson and Francis G. Castles (eds), *The Welfare State Reader* (Cambridge: Polity Press, 2000), p. 112. See Nancy Fraser, 'From redistribution to recognition? Dilemmas of justice in a "postsocialist" age' in Fraser, *Justice Interruptus* (New York: Routledge, 1997).

31. See Giovanna Procacci, 'Social economy and the government of poverty' in Burchell, Gordon and Miller (eds), *The Foucault Effect* (London: Harvester Wheatsheaf, 1991). The tricky part of these arguments is that they are as easily made on one side as on the other. Nancy Fraser shows how 'dependency' in the welfare state debate has been attacked on very similar grounds from both 'progressive' and 'conservative' authors, in Nancy Fraser and Linda Gordon, 'A genealogy of "dependency"' in Fraser, *Justice Interruptus*. For a general view on this, see the last section of Chapter 4.

32. Stauffer, 'After socialism: capitalism, development and the search for critical alternatives', in *Alternatives*, Vol XV, 1999. See also Moore, 'Development discourse as hegemony', p. 6.

33. Björn Hettne, 'European integration and world development', *EJDR*, Vol. 2, No. 2, Dec. 1990, p. 196.

34. See Anna Dickson, 'Development and international relations', *International Political Economy*, Vol. 5, No. 2, Summer 1998, pp. 362–77.

35. One can also follow McMichael's suggestion that 'development' is actually being replaced by 'globalisation'. 'The globalisation project succeeds the development project ... Whereas development was a public undertaking in the development project, it is viewed as a private undertaking in the globalisation project'; and, slightly less provocatively, 'In the past we understood development to be a process of economic growth organised nationally, but today, global economic integration is transforming development into a process of *globally organised economic growth*.' McMichael, *Development and Global Change* (Thousand Oaks: Pine Forge Press, 2000), p. 149 and p. xxxiii, respectively.

36. Hettne, 'European integration', p. 195. Preston puts it more forcefully in P. W. Preston, 'Development theory: learning the lessons and moving on', *EJDR*, Vol. 11, No. 1, June 1999, p. 16.

37. Robert H. Jackson, 'The weight of ideas in decolonisation: normative change in international relations' in Judith Goldstein and Robert O. Keohane, *Ideas and Foreign Policy* (Ithaca: Cornell University Press, 1993), pp. 115 and 119.

38. Attentively looking at 'actors' – the attention they pay at the critiques that actors mobilise and resist – is Boltanski and Thévenot's answer to a sociology that assumes a 'critical', external stance to the studied subjects. See Luc Boltanski and Laurent Thévenot, *De la justification* (Paris: Gallimard, 1991); Thomas Bénatouïl, 'A tale of two sociologies. The critical and the pragmatic stance in contemporary French sociology', *European Journal of Social Theory (EJST)*, Vol. 2, No. 3, 1999, pp. 379–96.

39. Ibid. and Luc Boltanski, *L'Amour et la justice comme compétences. Trois essais de sociologie de l'action* (Paris: Métailié, 1990), pp. 65–66.

40. However it is possible to disagree with a conceptualisation of violence as absolutely external to this framework, not only because violence can be other than physical and can thus be theorised (as in the form of tyranny) but also because such separation between justice and violence rests on a democratic-pluralistic understanding of justice (which is only one possible understanding).

41. Luc Boltanski and Laurent Thévenot, 'A sociology of critical capacity', *EJST*, Vol. 2, No. 3, p. 361.

42. The 'beings' of the orders of worth are retrieved from yet another 'source material'. More than bringing together classic philosophical texts and mundane texts, this move of Boltanski and Thévenot's must again be seen in the light of an insistence on specific 'situations'.

43. Boltanski and Thévenot, 'A sociology of critical capacity', p. 370.

44. Boltanski and Thévenot, *De la justification*, p. 256.

45. It can be argued that responsibility belongs, in a third instance, to the '*civic* order of worth'. If on the one hand, a meaning of responsibility that diverges from the current common understanding is envisaged, and if, on the other hand, we divest solidarity from its older common meaning, a new relationship between the two concepts is formed. The 'civic' order of worth can espouse this understanding of responsibility: it insists on the collective character of people's interactions, as well as on their statutory condition. The form of 'giving' that corresponds to it is not included in the Bourdieusian triptych, we can call it 'mutual debt' (civic exchange) so as to clarify the (long) time span it involves as well as its mutual character (that it shares with all forms of 'giving' but in a particularly pronounced form). Although 'mutuality' does not strictly correspond to 'equality', we will call this responsibility 'collective-egalitarian' (to be distinguished from individualistic-egalitarian responsibility).

46. Boltanski and Thévenot, 'A sociology of critical capacity', p. 374.

47. Boltanski and Thévenot did not conceptualise encounters of more than two 'orders of worth'.

48. Castoriadis, 'La "rationalité" du capitalisme', p. 75.

49. Ferguson, *The Anti-politics Machine*, p. xiv.

50. Boltanski and Chiapello, *Le nouvel esprit du capitalisme*.

51. Marc DuBois, 'The governance of the Third World: A Foucauldian perspective on power relations development', *Alternatives* 16, 1991, p. 1. See, for the same observation, Michael Cowen and Robert Shenton, 'The invention of development' in Crush (ed.), *The Power of Development* (London: Routledge, 1995).

52. Ferguson, *The Anti-politics Machine*, p. 15.

53. Gasper, 'Essentialism in and about development', p. 149. If this tension overlaps with the previous one, it is because ultimately, the actual usages of the term are always rooted in all of the conceptions at the same time.

54. Escobar, 'Discourse and power in development', p. 387.

55. Doug J. Porter, 'Scenes from childhood; the homesickness of development discourse', in Crush (ed.), *Power of Development*, p. 63.

56. W. B. Gallie, 'Essentially contested concepts' in Max Black (ed.), *The Importance of Language* (NJ: Prentice-Hall, 1962).

57. Albert O. Hirschman, *The Passions and the Interests. Political Arguments for Capitalism before Its Triumph* (Princeton: Princeton University Press, 1977), p. 86.

58. Escobar, 'Discourse and power in development', p. 387.

59. Escobar, 'Imagining a post-development era' in Crush, *The Power of Development*, p. 212.

60. See Moore 'Development discourse as hegemony'.

61. As Walzer defines tyranny, that is, as the illegitimate crossing of boundaries in distributive justice. See Chapter 13 of Michael Walzer, *Spheres of Justice* (Oxford: Martin Robertson, 1983).

62. And both are historically emancipatory movements.

63. An extract from Steve Biko's trial ascertains this:

'Judge Boshoff: Democracy, doesn't it pre-suppose a developed community, democracy where you have one man, one vote?

Biko: Yes, it does, and it is part of the process of developing the community. You cannot – My Lord, people in voting, when allowing them to vote, I think you have got to give them the vote, I think you may device (?) as the government in a way the means of ensuring a proper existence of that vote, but certainly you give them the vote.

JB: Yes, but democracy is really only a success if the people who have the right to vote can intelligently and honestly apply a vote?

Biko, Yes, My Lord, this is why Swaziland for instance where they have some people sometimes who may not read the names of the candidates, they use signs.

JB: Yes, but they do not know enough of the affairs of government to be able to influence it by a vote? I mean surely you must know what you are voting for, what you are voting about? Assuming now they vote on a particular policy, such as foreign investment, what does a peasant know about foreign investment?

Biko: I think My Lord, in a government where democracy is allowed to work, one of the principles that are normally entrenched is a feedback system, a discussion in other words between those who formulate policy and those who must perceive, accept or reject policy. In other words there must be a system of education, political education, and this does not necessarily go with literacy. I mean Africa has always governed its peoples in the form of various chiefs, Chaka and so on, who couldn't write.

JB: Yes, but the government is much more sophisticated and specialised now than in those days?

Biko: And there are ways of explaining it to the people. People can hear, they may not be able to read and write but they can hear and they can understand the issues that are put to them [...]'. Steve Biko, *I Write What I Like* (Oxford: Heinemann, 1979), p. 127. This is an intact extract of the court proceedings, including the parenthesis in the text.

4 THE VOCATION OF RESPONSIBILITY

1. 'Responsibility demands courage because it places us at the extreme point of the acting decision, because it entails a vocation', my translation. Vladimir Jankélévitch, 'La responsabilité en son for intérieur', *Revue Internationale de Philosophie*, No. 39, Tome 11, 1957, pp. 69–74. A modified version of this chapter appears, under the title 'Preceding "global responsibility": autonomy, knowledge, power', in Mike Davis et al. (eds), *International Intervention in the Post-Cold War World* (NY: M. E. Sharpe, 2003).

2. Richard McKeon, 'The development and the significance of the concept of responsibility', *Revue Internationale de Philosophie*, Vol. 39, Tome 11, 1957, p. 10. However, ευθύναϛ (the account of one's actions), which becomes the governors' account of their deeds in the hellenistic years (ευθύνη), exists in Ancient Greece.

3. Or, as it will be put in this chapter, responsibility *entails* such relationships and can be understood as something different from what characterises the autonomous individual.

4. One more classical view holds that ethical/moral responsibility is only about the question 'For what is A responsible?' and political responsibility is also about the question 'To whom is A responsible?' Another classical view – a different formulation of the same idea – holds that ethical responsibility concerns the individual level while political responsibility concerns the collective level. Different objections are possible, starting with the collective character of ethical life and continuing with the refusal to adopt the free will versus determinism divide which both of these views recreate. Once it is admitted that Kantian autonomy is all but an impossibility (or a tautology, according to Hegel's criticism of the categorical imperative) and once God or an overarching idea of Nature is ruled out as a source to which we might respond, ethical and political responsibilities cannot be separated. However, later, we will see the practical limits of the extension of ethical reasoning to the collective level.

5. See Denys de Béchillon, 'L'imaginaire banal de la responsabilité', *Critique*, Nov. 2000, Tome LVI, No. 642.

6. This is one reading of Antigone's revolt. Romantically (and we have largely inherited this interpretation), she has been seen as the emblem of the revolt of the individual against the oppression of the state.

7. Smiley's interpretation in Marion Smiley, *Moral Responsibility and the Boundaries of Community. Power and Accountability from a Pragmatic Point of View* (Chicago: University of Chicago Press, 1992).

8. Ibid., p. 55.

9. 'A strengthening of the multilateral dimension is also necessary to ensure adequate sharing of the financial, commercial and political burdens which the North needs to shoulder *vis-à-vis* the South.' 1997, 31.

10. Hannah Arendt, *The Human Condition* (Chicago: University of Chicago Press, 1998 [1958]), p. 16. This is interesting both because it gives charity the status of a necessary nuisance and because it separates it from the realm of (higher) knowledge. But, on the one hand, insofar as responsibility relates genealogically to charity, it cannot be perfectly separated from knowledge, as we will see. On the other hand, under this light, Christian charity may be seen as one version of an *attenuation* of the perhaps overburdening Derridean understanding of responsibility that we will examine. But see Jankélévitch's view: 'nul ne peut prétendre que son essence morale lui soit littéralement un fardeau: car mon essence morale, comme mon être tout court, considéré simplement ... me pèse encore bien moins que l'air atmosphérique ... Notre être moral n'est ni un "avoir" ni un dépot qui nous serait commis, er cependant nous en prenons conscience comme d'une charge! Le sens commun tente maladroitement, par des analogies métaphoriques ou même mythologiques, de s'expliquer ce paradoxe d'un "onus ethicum" ... ', Jankélévitch, 'La responsabilité en son for intérieur'.

11. Arendt, *The Human Condition*, p. 53. In anticipation of Chapter 5 on efficiency, see the following extract from the European development discourse and how it denigrates charity: 'These economic realities are not the only *reasons* for the Community's cooperation policy, but they do demonstrate why cooperation is necessary *to all those in Europe who might be tempted to regard it as nothing more than charity or even a waste of money.*'

12. For an ironic reversal of ethnological observation, see this extract of African literature: 'I went along with the Commandant to the Headmaster of the Dangan School, where he had been invited for cocktails. I carried the parcel he was going to give to Mme Salvain. This is a native custom that Europeans have as well, taking something for their hosts.' Ferdinand Oyono, *Houseboy* (Johannesbourg: Heinemann, 1990 [1960]), p. 30.

13. McKeon, 'The development and significance', p. 13.

14. We must remember that responsibility as such only becomes an issue of philosophical debate a century later than Kant. However if the third 'modern' understanding is broadly understood to emerge already from the seventeenth century on, it is important to make a clear distinction between those who, like Hobbes, Locke and Hume, believe that 'human actions are determined by causality or necessity similar to that which determines physical change, [that] no special moral cause or imputation is needed' and those, like Pufendorf or Kant, who believe that 'the causality of human actions is free (as distinguished from physical necessity), since action depends on will and intellect ... and [that] the external accountability imposed by power or judged by pragmatic utility must be judged by an internal law recognised by conscience or reason'. McKeon, 'The development and significance', pp. 14–15.

15. It might also be useful to note that in *Metaphysics of Morals*, Kant explicitly objects to the domestic (paternalistic) understanding of the

state; this could possibly apply to colonialism: 'A government that was also legislative would have to be called a despotic as opposed to a patriotic government, but by a patriotic government is understood *not a paternalistic one (regimen paternale), which is the most despotic of all (since it treats citizens as children)*, but one serving the native land ...' but he adds: 'In it the state does treat its subjects as members of one family but it also treats them as citizens of the state.' In Immanuel Kant, *The Metaphysics of Morals* (Cambridge: Cambridge University Press, 1996 [1797]), p. 94. I have not used the italics of the text and the italics here are mine. See Chapter 6 for more on the 'domestic world'.

16. Smiley, *Moral Responsiblility*, pp. 50–1.

17. In a passage that is significant of a whole era and that is situated in the famous essay devoted to 'Liberty', John Stuart Mill says: '(...) *It is, perhaps, hardly necessary to say that this doctrine is meant to apply only to human beings in the maturity of their faculties. We are not speaking of children*, or of young persons below the age which the law may fix as that of manhood or womanhood. Those who are still in a state to require being taken care of by others, must be protected against their own actions as well as against external injury. *For the same reason, we may leave out of consideration those backward states of society in which the race itself may be considered at its nonage.* The early difficulties in the way of spontaneous progress are so great, that there is seldom any choice of means for overcoming them; and a ruler full of the spirit of improvement is warranted in the use of any expedients that will attain an end, perhaps otherwise unattainable. *Despotism is a legitimate mode of government in dealing with barbarians, provided the end be their improvement, and the means justified by actually affecting that end.* Liberty, as a principle, has no application to any state of things anterior to the time when mankind have become capable of being improved by free and equal discussion' (my italics). There is not much need for comments here, perhaps we can just underline the issue of the name: Barbarians are those who cannot speak or better whose language cannot be heard – they don't have names – they don't even have a name showing where they come from. On Barbarians and Hellenes as a couple of asymmetrical counter-concepts, see Reinhart Koselleck, 'The historical-political semantics of asymmetric counterconcepts' in Koselleck, *Futures Past. On the Semantics of Historical Time* (Cambridge: Cambridge University Press, 1985). But to avoid being unfair to Mill, we must dissociate him from Christianity which he disliked and note his defence of Black Jamaicans in a massacre of his time ('la forme affaire' of Boltanski) that Said notes in Edward Said, *Culture and Imperialism* (NY: Vintage, 1993), p. 130.

18. Dependency – as opposed to autonomy – has generally carried a negative understanding; and it has been attacked both from the right and from the left. I have given the examples from the work of Giovanna Procacci, 'Social economy and the develoment of poverty' in Burchell, Gordon and Miller (eds), *The Foucault Effect: Studies in Governmental Rationality*, (London: Harvester Wheatsheaf, 1991) and Lawrence M. Mead who make, concerning different periods, a similar argument concerning

welfare measures. For an overview, see Fraser and Gordon, 'A genealogy of "dependency"' in Fraser, *Justice interruptus* (New York: Routledge, 1997).

19. The discussion on blameworthiness is inspired by Smiley, *Moral Responsibility*, pp. 4–14, 72–92.

20. See Smiley, *Moral Responsibility*, p. 91.

21. That is, for instance, Cornelius Castoriadis's view: 'But we cannot enough reiterate that the question will remain intractable so long as autonomy is understood in the Kantian sense, that is, as a fictively autarchic subject's conformity to a "Law of Reason", in complete misrecognition of the social-historical conditions for, and the social-historical dimension of, the project of autonomy.' Cornelius Castoriadis, 'Individual, society, rationality, history' in Cornelius Castoriadis, *Philosophy, Politics, Autonomy* (Oxford: Oxford University Press, 1991), p. 75.

22. See Wagner, *Theorizing Modernity* (London: Sage, 2001), Chapters 1 and 2.

23. 'Saying that a responsible decision must be taken on the basis of knowledge seems to define the condition of possibility of responsibility (one cannot make a responsible decision without science or conscience, without knowing what one is doing, for what reasons, in view of what and under what conditions), at the same time as it defines the condition of impossibility of this same responsibility (if decision-making is relegated to a knowledge that it is content to follow or to develop, then it is no more a responsible decision, it is the technical deployment of a cognitive apparatus, the simple mechanistic deployment of a theorem).' Jacques Derrida, 'Secrets of European responsibility', in Jacques Derrida, *Given Time: I. The Counterfeit Money* (trans. Peggy Kamuf) (Chicago: University of Chicago Press, 1992), p. 24. See also Jacques Derrida, 'Force of law: The '"mystical foundation of authority"', in Drucilla Cornell, Michel Rosenfeld and David Gray Carlson (eds), *Deconstruction and the Possibility of Justice* (New York: Routledge, 1992), pp. 3–67.

24. Even Zygmunt Bauman illustrates his discussion of responsibility and development with an example in which a child asks his mother what to do. See Zygmunt Bauman, 'On universal morality and the morality of universalism', *European Journal for Development Research*, Vol. 10, No. 2, Dec. 1998, pp. 7–18. By contrast to the relation between responsibility and autonomy, that between autonomy and knowledge is as old as the Old Testament and not characteristic of a secular context. In addition, how are we to take in account that '*ignorantia legis no excusant*', a principle that takes the form of adage or even law in many contexts? The necessity of this principle in the face of the possibility of dubious excuses is clear. It implies that whether one ignores or not something that one is supposed to know is irrelevant: the law is applicable, and responsibility at stake. But this is not equivalent to saying that ignorance/uncertainty is always part of the decision and that it is also on the basis of this ignorance/uncertainty that the decision is taken. And that, therefore, responsibility ensues.

25. See Derrida, 'Force of law'; David Campbell, 'The deterritorialization of responsibility, Levinas, Derrida, and ethics after the end of philosophy' in *Alternatives*, Vol. 19 (1994), pp. 455–84.

26. Primo Levi, *Moments of Reprieve* (London: Abacus, 1987), pp. 149–60. A normative horizon of emancipatory knowledge can be maintained, as was done with autonomy. See Boaventura de Sousa Santos, 'On oppositional postmodernism', in Munck and O'Hearn (eds), *Critical Development Theory* (London: Zed, 1999), pp. 36.

27. Jacques Derrida, *Politics of Friendship* (trans. George Collins) (London: Verso, 1997), p. 250.

28. Ibid.

29. Daniel Warner, 'An ethic of responsibility in international relations and the limits of responsibility/community', *Alternatives*, Vol. 18 (1993), pp. 431–52.

30. R. B. J. Walker, *Inside/Outside: International Relations as Political Theory* (Cambridge: Cambridge University Press, 1993), p. 58.

31. Gerrit W. Gong, *The Standard of 'Civilization' in International Society* (Oxford: Oxford University Press, 1984).

32. Heteronomy is at play in this alterity, not because it is in any way the absolute law 'of the other' (with all the tyrannical potential that it carries) that is at play. On the contrary, it is perhaps even a prerequisite that this possibility of demand-response be instituted in a social-imaginary way. But exactly because of this (imaginary) moment of institution of society, the 'other' is defined strictly as the other for whom the law exists, whom the law protects. It is in this sense that in the situation where responsibility is at stake, the law will be the other's. This is confirmed by Derrida's example of institutional alterity, which is – as we will see – precisely, law. From a strategic point of view, heteronomy can be conceived as the condition of response, because if responsibility (as accountability) is instituted to counter unlimited power, then, it must be the law of the weaker (the one who demands) that is operating. In this respect, see Derrida's own words: 'I would be tempted, up to a certain point, to compare the concept of justice – which I'm here trying to distinguish from law – to Levinas's … *because of the heteronomic relation to others*, to the faces of otherness that govern me, whose infinity I cannot thematize and *whose hostage I remain*.' Derrida, 'Force of law', p. 22, my emphasis.

33. Denise Egea-Kuehne, 'The challenge of freedom in eastern Europe: Derrida's ethics of affirmation and educational responsibility', in Ursula E. Beitth (ed.), *The New Europe at the Crossroads* (NW: Peter Land, 1999), p. 28.

34. David Campbell, 'The deterritorialization,' p. 468. But as Campbell underlines in his discussion on the 'deterritorialization of responsibility', both authors see in alterity the basis for ethics and responsibility.

35. Derrida, 'Force of law', p. 252.

36. This remark's fruitfulness should not be ignored just because of the long-standing discussion between communitarians and their opponents. Abandoning the crucial concept of community, in the sense of Arendt's common world, because it has been used in infelicitous ways seems an unfortunate choice: this has implications in the advocacy of a solidaristic development world. On the relation between individual and state in Kant, see Fernando R. Teson, 'Kantian international liberalism' in David

R. Mapel and Terry Nardin (eds), *International Society, Diverse Ethical Prespectives* (Princeton: Princeton University Press, 1998), pp. 103–13.

37. This is all the more relevant since at the historical origins of development, we find the Saint-Simonian idea of trusteeship whereby property would be placed in the hands of 'trustees' 'chosen on the basis of their ability to decide where and how society's resources should be invested'. See Cowen and Shenton, 'The invention of development' in Crush, *Power of Development*, p. 34.

38. A crucial difference exists with Levinas who, as Campbell notes, has casually and in repeated instances restricted the notion of the other to the neighbour, and, in one case, shockingly excluding Israeli responsibility for Palestinians. Apart from every other implication, this is radically at odds with the Levinasian proclaimed fusion of the other and 'I'. See Campbell, 'The deterritorialization', p. 466. It may be added that Derrida's insistence of keeping one and the other separated, as mentioned earlier, can be thought of, as part of the more general anti-totalitarian effort of deconstruction.

39. Luc Boltanski, *La Souffrance à distance* (Paris: Métailié, 1993), pp. 32–3.

40. Ibid., pp. 114–15.

41. Walzer, *Just and Unjust Wars* (New York: Basic Books, 1977) p. 298.

42. Ibid, p. 290. For a reflection on 'in the name of', see B. Honig, 'Declarations of independence: Arendt and Derrida on the problem of founding a republic' in *American Political Science Review*, Vol. 85, No. 1, March 1991.

43. In fact, Walzer even brings in the question of distance but as a factor in the domestic relationship between the representative ('officials' is his term) and the represented that must be taken into account. Having briefly acknowledged the basic pattern of differentiation that can be operated within collective responsibility, we will leave it aside until the last section of this chapter.

44. Hierarchical responsibility, however, co-exists with Marxist undertones; 'It is in the interests of *us* Europeans, *small and weak* amongst the industrialised *giants*, to work together with *the proletariat of the world* to stop wild price fluctuations ... It is clear here and now that countries with limited resources like *our own* cannot make an independent voice heard by the great powers of this world, nations amd multinational companies, unless we link forces to provide a big enough production and a sufficiently large market.' 1979 9, my emphasis. The temptation to think that 'western' development discourse is identical to American development discourse is shaken much earlier than the current rift.

45. '[U]ne politique de coopération qui doit permettre *à la Communauté d'assumer à l'avenir ses responsabilités de grand ensemble économique à vocation politique* avec une cohérence et une efficacité accrues.' 1972 9, my emphasis.

46. 'It is thus not only a duty but a matter of self-interest to do everything to assist these countries in their development.' 1979 66. More shockingly, however: 'The whole history of the industrialised nations now helping the Third World to achieve a state of economic well-being shows that

material considerations alone are no justification for past conquest – whether good or bad – nor for any action the developed countries may take in the Third World now or in the future. It would seem that culture, although not a cause for slavery was often seen as a justification for colonialism. *And there is a positive side to cultural colonization, since it has provided the basic links that can unite the countries of western Europe and the vast majority of the Third World, particularly the ACP group.'* 41 1977 45, my emphasis.

47. In every sense, also of blameworthiness which is mitigated, like here: 'Even if the Community sometimes has restrictive reactions when its partners apply for preferential arrangements ... these minor offences are not enough to get it convicted of protectionism or to explain the failure of the ACP to improve.' 1988 33. Also in sentences referring to '[the Community's] desire to take an increasing share of responsibility towards all the developing countries.' 1988 26.

48. See, for a reappearance of the theme of the colonial ties, but only so as to reject its relevance: 'After decades of *blaming the colonial heritage* of the Northern domination of an unjust international economic system for most of their *problems*, developing countries now increasingly *accept* that development depends primarily on the policies they adopt and implement ... While elites and pressure groups in many developing countries still resist necessary changes, they are no longer protected by a benevolent [!] superpower and face increasing pressures from both their own populations and the international community to face up to their *responsibilities*.' 1997 74, my italics.

49. 'In the final analysis, *assuming global responsibility means the acceptance of the concept of a global society* in which each actor has to make his (sic) contribution towards the promotion of common welfare and collective security ... .' 1997 76. See also Romano Prodi, President of the European Commission: 'L'Europe assume ses responsabilités, mais cela ne suffit pas. Les Africains ne demandent pas la charité à l'Europe et aux Etats-Unis', in 'Les responsabilités de l'Europe *vis-à-vis* de l'Afrique', *Le Monde*, 11 July 2003.

50. 'Managing the world economy as a singular entity' and, generally, the idea of the global market as uniting the world is an idea that combines both the (otherwise positive) element of a world that brings people together and an individualised, 'egalitarian' responsibility. For a critique of this economic entity that is the globalised world, see McMichael, *Development and Social Change*, p. 165.

51. See David Chandler, 'International justice', *New Left Review*, Vol. 6 (November/December 2000), pp. 55–66.

52. Epitomised by the responses to the attacks on New York and Washington in 2001.

53. But currents as influential as Foucauldian post-structuralism or Gramscian Marxism have insisted on the possibility of thinking of society not as 'fixated on notions of the state'. See Laura Chrisman and Patrick Williams, 'Colonial discourse and post-colonial theory. An introduction', in Patrick Williams and Laura Chrisman (eds), *Colonial Discourse and Post-Colonial Theory, A Reader* (New York: Harvester Wheatsheaf, 1995), pp. 1–20.

54. Zygmunt Bauman, 'Wars in the globalization era', *European Journal of Social Theory*, Vol. 4, No. 1 (February 2001), pp. 11–28.
55. David Chandler, 'International justice'.
56. Cornelius Castoriadis, 'Le cache-misère de l'éthique'; Michael Walzer, *Just and Unjust Wars*.
57. Which, as Schmitt notes, is not the correct citation by Clausewitz who said: 'War is nothing but a continuation of political intercourse with a mixture of other means.' See Carl Schmitt (trans. Georg Schwab), *The Concept of the Political* (Chicago: University of Chicago Press, 1995 [1932]), p. 34.
58. The expression is in Richard K. Ashley, 'Living on border lines: man, poststructuralism and war' in James Der Derian and Michael Shapiro (eds), *International/Intertextual Relations: Postmodern Readings of World Politics* (Lexington: Lexington Books, 1989).
59. Veblen's term in Albert O. Hirschman, 'Morality and the social sciences: a durable tension', in Albert O. Hirschman, *Essays in Trespassing, Economics to Politics and Beyond* (Cambridge: Cambridge University Press, 1981), p. 304.
60. Arendt, *The Human Condition*, p. 237.
61. Ibid., p. 241.
62. This might seem a very hard ethic, and it probably is too hard for life to go on. Examples are there to testify this: the real difficulties facing the initial functioning of the International Tribunal for Rwanda or the repeated promises made to Robert Mugabe that his possible involvement in the 'massacres' in Matabeleland would not be investigated if he stepped down.

5 THE PASSION OF EFFICIENCY

1. Joseph Conrad, *Heart of Darkness* (London: Penguin, 1902).
2. For a post-colonial critique of *Heart of Darkness* see Chinua Achebe, 'An image of Africa: racism in Conrad's "Heart of Darkness", *The Massachusetts Review*, 18, 1977, pp. 782–94. Marlow's position is more ambiguous *vis-à-vis* the justification of efficiency. See Robert Hampson's enlightening introduction in the Penguin edition.
3. I owe this story to Robert Cryer, 'Human rights and the question of international criminal courts and tribunals', paper presented at an HRC/IPSA Conference on 'International intervention: from power politics to global responsibility', Vienna, August 2001.
4. This definition is due to Michael Stingl, 'Equality and efficiency as basic social values' in Christine Koggel (ed.), *Moral Issues in Global Perspective* (Ontario: Broadview Press, 1999), p. 607.
5. This expression is from Boaventura de Sousa Santos, 'Towards an epistemology of blindness: why the new forms of "ceremonial adequacy" neither regulate nor emancipate', *European Journal of Social Theory*, vol. 4, No. 3, August 2001.
6. That takes things that should be assumptions for granted, such as efficiency. Also see Brohman, 'Economism and critical silences in

development studies', *Third World Quarterly*, vol. 16, 1995; and John Dewey, 'The construction of good' in Thayer, *Pragmatism* (Indianapolis: Hackett Publishing Comany, 1982), p. 313.

7. For instance: 'There remain tensions between economic efficiency, social justice and ecological sustainability which cannot be fully resolved at the theoretical level, and in any event, reflect important conflicts or interests.' 1997 78.

8. Weber, *The Theory of Economic and Social Organisation* (trans. Talcott Parsons) (NY: The Free Press of Glencoe, 1964), p. 117.

9. Ibid., p. 115.

10. Cornelius Castoriadis, 'Individual, society, rationality, history' in Cornelius Castoriadis, *Philosophy, Politics, Autonomy* (Oxford: Oxford University Press), 1991.

11. Ibid., pp. 51–2.

12. Ibid., p. 52 and Wagner, 'Choice and decision-making' in Peter Wagner, *A History and Theory of the Social Sciences* (London: Sage, 2001), p. 102.

13. Castoriadis, 'Individual, society, rationality, history', p. 66.

14. Theodor Geiger, *Welfare and Efficiency. Their Interaction in Western Europe and Implications for International Economic Relations* (Washington: NDA, 1978), p. 15.

15. Andrew R. Schotter, *Microeconomics. A Modern Approach* (London: HarperCollins, 1994), p. 463. But Pareto efficiency also has a particular characteristic by comparison with the 'conventional sense', it serves to avoid comparative calculation.

16. The division between rational and irrational action originally served to distinguish between the objects of study of economics and sociology.

17. As the concept of interest transformed itself from a political into an economic one, efficiency became closely linked to it. Heilbron's concise history of the concept shows that 'interest' presents us with three ambiguities that concern its descriptive/prescriptive nature, the possibility of calculating its maximisation and whether it expresses 'rational' behaviour or not. See Johan Heilbron, 'Interest: history of the concept' in Neil J. Smelser and Paul B. Baltes, *International Encyclopedia of Social and Behavioral Sciences* (Oxford: Elsevier, 2001).

   Hirschman gives the following definition of 'interest': 'the disciplined understanding of what it takes to advance one's' ends. There is only one difference between this definition and the one of efficiency: the 'interest' is very clear as to the ultimate ends. Indeed, in the interest 'as it had been developed by the political literature since Machiavelli', the end was to promote 'one's power, influence and wealth'. Albert O. Hirschman, *The Passions and the Interests* (Princeton: Princeton University Press, 1977), p. 39. The transformation of 'interest' from a political to an economic concept is partly explained by 'the special affinity of rational calculation implicit in the concept of interest with the nature of economic activities'. As this transformation takes place, however, and as 'ends' that had been ascribed to the 'political' interest are lost, the economic interest becomes strictly a modality. The dissociation and the ultimate irrelevance of the previous 'political' ends from the 'economic interest' account for the opposition of interests and passions. In fact, what is argued is that the political 'passions' will take care of themselves, provided that everyone acts in an economically sound way, i.e. looking at their individual economic interests. In other words, the political does not involve choices to be made: the 'questioning on the fate of the community' is closed.

This process is also what transforms interest into economic efficiency. More explicitly, such an understanding of interest 'advocate[s] the injection of an element of calculating efficiency, as well as of prudence, into human behaviour *whatever might be the passion by which it is basically motivated*' (ibid., p. 40). Interest is reduced to an efficiency calculation, a modality, that is 'what is important', from the latin *interesse*. Efficiency is regarded as a dispassionate element that allows human behaviour to be based on rational calculation: we are close to instrumental rationality. Another factor that has influenced this transformation is that interest also meant (and means) the price of the loan, something which is useful to keep in mind when considering the debt/loan as a form of giving.

18. Hirschman, *The Passions and the Interests*, p. 40.
19. Louis Dumont, *Homo aequalis* (Paris: Gallimard, 1977), Chapters 1 and 2. Lefort underlines the assumption on which the mere idea of separating the domains of the social rests: the assumption of 'the primal dimensionality of the social'. When we talk about the 'economic' as separate from the 'political', for instance, we inevitably bring in a greater whole that we imagine to exist (the social) and even an idea about how this greater whole has come about, the origins of society. The fact that entities such as the 'economic' are unreflectively assumed to exist in a separate way hides the adoption 'of a notion of a pre-social society'. Lefort, 'The permanence of the theologico-political', in Claude Lefort (trans. David Macey) *Democracy and Political Theory* (Cambridge: Polity Press, 1988).
20. The signal of this emergence is given by the result of a slow evolution in the perception of exchange, when exchange is no longer thought to entail the gain of one partner and the loss of the other but as leading to a gain for both.
21. Lefort, 'The permanence of the theologico-political', p. 217.
22. Brohman, 'Economism and critical silences', p. 301.
23. Kevin P. Clements, *From Right to Left in Development Theory. An Analysis of the Political Implications of Different Models of Development* (Singapore: Institute of Southeast Asian Studies, 1980). Also see Goodin: 'Morally as well as economically, the fundamental justification of the market is simply that under certain, tightly specified conditions, the operations of the market will serve to maximise social welfare.' Robert E. Goodin, 'Reasons for welfare. Economic, sociological, and political – but ultimately moral' in J. Donald Moon (ed.), *Responsibility, Rights and Welfare. The Theory of Welfare State* (Boulder: Westview Press, 1988), p. 24.
24. The idea of the economic, more broadly than efficiency, determining what is possible 'on the level of the superstructure' is also a Marxist idea. See Nicos Mouzelis, 'Sociology of development: reflections on the present crisis', *Sociology*, Vol. 22, No. 1, p. 36.
25. Clements, *From Right to Left*, p. 13.
26. Ibid.

27. Hirschman, *The Passions*, p. 104. Rules against debates: the choice was easy for Adam Smith who praised the reasonableness of the economic against the folly of the political.

28. Karl Polanyi, *The Great Transformation* (Boston: Beacon Press, 1944), p. 139.

29. The minimal definition chosen by Boltanski and Chiapello, *Le nouvel esprit du capitalisme* (Paris: Gallimard, 1999) p. 37. Boltanski and Chiapello (ibid., p. 39) underline the importance of dissociating capitalism and market economy. Thus: (a) market economy has come into existence step by step and precedes capitalist accumulation, (b) capitalist accumulation obeys the rules of market economy only when there are not more direct ways to profit. Additionally, it is important to dissociate the question of justification (where efficiency is central) and the question of the motivational force (of capitalism or development).

30. Ibid., p. 50, for one instance. The other two pillars are progress and liberation.

31. Polanyi, *The Great Transformation*, p. 144.

32. In Boltanksi and Thévenot, *De la justification* (Paris: Gallimard, 1991). See Chapter 6.

33. Hirschman, too, identifies efficiency as an element brought about by the capitalistic 'commerce' or 'the economy'. In the political arguments for or against capitalism, efficiency is sometimes thought to threaten despotism and at other times to strengthen it. Hirschman, *The Passions and the Interests*, p. 122.

34. Pierre Bourdieu, 'The myth of "globalisation" and the European welfare state' in Pierre Bourdieu, *Acts of Resistance. Against the New Myths of Our Time* (trans. Richard Nice) (Cambridge: Polity Press, 1998), p. 40.

35. This criticism need not come from the left. Conservative approaches have also pointed out the 'contradiction' between the intended objectivity of positivism and the inescapable involvement of social values in efficiency (do 'better' means that one knows what is 'good' in the first place).

36. This is not so different from Marx's critique of the colonial rule in Britain, a critique notorious for its ambiguity: on the one hand, he expresses moral condemnation; on the other hand, he sees foreign oppression in India as politically and historically necessary for a social revolution. Concerning efficiency, Marx's position is interesting because although he sees British rule as highly inefficient, he also thinks that it is irrelevant for the outcome of the 'revolution' to come. See his letter to Engels on 14 June 1853; and two articles in the *New York Daily Tribune* on 25 June, 1853. Schlomo Avineri (ed.), *Karl Marx on Colonialism and Modernisation* (NY: Doubleday & Company, 1968).

37. Wagner, *Theorizing Modernity*, p. 32.

38. For a different use of this story, see Michel Foucault, 'Language to Infinity' in Michel Foucault, *Aesthetics, Method and Epistemology* (James Faubion, ed.) (NY: The New Press, 1998). I saw the story as related to the limit of the domus, or the space in which time can be limited. Indeed, 'domesticated' is another word for 'mastered': the occasion can be grasped to underline the relation, under colonialism and also still now in some places, between the 'master' and the 'domestic'. In Nigeria, 'master' is still used, as is

'baas' in southern Africa. 'Domestics' or 'domestic workers' ('maids' and 'gardeners'), that is, people working for, and living in, the household are expressions of everyday use in Zimbabwe. 'Masters', 'bosses'/baasses and 'madams' who employ people in these positions frequently explain that 'they could not live' without them. Beyond a mere exaggeration, we must see in this a very solid paternalistic frame of relations that reflects a Hegelian interdependency. Historically, this must also direct our gaze to the Roman 'domus' and the live-in personnel (slaves) and preceding this, to the Greek roots of 'economy', the law of the household. For examples of the above expressions in post-colonial literature, see Buchi Emecheta's *The Slave Girl* (Oxford: Heinemann, 1995 [1977]) and Chinua Achebe's *No Longer at Ease* (Oxford: Heinemann, 1987 [1960]).

39. Indeed, as Santos underlines, 'mainstream economics operates and intervenes in social life in a coarse-grain mode but manages to legitimise its operation and interventions as if it were of fine-grain resolution quality'. 'Coarse-grain resolution' stands for a poor capacity of correspondence between 'reality' and the information that is given about it, while 'fine-grain resolution' stands for the opposite. Neo-classical or mainstream economics has relied on theories whose resolution is lower than the resolution of its methods but has managed to present itself as relying on methods. Such confusion of genres has also presided over efficiency which is a theoretical (political and moral) fiat, rather than a mere instrument of instrumental rationality. Santos, 'Epistemology of blindness', *European Journal of Social Theory*, 2001, pp. 261–2.

40. Carlson shows this happening in the case of classic price theory. David Gray Carlson, 'On the margins of microeconomics' in Cornell, Rosenfeld, and Carlson, *Deconstruction* (New York: Routledge, 1992) p. 265.

41. 'Technical efficiency' has been a pervasive theme of structuralist economics, which are 'reformist' *vis-à-vis* capitalism, since they underline political will. In structuralist economics, technology is a determinant factor of growth and development and the state must use technology in the most efficient way. The discussions on technological transfer in the European development discourse bear this influence.

42. Concerning foreign policy, see David Campbell, 'Global inscription: how foreign policy constitutes the United States', *Alternatives*, Vol. XV, No. 3, Summer 1990, p. 278.

43. 'Empirical inadequacy', non-desirability', and the question of necessity are the three critiques that Wagner addresses to rational choice. Wagner, 'Choice and decision-making' in Wagner, *History and Theory of the Social Sciences* (London: Sage, 2001).

44. Derrida cited in Carlson, 'On the margins'.

45. Colin Leys, *The Rise and Fall of Development Theory*, p. 103.

46. And for a moment, we can thus adopt the explanation of development as myth: 'in a world dominated by reason, it is the 'imaginary' which generates efficiency': Rist, '"Development" as part of the modern myth', *European Journal of Development Research*, 1990, p. 14.

47. 'So the industrialised and the developing countries have every interest in encouraging more rational use so that, in the long term, they both have easier access to the world energy market. The industrialised world,

particularly the Community, can help the developing countries ... promote more rational ways of utilisation.' 52 1978 11.

48. 1979 98; 1986 15, 1979 86; 1997 38, respectively.

49. Laurent Thévenot, 'Equilibre et rationalité dans un univers complexe', *Revue économique*, No. 2, 1989, pp. 147–97.

50. Ferguson, 'From African socialism to scientific capitalism' in Moore and Schmitz, *Debating Development Discourse* (London: Routledge, 1994).

51. For example, see Mathur, 'The current impasse', *Alternatives*, 1989.

52. 'L'échelle communautaire est *objectivement* plus appropriée pour mener plus *efficacement* certaines actions de coopération, que l'échelle nationale ... .' 1972 36, my emphasis.

53. 'The objective validity of all empirical knowledge rests exclusively upon the ordering of the given reality according to categories which are subjective in a specific sense, namely, in that they present the presuppositions of our knowledge and are based on the presupposition of the value of those truths which empirical knowledge alone is able to give us.' Max Weber, '"Objectivity" in the social sciences', in Max Weber, *The Methodology of the Social Sciences* (H. H. Gerth and C. Wright Mills, eds) (London: Routledge, 1991 [1948]), p. 110.

54. 'More important, structurally speaking, is the transformation of the farms, the modernisation of their equipment and the introduction of more efficient techniques ... .' 80 1983 77.

55. 'Whenever necessary, attention can be drawn to delays and cumbersome practices in order to improve efficiency.' 89 1985 22.

56. 'This [an effective industrial sector] in turn can lay the foundation of the transformation of an economy based on traditional and outmoded technologies into a more modern economy based on efficient and updated technologies.' 146 1994 65.

57. Linklater, 'The problem of community in international relations', *Alternatives*, 1990, p.144.

58. Gerald Berthoud, 'Modernity and development', in *European Journal of Development Research*, Vol. 2, No. 1, 1990, p. 23. Typical of this trend of thought and showing the link to capitalism, the following statement of Furtado: 'control of technology constitutes the cornerstone of the international power structure at the present time. In the final analysis, the struggle against dependence becomes an effort to neutralise the effects of the technological monopoly held by the central countries ... modern technology, the key ingredient of the accumulation process.' Celso Furtado, 'Dependence in a unified world', *Alternatives*, VIII, 1982, p. 277.

59. 'There is no way that the viability and efficiency of projects in *these* countries can be ensured without general or sectoral reforms and structural adjustment is the result of the need to strike all the balances again ... It is important to remember that the Community's opening to the problem of economic rationalisation does not replace the traditional long-term development schemes ... .' 120 1990 13.

60. 'Si ce régime de libre échange n'a pas porté, bien au contraire, préjudice aux pays tiers, il représente pour l'association une dimension irremplaçable

parce qu'il détermine dans une grande mesure son efficacité économique et surtout sa portée politique ... .' 1972 34.

61. An example of the 'methodological' precedence of the political over the economic: 'Political steps must also be taken and we need an agreement with the ACP to make this beginning possible. Then comes the operational stage. Energy saving techniques will have to be transferred and we must contribute to prospection and the more rational use of oil, uranium and coal resources.' 51 1978 68.

62. See Hirschman, 'The rise and decline', and Gasper, 'Culture and development ethics'.

63. Hirschman, 'The rise and decline' in Hirschman, *Essays in Trespassing*, (Cambridge: Cambridge University Press, 1981), p. 21.

64. 'Now that developing countries are no longer pawns in the geostrategic power game between opposing blocs, the main donors are increasingly requiring the aid they give to be used effectively, particularly since the resources available are becoming more scare [sic].' 141 1993 55. But geopolitics is not indifferent towards efficiency, as the texts and instrumental rationality show.

65. 'More important, structurally speaking, is the transformation of the farms, the modernisation of their equipment and the introduction of more efficient techniques, which means an increase in the farmers' ability to adapt to the changing conditions of the market and to absorb such new techniques.' 80 1983 77.

66. 'The new agreement has made it possible to improve the structure of the private sector and set up a proper development support strategy for it in the ACP countries. The challenge facing everyone is a daunting one. It will require exceptional flexibility, and a new partnership between the public sector and private operators based on mutual sympathy and understanding.' 181 2000 23.

67. Hirschman, *The Passions and the Interests*, p. 122 and Hirschman, 'The rise and decline', p. 21.

68. 'The main problem we have encountered over the last 18 months is that we have been proposing a radical reform of the mechanisms and instruments to make cooperation more efficient and to ensure a greater impact. The ACPs have got used to 30 years of cooperation on another basis and have found it hard to accept that resources will in future be allocated not just on the basis of their needs but on performance, nor did they like having some instruments removed.' 179 2000 6.

69. It is interesting to note that 'performance' was one of the two outcomes of the post-68 double demand for autonomy and security in France. See Boltanski and Chiapello, *Le nouvel esprit du capitalisme*, p. 248. It originated in the demands of the younger employees of firms, i.e. those who could not ask for statutory security since they had not been employed for long enough. It provides an interesting parallelism with the relation between more economically developed and less economically developed countries. In a sense, arguing for 'needs' and the existing contractual security was for the ACP a 'statutory' demand. The EU answered by a 'performance' solution. This points to the inescapable logic of parents-children.

70. See Chapter 6.

71. '[T]he Community's cooperation policy should help establish genuine democracy in the developing world and make these countries work more transparently, more openly and more efficiently.' 128 1991 51. Further, conditions are created so as to enhance efficiency: these are the famous conditionalities: '... efforts towards more efficient development coopera- tion policies on the basis of increased conditionalities'. 1997 51

72. 'The Community's development cooperation policy has logically to steal a march on this process from the recent past of former colonies, on whatever is negative and positive. At the moment, *efficiency dictates* that the general development policy has to come from the Community.' 128 1991 59–60, my emphasis. In a remarkable twist, this extract presents efficiency as its own author. It is remarkable in the sense that although it starts by setting the Community's policy as the 'actor' – a position encountered previously – and it finishes by doing the same, efficiency is centrally introduced as a necessity device. The verb 'dictates' helps to perceive efficiency as something with a strong capacity to direct and to order, as something endowed with a will. Overall, the impression is that the general policy must be a Community policy because efficiency orders it. In this portrayal, efficiency is an 'imperative'.

73. 'Orders' can be 'orders of worth' or 'orders of justice': within each order, a particular set of rules and general configuration of beings and things is valid, which is not similarly valid in another order.

74. Quoted in Rist, '"Development" as part of the modern myth', p. 12.

75. See Claus Offe, 'Some contradictions of the modern welfare state' in Christopher Pierson and Francis G. Castles (eds), *The Welfare State Reader* (Cambridge: Polity Press, 2000), p. 69. The differentiation between national welfare-states is important, just as it is in development: there are different compromises between considerations of equity and justice and 'the liberal obsession with market efficiency and commodification'. See Esping-Andersen, Gøsta, 'Three worlds of welfare capitalism' in Pierson and Castles, *The Welfare State Reader* (Cambridge: Polity Press, 2000), p. 162.

76. Offe, 'Some contradictions'. The market is thought by some as all-encompassing. See, for example, Etienne Balibar, 'Inégalités, fractionnement social, exclusion' in Joëlle Affichard and Jean-Baptiste de Foucauld, *Justice sociale et inégalités* (Paris: Esprit, 1992); an argument reminiscent of Procacci's observation on the change between political economy (that accepted exclusion) and social economy (that included the poor).

77. See an economist's exposition of the problem: 'The term "economic efficiency" ... entails a norm by which alternative economic situations may be ranked. And since alternative economic organisations are agenda that affect the welfare of the members of society, the norm has to be one that is acceptable to the members of that society. One way of expressing society's will with respect also to alternative economic organisations is through the political process, in a democratic state through the voting mechanism. Yet, the outcome of a political decision, democratic or otherwise, about a set of economic alternatives is not regarded as necessarily efficient by the economist. Indeed, he often is highly critical

of democratic legislation. It follows that the norm of economic efficiency is distinct from an expression of political will and, therefore, that it may be properly criticised by reference to the adopted norm of economic efficiency.' E. J. Mishan, *Economic Efficiency and Social Welfare. Selected Essays on Fundamental Aspects of the Economic Theory of Social Welfare* (London: George Allen and Unwin, 1981), p. 258.

78. Boltanski and Thévenot, *De la justification*. See Chapter 6.

79. One could play with words here and use 'the diktat' of efficiency as it opposes democracy. Fritz Scharpf, *Governing in Europe: Effective and Democratic* (Oxford: Oxford University Press, 1999).

80. Thus, the complicated procedures of implementation of the Lomé Convention have often been criticised in the name of efficiency. It must be clear that the 'making' of a decision that I refer to is different from the 'fabrication' of politics of which Hannah Arendt has warned us.

81. Jacques Derrida, 'The mystical foundation of authority' in Cornell, Rosenfeld, Carlson, *Deconstruction* (New York: Routledge, 1992), p. 46 and 47 or Judith Butler, 'Dynamic conclusions' in Judith Butler, Ernesto Laclau and Slavoj Žižek, *Contingency, Hegemony, Universality. Dialogues on the Left* (London: Verso, 2000).

82. There are numerous examples in the EU development discourse, going from the improvement of the efficiency of the agricultural production (115 1989 78) to more efficient social sectors (111 1988 72) or more efficient small and medium enterprises (65 1981 96).

83. See Arundhati Roy's recent article on the Iraq war: Roy, 'The day of the jackals. On war and occupation', 2 June 2003, *Counterpunch* Internet site.

84. Brohman, 'Economism and critical silences', p. 301.

85. 'Government intervention seems necessary to initiate and nurture the modernisation process ... it could actually be argued that the more backward a country is, the more radical should government intervention be in promoting trade and industry.' 53 1979 65.

86. For an example: 'The ACP cannot for the moment determine or control the instruments that are vital to their development policies both for historical and operational reasons.' 111 1988 50.

87. See Johannes Fabian, *Time and the Other. How Anthropology Makes its Object* (NY: Columbia University Press, 1983).

88. Ibid., p. 31.

89. 'Can we really make civilizations and areas of production that are at different stages of development complementary and avoid keeping the poor dependent on the others by helping them to catch up?' 48 1978 46.

90. Santos, 'An epistemology of blindness'.

91. See Bauman, 'On universal morality', *EJDR*, 1998.

92. Cases like Samuel Huntington's are revealing: in his 'clash of civilisations' the hybrid object that 'African civilisation' is, was completely absent: Huntington, *The Clash of Civilisations and the Remaking of the World Order* (NY: Simon and Schuster, 1996). But Boltanski and Chiapello also inform us that both in the management literature of the 1960s and in that of the 1990s, Africa is nowhere to be found. Boltanski and Chiapello, *Le nouvel*

esprit du capitalisme. Events like the recent tour of George W. Bush in some African countries (advertised as a tour in 'Africa') in July 2003, exactly following the end of organised American military operations in Iraq, are entirely constructed on such rhetoric of forgetting and 'resurrection' by the powerful.

93. *Hugh Selwyn Mauberley.*

6 PANDORA'S BOX: GIVING DEVELOPMENT

1. Hesiod's notoriously misogynist account differs slightly from the one above. In the light of the importance of the gift in Christian charity, it is interesting to note that Pandora's myth is a version of Biblical Eve's: the woman, directly or indirectly created by the gods and God out of earth, who is at the root of humanity's problems is also the inevitable Mother (Earth).

2. Lewis Hyde, *The Gift. Imagination and the Erotic Life of Property* (NY: Vintage, 1979).

3. Moore, 'Development discourse' in Moore and Schmitz, *Debating Development Discourse,* (London: Macmillan, 1994), p. 17.

4. Torfing, *New Theories of Discourse,* (Oxford: Blackwell, 1999), p. 298.

5. See, for example: '[C]ooperation with the Third World is more than a moral duty or a political imperative. It has become a vital economic necessity for the Community.' 52 1978 10.

6. Doty, *Imperial Encounters* (Minneapolis: University of Minnesota Press, 1996). Also in Doty: 'Foreign aid enables the administration of poverty, the surveillance and management of the poor. Foreign assistance does what welfare institutions do at the domestic level', p. 129. See also Lumsdaine, *Moral Vision in International Politics.*

7. Lumsdaine, *Moral Vision,* p. 186.

8. Boltanski's expressions in inverted commas from *La souffrance* (Paris: Métailié, 1993), in the title of the book and p. 16 for the first use of the second expression.

9. I cannot do justice to the subtle but significant differences between these concepts.

10. However, note the Athenian and Jewish communities' communal provision. See Walzer's *Spheres of Justice,* pp. 60–71.

11. François Ewald, *Histoire de l'Etat providence. Les origines de la solidarité* (Paris: Grasset, 1986), p. 24.

12. According to the criticism of responsibility in Chapter 4, this argument cannot hold. Responsibility is by definition interactive and there is, therefore, no such thing as a valid opposition between an obligation and a free responsibility, except if one wishes to adopt a Levinasian understanding of responsibility (one where indeed the Other always *obliges* to a response). From an international politics perspective, see Campbell, 'The deterritorialization of responsibility', *Alternatives,* 1994.

13. Albert O. Hirschman, *The Rhetoric of Reaction: Perversity, Futility, Jeopardy* (Cambridge: Belknap Press, 1991), Chapter 2 and in particular pp. 27–35.

14. See Offe, 'Some contradictions' in Pierson and Castles (eds), *The Welfare State Reader*, 2000, p. 73.

15. Procacci, 'Social economy' in Burchell et al., *The Foucault Effect*, pp. 156–7. For a further understanding of *savoir* and, particularly, its conceptual roots see Colin Gordon, 'The soul of the citizen: Max Weber and Michel Foucault on rationality and government' in Scott Lash and Sam Whimster (eds), *Max Weber, Rationality and Modernity* (London: Allen and Unwin, 1987), p. 307.

16. Despite Marx's assertion that colonialism is an outlet for the western bourgeoisie's progeny, the fact that colonies were directed strongly to the production of raw materials, made labour (and thus the maintenance of these men and women at an acknowledged level of health, for instance) a 'necessary evil'. The colonised were crucial in producing the colonisers' wealth. Additionally, in many situations (in particular in Africa), colonisers were not from the bourgeoisie but on the contrary came from working class or rural backgrounds, something that has borne strong consequences in terms of today's land distribution. However, this remark from Marx can serve as a guiding idea for understanding what goes on with the export of international organisation or NGO staff in these 'developing countries' where the former live, in principle, as an inaccessible, untouchable (thus, for example, protected from violence) and very wealthy elite.

17. Procacci, 'Social economy', p. 166.

18. Walzer, *Spheres of Justice* (Oxford: Martin Robertson, 1983) p. 68.

19. Boltanski, *La souffrance*, pp. 17–18.

20. As Holmes notes in Stephen Holmes, 'Liberal guilt. Some theoretical origins of the welfare state' in Moon, *Responsibility, Rights* (Boulder: Westview Press, 1988), p. 90. The case of Zimbabwe is a telling example.

21. The example *par excellence* is the case of technology transfer.

22. We must nevertheless note the momentary hesitation over full acceptance of neo-classical economics in the 1990s. The problem was that in the early 1990s, when the 'science' of neo-classical economics fell out of favour with the development discipline partly forging the European development discourse, the equivalent of 'social economy' had already been tried in the form of *ad hoc* applications of interventionist principles mixed with 'regionalism' or 'special relations' stemming from a shared colonial past as well as the remnants of by then classic modernisation theory, whose epitome we find in the 1970s European development discourse. The ensuing and current focus of development studies and policy on more specific issues such as gender, environment, human rights, but also the intention of reducing the scale of intervention to 'micro-projects', are the result of a particularly self-reflective type of 'social economy' associated with a scientific pretension to efficiency, one that is ironically both trying to avoid the previous problems but necessarily stumbling on them.

23. Bourdieu, *Esquisse* (Paris: Seuil, 1972) p. 339.

24. This is restricted to an 'inspiration', because Bourdieu is actually interested in different forms of *exchange*, not of giving.

25. Schematising the different forms of giving entails operating two necessary reductionisms. The first one involves ignoring the Maussian complexity of the gift-form, precisely as it may comprise loan/debt/credit and *donnant-donnant* elements, but also as a 'total social phenomenon'. The fuzziness of the gift, including its spiritual and emotional elements, are suspended. The second reductionism restricts the relation among the people/institutions in these forms of giving to a dualistic form. This is a significant reductionism because it effaces the place of the 'third instance', God in medieval charity, and responsibility, or the international community in more recent occurrences.

26. '*La période post-coloniale est révolue et la logique donateur-receveur est dépassée*. L'UE et les ACP ont des intérêts communs à développer et une opportunité stratégique à saisir. Il nous faut un partenariat revalorisé sur des bases nouvelles et ambitieuses.' 1998 167 5, my emphasis.

27. In 'L'ordre du discours', Foucault has proposed that 'condition of possibility' is a more fruitful category of historical/discursive analysis than 'signification' or 'meaning'. This sprang from an attempt to distance his work from what he saw as the characteristics of the traditional history of ideas. 'Condition of possibility' was an enabling device, meant to avoid references to hidden meanings (or to a general hidden meaning as, for instance, a collective unconscious).

28. Derrida, 'Secrets of European Responsibility' in Derrida, *Given Time* (Chicago: Chicago University Press, 1992) p. 40. The same insight is expressed by Boltanski and Thévenot's account of the role of gifts in relations in the domestic world, a world in many ways related to development, as we will see.

29. 'Lastly, *there are forms of credit* offered on such favourable terms that they *are tantamount to gifts*. Indeed, the richer countries are beginning to give such aid *as outright gifts*. This money goes principally to the countries which lack the raw materials and the educational skills necessary for development. These sums go to the poorest ....' 1979 91, my emphasis.

30. The parallel with the welfare state discourse is once more striking. F. Ewald (*Histoire de l'Etat providence*, Paris: Grasset, 1986, p. 73) quoting a French author of 1906 is himself worth quoting: '"Noblesse oblige". Il faut élargir cette belle devise, aussi bien aux dons de la fortune, du talent, de la beauté, de l'intelligence qu'à ceux de la naissance. "Toute superiorité oblige". Toute superiorité doit s'expier par le dévouement social. Autant de formules qui reprennent les principes du *régime de patronage*, c'est-à-dire l'ensemble des règles de conduite selon lesquelles le patronat, du moins le grand patronat, prétendait qu'il convenait de gouverner l'industrie et qui forment en opposition à l' "économie politique", la doctrine de l' "économie sociale".' One cannot but note here the triple interest: the first interest resides in the responsibility that is entailed by superiority; the second in that the gifts bestowed upon the superior ones (presumably by nature) are themselves a cause of responsibility, thereby forming an unbroken chain of gift-responsibility-gift and so on; the third interest resides in the observation that it is the *savoir* of 'social economy'

– the closest to development studies – that prescribes such responsibility to giving (or assisting etc.) and not the 'science' of political economy (that would doubtlessly limit the gift's excesses by applying a concept of efficiency).

31. Last italics mine but 'responsible' was already italicised. The end of the extract is as follows: '... and what one receives'. We see how the possibility of an egalitarian responsibility is thus allowed. Derrida, 'The madness of economic reason: a gift without present' in Jacques Derrida, *Given Time: I The Counterfeit Money* (trans. Peggy Kamuf) (Chicago: University of Chicago Press, 1992), p. 63.

32. On the other hand, somewhere else, Derrida has noted how a response, responsibility may be left aside, precisely also to avoid excess. Jacques Derrida, *On the Name* (Stanford: Stanford University Press, 1993).

33. Derrida, 'The madness of economic reason', pp. 61–2.

34. For more on 'calling', see section 6.3.

35. See Benveniste's etymological exploration of owing and debt: owing implies having to give something back that belongs to somebody else but which I didn't necessarily borrow. The loan and the debt are two sides of the same coin. The relation between debt and duty is most significant. I will always take Bourdieu's *prêt* (loan) to be, conversely, a debt. Of course, the difference between the two is significant since it lies in the initiative taken, to provide a loan or to contract a debt. Derrida notes that Malamoud makes the Nietzschean link: 'In debt are combined duty and fault ... a connection for which the history of the Germanic languages provides evidence.' See Derrida, *On the Name*, pp. 135–6.

36. Debt has a different way of dealing with uncertainty than the gift. In the gift, there is trust; and the breach of the circle would simply and inexorably mean (and has meant) a breach of community. The contrast between certainty and uncertainty is stark. On the other hand, in the debt, uncertainty is trapped in the contract. Because trust is – always in the ideal-typical debt – absent, there existed, in the middle ages, the institution of the *surety* (Hyde, *The Gift*, p. 123). It is not different from today's guarantor.

37. Ewald, *Histoire de l'Etat providence*, p. 46.

38. As Susan Strange says: 'The phenomenon of borrowing – getting money today in exchange for money tomorrow – is economic. But how such transactions are managed is political.' Susan Strange, 'The new world of debt', *New Left Review*, 230, 1998, p. 92.

39. 'It appeared essential, politically, to maintain the *"acquis"* of Lomé II in order to ensure the security of our relations ... So that the *spirit* of Lomé may live (...).' 89 1985 11.

40. 'Because we are in the Lomé Convention, we *commit* ourselves outside it to a *different fight, an endless fight*, one *we shall wage to the end* at international level to see that the stabilisation of raw materials prices is accepted as a *vital* target, that *the problem of debt* is considered as a *burden, an unjust almost*, on the developing countries – *and if it is not an unjust one, then a paralysing one*. If the *debt burden* stayed unchanged, the developing countries could not go on borrowing.' 79 1983 12, my emphasis.

41. The following excerpt is an explicit example of the construction of a common universe. 'For the first time in the history of our cooperation, our negotiators have agreed to deal fully and explicitly, in the Convention with the question of human rights and respect for human dignity ... we are making this *commitment* a part of our *common heritage*.' 89 1985 9, my emphasis.

42. Chapter 23 of Deuteuronomy has two verses: '19: Thou shalt not lend upon usury to thy brother; usury of money, usury of victuals, usury of anything that is lent upon usury. 20: Unto a stranger thou mayest lend upon usury: but unto thy brother thou shalt not lend upon usury, that the Lord thy God may bless thee in all that thou settest thine hand in the land whither thou goest to possess it.' Cited in Hyde, *The Gift*.

43. For example, see Weber's references in *The Protestant Ethic and the Spirit of Capitalism* (London: Allen and Unwin, 1976).

44. We have seen that a second understanding of an 'egalitarian' responsibility (collective egalitarian) is a more social-democratic one, where solidarity is responsibility's substantive filling. The difference is that in the latter, a community of interests is assumed whereas it is opposition of interests in the former.

45. Schematically, the two movements can be drawn as one of vertical expansion (responsibility) and one of horizontal expansion (efficiency).

46. Which Marcel Mauss tried, in a certain way, to keep apart from the gift, according to Derrida, 'The madness of economic reason', p. 42.

47. To be distinguished from the welfare state resulting from the corporatist-statist legacy and the 'social-democratic welfare state'. The liberal welfare state is 'obsessed' 'with market efficiency and commodification' and is characterised by modest universal transfers. Esping-Andersen, 'Three worlds' in Pierson and Castles, *The Welfare Reader*, 2000, p. 162.

48. This uncontrollable acceleration is globalisation and '[Europe] cannot afford to think of itself as *an island of stability in a world in disarray*' (1997 3). The questioning of structuralist thinking in development policy is exemplified by something which sounds very much like a determinism, too, only one of disorder. Possibilities of resistance are limited, and even dismissed. '[R]esisting the process of globalisation is therefore *quixotic and suicidal* for any country.' 1997 74. 'Globalisation' does not only affect the rhythm of time but also the 'slices' of time: thus, although, in the 1990s, the colonial past is a theme that fades away (to come back through critique at the end of the 1990s, although it still hasn't penetrated again the European development discourse), Europe's own past re-emerges: '[T]he Community entered a *drastically different context* after the fall of the Berlin Wall ... problems that have been *buried* for decades in Europe's *past* and were mainly associated with today's Third World are becoming facts of life in Europe again ....' The same type of concern is found in the American foreign policy discourse of the 1960s. 'Fear was generated by widespread poverty in Europe after World War II, but the danger of poverty associated with "the third world" was of an essentially different nature. In the case of Europe, poverty itself was the object of concern, the thing to be eliminated. In the case of "the third world", the subjects

who personified poverty were the objects of concern.' Doty, *Imperial Encounters*, pp. 129–30.

49. The big difference with the welfare discourse is that international politics lacks a Leviathan.

50. See particularly on charity and dependency, Walzer, *Spheres of Justice*, pp. 91–4.

51. Goodin, 'Reasons for welfare', pp. 39–41 and Procacci, 'Social economy' make a similar argument with regard to the problem of dependency in welfare. Goodin suggests that there are two solutions to dependency, both involving extra-market provisions: the first leaves the dependent still exploitably dependent and precluded from participation in the markets, the other renders them independent and hence qualified to participate in markets 'and quasi market politics'. And he continues: 'Historically, the former was the option customarily pursued. Those in need of extra-market assistance were branded "paupers", stripped of their rights of citizenship ... .' As noted earlier, Procacci builds her argument on the different treatment of poverty by political economy, which excludes poverty as extraneous to its natural order and aims at its elimination, compared to social economy which, finding the utility of a politics of poverty, transforms poverty into pauperism and consequently includes it as a perversion of a specific moral order.

52. See Derrida's note on Heidegger's 'thinking of the *call* as thinking of the gift' in Derrida, 'The madness of economic reason', p. 51.

53. 'The EEC has an obligation to the ACP countries and to itself to do its utmost to see that these hopes are realised.' 51 1978 69.

54. Evident in Commissioner Marin's debatable view of history. 'What I cannot accept is the idea that a more united, politically stronger Europe which plays an international part with more united and more structured institutions will automatically *forget its responsibilities* towards the Third World. History suggests the opposite, when Europe has flourished, it has played its part and the consequences have been favourable to the Third World. ... But the *responsibility is shared*. They too *must* make an effort.' 121 1990 3, my emphasis.

55. See the defence of the introduction in the EU policy of the structural adjustment approach: 'There is no way that the viability and efficiency of projects in these countries can be ensured without general or sectoral reforms and structural adjustment is the result of this need to strike all the balances again ... .' 120 1990 13.

56. '[A]u cours des années 1970, la priorité absolue portait sur les grandes infrastructures. L'accent a été mis ensuite sur l'agriculture.' 154 1995 76.

57. From the viewpoint of the radical fringe of ACP discourse, such links must be kept in mind today and continue to justify an EU preferential policy.

58. 'La politique d'ouverture préferentielle que la Communauté pratique à l'égard de certains pays en voie de développemént répond à des obligations et à des intérêts particuliers, créés aussi bien par l'histoire et la géographie que par une complémentarité économique évidente et un ensemble de rapports traditionnels qui ne sont pas seulement d'ordre commercial.' 1972 35.

59. As Rosalind Thomas says: 'Certainly the ACP need to realise that non-reciprocal and differentiated schemes are not *per se* the problem.' But she immediately adds: 'Provided they apply to all developing countries and least-developed countries, they are indeed compatible with the GATT Agreements.' See *The WTO and Trade Cooperation Between the ACP and the EU: Assessing the Options* (Maastricht: ECDPM, 1997), pp. 38–45.

60. In its mandate for Cotonou, the EU prefers 'dialogue, contract rather than conditionality and the fulfilment of mutual obligations'. *Comparing the ACP and EU Negotiating Mandates* (Maastricht: ECDPM 1998). On the opposition between dialogue and conditionality, see D. Frisch, 'Lomé passé? – The floor to the ACP partners' (http://www.inzet.nl, Amsterdam, 1997), pp. 5–11. On the opposition between contractuality and conditionality, see L. Box, J. von Braum and J.J. Gabas, *Looking Beyond Lomé IV. Towards Practice-oriented Policies* (Maastricht: ECDPM, 1999).

61. 'Global governance ... may imply new forms of conditionality and intervention into what has traditionally been considered the internal affairs of states. However, it must be based on the rule of law and legitimised within fully representative institutional structures. As a consequence, law will have to be developed considerably.' 1997 76. In *Le nouvel esprit du capitalisme*, p. 500, law is the location *par excellence* of the compromise.

62. In his excellent *Commentary on the Green Paper on Relations between the European Union and the ACP countries* (Maastricht: ECDPM, 1997), George Huggins writes: 'Democracy and good governance have been among the main principles of Lomé from the outset, but are expected to assume an added significance in the light of the experience of the past decades. A principle of efficiency in the use of resources and in their results is to be given greater prominence. This is perceived as a means of addressing two antagonistic considerations: EU responsibility towards European citizens for the resources applied in international development efforts without necessarily removing from the ACP countries the primary responsibility for controlling and monitoring their own development. It is also a double-edged tool in that it seeks to impose a development discipline on the ACP countries.' Efficiency as a means of both EU internal accountability and ACP individual egalitarian responsibility is a double instance of articulation.

63. Thus, in their mandate for the draft of the Cotonou Agreement, the ACP declare that 'a true partnership cannot be characterised by conditionalities', making clear that equality is not what is involved in the conditionalities, and hence, responsibility is hierarchical. On 'partnership', look under the last compromise.

64. 'In sum, political (as well as economic) participation is in principle supportive of development. However, imposing western-style political pluralism, irrespective of the cultural traditional and historical evolution of particular societies is potentially counterproductive.' 1997 38.

65. 'C'est donc à l'Europe, car elle est la seule à pouvoir le faire et c'est sa responsabilité historique et son intérêt géopolitique bien compris, de prendre l'initiative d'une vraie politique de coopération avec l'Afrique

noire qui soit à la fois responsable, cohérente, juste et efficace.' 154 1995 82.

66. 'Europe needs the enterprise to succeed because development policy helps shape its own identity; because a part of its strength in international affairs comes from its special relations with the Third World; because it depends on the African, Carribean and Pacific States ... .' 79 1983 13.

'The Commission document contains an appeal for a new deal aimed at giving an economic, social and cultural dimension to political interdependence. It is a matter of the greatest urgency, for thanks [sic] to food shortfalls and debt the majority of ACP states are more economically dependent today than they were in colonial times.' Ibid.

67. 'For the past 20 years we have been supplying the developing countries with the instruments of development, with roads, hospitals, factories and so on. Some countries have benefited, those which were best prepared, and some have not because the people were not willing to use the tools, not having been prepared to do so.' 79 1983 14.

68. Commissioner Pinheiro declared in 1997 (Inzet website, pp. 3–7): 'To make decentralised cooperation efficient and effective, many have told us that there should be provision for assistance for capacity-building among the institutions of civil society. I am persuaded by these arguments.' It is worth noting the focus of capacity-building on civil society, whether this is a 'bottom-up' or 'top-down' approach is uncertain.

69. 'This part [introductory of *Lomé* III] ... constitutes the political expression of what has been achieved by reinforced and renewed cooperation over a quarter of a century, an "*acquis*" that was described during the negotiations as the "common heritage" of the partners.' 89 1985 22.

'The fact that we, as partners, agreed to found our future relations on something essential – the fulfilment of man as the agent of development and the subject of all our cooperation efforts is a moral and "developmental" choice – is not political in the usual meaning of the word. What it is in fact is a return to the source and the very foundations of development ... the idea some people might have that the reference to human rights means the Community can set itself up as the watchdog of its partners' political ethics is not in the Convention.' 105 1987 6.

70. Says Huggins, 'Commentary on the Green Paper'. For a revealing understanding of the 'Lomé culture', see D. Frisch, *The Future of the Lomé Convention* (Maastrich: ECPM, 1996).

71. 'The two main aims of what some people have called the new orthodox economic policy are to make the economy more efficient, obviously, and to take the pressure off public finance. The economic efficiency which privatisation is supposed to bring about is not just produced by transferring ownership. It all depends on how interested the new owners are in proper business management in a context of economic liberalisation.' 146 1994 53.

72. 'No one denied that future cooperation should be based on a much fuller degree of partner country "ownership", initiative and responsibility for performance', as Pinheiro says in 1997 (Inzet website). Apart from the link with egalitarian responsibility, we see here the profile of the theme of trust.

73. For an exception to this, this passage is also interesting because of the direct link between colonial past and hierarchical responsibility (moral duty). 'But the EU must never forget our colonial past brings with it a moral duty.' 178 1999–2000 8.

74. 'After decades of blaming the colonial heritage of the northern domination of an unjust international economic system for most of their problems, developing countries now increasingly accept that development depends primarily on the policies they adopt and implement.' 1997 74.

75. 'However, it had to be recognised that unconditional assistance did not help developing countries to become fully accountable for their policies, allowed economic dependence to continue under the guise of a convenient safety net and caused many countries to become addicted to aid.' 1997 14. This extract is very interesting because it brings several elements of the compromises between the different types of giving: the condemnation of unconditional aid (the gift) and consequently the issue of the conditionalities, the responsibility (egalitarian individual) of the developing countries that was not 'helped' (hierarchical responsibility), the economic dependence and the safety net (aspects of the debt), the addiction to aid (an ungratefulness, the absence of an awaited counter-payment?).

76. 'Dans le même temps, la coopération au développement tire les leçons du passé afin d'améliorer son approche. Elle se détache progressivement de l'aide classique au développement pour adopter une "approche contractuelle". Les relations futures de la Communauté sont appelées à se fonder sur un contrat de confiance aux termes obligatoires pour les deux parties ... la démarche s'applique également aux pays les plus défavorisés où l'aide sera toujours davantage liée à une obligation de résultats.' 1995 154 77.

77. 'This mutual confidence is of even greater importance in cooperation between Europeans and our partners in Africa, the Caribbean, and the Pacific, because human questions mean even more to them than they do to us.' 51 1978 17.

78. See Gerald Berthoud, 'Market' in Sachs, *The Development Dictionary* (London: Zed, 1992).

79. 'Lomé IV is the realisation of the will to consolidate, improve and strengthen the ties of a cooperation contract founded on solidarity and mutual interest, which the two parties have been expressing ever since the negotiations began.' 120 1990 12.

    'This is the culmination of both sides' desire, expressed at the opening of the negotiations, to "continue, intensify and increase the effectiveness" of cooperation based on solidarity and mutual interest.' 89 1985 21.

80. 'In all the Community languages, we always used to talk about development aid. Now we talk about development policy. (...) relations between the EEC and the developing countries went from financial aid to cooperation policy and to partnership ... to something more political.' 51 1978 15. Note the date of the extract and, once again, the hesitations and ambiguities about whether the whole Lomé system is political.

    But: '[T]he equality between the two partners is a fiction.' Kouleimah-Gabriel, *The Geographic Scope ...*, pp. 10–17.

81. '[W]e owe it to the developing countries to ensure that they have room for growth. Just as we owe it to future generations to ensure that our present lifestyle does not destroy the foundations of their very existence.' Frisch, 'The future of the Lomé Convention', pp. 7–15.

82. 'The most important impetus to change towards more democratic rule has been the globalisation and intensification of communication … and the effects of international economic exchange which cannot be stopped at borders and lead people to demand more representational government structures and freedom oriented policies.' 1997 22.

83. 'However, past experience does not provide a conclusive answer to the question of the relationship between democratic government and economic development. It can neither be maintained that democracy is a necessary precondition to economic development nor that it is an obstacle to it ….' 1997 38.

7 EUROPE'S QUEST

1. Dambudzo Marechera, *Black Sunlight* (Oxford: Heinemann, 1980). Marechera has narrated his life in his books; the archival work of Flora Veit-Wild has made other aspects of it accessible.

2. But also of black Africans, more generally. A person from Cameroun, explaining to me his shock at being brought to a restaurant where the only black people were those serving – an overwhelming feature in Harare's geography – told me: 'Il n'y avait que des Européens': he meant white Zimbabweans.

3. However, the radio and TV programmes, mainly emitted in Shona, talk of *varungu* and *vachena* (both words mean 'white'; the first is derived from *chirungu*, the Shona word for English) instead of 'Europeans', which is the word used in the English-language newspapers. Thanks to Kudakwashi G. for answering my questions.

4. As he notes with regard to Orientalism, 'Orientalism is never far from what Denys Hay has called the idea of Europe, a collective notion identifying "us" Europeans as against all "those" non-Europeans, and indeed it can be argued that the major component in European culture is precisely what made the culture hegemonic both in and outside Europe: the idea of European identity as a superior one in comparison with all the non-European peoples and cultures.' Edward Said, *Orientalism. Western Conceptions of the Orient* (London: Penguin, 1978), p. 7. As was objected after the publication of this book, Orientalism (or Occidentalism) is created by both sides.

5. Blair Rutherford, *Working on the Margins, Black Workers, White Farmers in Postcolonial Zimbabwe* (London and Harare: Zed Books and Weaver Press, 2001).

6. Ibid., p. 64.

7. Ibid., p. 80. It is interesting that Rutherford uses the past tense: given that his research took place only two years ago, this seems more than a strategic literary device. It could be speaking of a certain unavoidable anthropological trap – that has set itself as a disciplinary rule – that distances (behind, in the past) the anthropologist from the subjects of

her/his study: Fabian's chronopolitics to which Rutherford nevertheless refers. But we must add the author's immediate cautionary note that 'European' and 'African', though they carry the stereotypes of late nineteenth- and twentieth-century colonial discourses, are used more pragmatically and within a negotiated framework.

8. Ibid., p. 86. In particular in relation to responsibility, Rutherford does not seem to notice the contradiction between what we called 'hierarchical' and 'egalitarian' responsibility. However, in different moments he refers to both. 'Rural white Zimbabweans that I met consistently contrasted themselves with Africans. They continually explained how this difference required, and conferred, a certain responsibility to edify Africans' and 'The pervasive theme – from AIDS to conservation, from sex to firewood – was that Africans did not recognise their responsibility for future consequences since their value system promoted endless consumption in the present.' In any case, Rutherford's book is a very welcome corrective to writings on development or capitalism that overlook environments where development/capitalism express themselves in other forms than in Europe. Thus although, for instance, Boltanski and Chiapello's book is full of valuable insights and original propositions, it crucially misses the point concerning 'African' or, at least, 'Zimbabwean' capitalism where the first spirit of capitalism unencumberingly co-exists with connectionist capitalism. Boltanski and Chiapello, *Le nouvel esprit du capitalisme*.

9. This stems from a discussion with Mayamiko Kachingwe.

10. Derrida, *The Other Heading* (Bloomington: Indiana University Press, 1992). As in the introduction, it is used strategically, both to underline a necessary interrogation on who are 'Europeans' but also, from a different perspective, as a call to acknowledge that in front of 'the other' that the ACP countries are, Europeans represent a unity, and a unity that must bear responsibility.

11. Edmund Husserl, 'The Vienna lecture' in Edmund Husserl (trans. David Carr), *The Crisis of the European Sciences and Transcendental Phenomenology* (Evanston: Northwestern University Press, 1970), p. 299.

12. Paul Valéry, 'The intellectual crisis' in Paul Valéry, *Variety*, 1954.

13. Hans-Georg Gadamer, 'The future of the European humanities', in H. G. Gadamer, *On Education, Poetry and History* (State University of New York Press, 1992), p. 208.

14. Derrida, *The Other Heading*, pp. 69–70.

15. Gadamer, 'The future of the European humanities', p. 201.

16. Ibid.

17. See Chapter 6.

18. The European development discourse is only one expression of the 'trade not aid' effect that has been regaining saliency periodically, ever since the British colonial rule in India.

19. Jacques Donzelot has shown how, at the national level, solidarity was an answer elaborated to respond to the fears created by sovereignty among both revolutionaries and conservatives under the French Third Republic. Solidarity was a 'strategic invention' mediating between the individual as principle of intelligibility of the social reality and the class struggle as motor of history. See Jacques Donzelot, *L'invention du social. Essai sur*

le declin des passions politiques (Paris: Fayard, 1984). At the international level, Walker has proposed that any relaxation of the exclusionary logic of the state (sovereignty principle) produced an immediate temptation towards the universal, towards 'progress' and 'development', a move that we can attribute to the workings of solidarity. Walker, *Inside/Outside* (Cambridge: Cambridge University Press, 1993).

20. Paul Gilroy, 'Urban social movements, "race" and community', in Williams and Chrisman (eds), *Colonial Discourse* (New York: Harvester Wheatsheaf, 1995).

21. For the distinction between emancipatory and regulatory knowledge, see Santos, 'Towards an epistemology of blindness', *EJST*, 2001.

22. See, for an extended discussion of these issues, Nathalie Karagiannis, 'Giving Development: Responsibility and Efficiency in the European development Discourse towards the ACP countries (1970–1990s)' (PhD thesis, Florence: EUI, 2002), Chapter 2 in particular. In this text, the fourth type of 'giving' – the mutual debt – is insisted upon, because it speaks of the reciprocal constitution of 'Europe' and 'Africa', an equality to be found otherwise only in the market exchange. In addition, this form of giving retains a sense of the past while circumscribing its relevance (and thus, it avoids the somehow oppressive, domestic and hierarchical, connotation of the gift).

23. William H. Sewell, *Work and Revolution in France, the Language of Labour from the Old Regime to 1848* (Cambridge: Cambridge University Press, 1980).

24. Although Marechera also somewhat ironises on authenticity when he describes Blanche's 'object of study', one can also think of this passage by Marechera as encapsulating perfectly chronopolitics at work, the resistance to it and the falling back onto a 'jargon of authenticity'.

25. Gadamer, 'The future of the European humanities', p. 207.

26. This refers to the post-Second World War development discourse, not the one stemming from nineteenth-century colonialism and which had, famously, a strong explicit 'civilisational' message to spread. But even then, the recent development discourse, too, is soaked in such 'civilisational messages', the preceding chapters showed this.

27. In winter 2001, a South African supermarket chain operating in Zimbabwe, OK, ran an advertising campaign based on the slogan 'empowering the consumer', a non-ironical pastiche of the latest developmentalist jargon.

Index